Scattered Shadows

Scattered Shadows

A Memoir of Blindness and Vision

John Howard Griffin

ORBIS BOOKS

Maryknoll, New York 10545

Founded in 1970, Orbis Books endeavors to publish works that enlighten the mind, nourish the spirit, and challenge the conscience. The publishing arm of the Maryknoll Fathers and Brothers, Orbis seeks to explore the global dimensions of the Christian faith and mission, to invite dialogue with diverse cultures and religious traditions, and to serve the cause of reconciliation and peace. The books published reflect the views of their authors and do not represent the official position of the Maryknoll Society. To learn more about Maryknoll and Orbis Books, please visit our website at www.maryknoll.org.

Manufactured in the United States of America

Library of Congress Cataloging-in-Publication Data

Griffin, John Howard, 1920-
    Scattered shadows : a memoir of blindness and vision / John Howard Griffin.
        p. cm.
    ISBN 1-57075-539-6
    1. Griffin, John Howard, 1920- 2. Blind—United States—Biography.
3. Blindness. 4. Vision. I. Title.
HV1792.G75 A3 2004
362.4'1'092—dc22
                                                                2003024213

In Memory of
Clyde Parker Holland and
Elizabeth Ann Griffin-Bonazzi

Contents

Introduction
Robert Bonazzi

Certainly nothing, no other art, no other form of communication is capable of possessing my heart and literally transforming me into the core of harmony as completely and magically as music.

—

A man loses his sight then, but let it be understood that he loses nothing else. He does not lose his intelligence, his taste, his sensitivity, his ideals, his right to respect. It is a grave mistake to think that blindness places a person into a given category of behavioristic patterns or psychological reactions. One remains as much an individual as always. There is no doubt, however, that one is obliged to lead a different, more complex, and often a more vital life.
—From the *Journals* of John Howard Griffin

I

John Howard Griffin's memoir, *Scattered Shadows*, under contract with the Boston firm that published *Black Like Me*, did not appear in book form during his lifetime, although selections saw print in the fifties and sixties. The reasons why it remained unfinished are complex, but the basic truth was that the ground of Griffin's focus had shifted abruptly from being a solitary novelist in the fifties to becoming a human rights activist on the lecture circuit during the sixties and early seventies.

Scattered Shadows

Black Like Me was a bestseller in 1961, has remained in print as a paperback since 1962 (in English and French), selling over eleven million copies in fourteen languages to date. *Scattered Shadows* has suffered the very opposite fate, but the thematic parallels of the two memoirs are striking and profound. In the modern classic on racism, a white novelist disguised as a "Negro" travels through the segregated South, returning to the middle-class world of privilege after six weeks. In the little-known story of *Scattered Shadows*, a soldier injured by forces beyond his control, gradually goes blind, then unexpectedly recovers his eyesight a decade later.

Both experiences concern the same man, misperceived as a stereotype and reduced to the "inferior" status of the *Other,* who discovers a greater humanity in *otherness.* Griffin realized that blindness was judged by the sighted to be a tragic handicap, an intrinsically different condition that had no relation to the inner life of the blind—exactly as whites prejudged black people as intrinsically *Other* based entirely on skin color, with no consideration of their qualities as individuals.

The memoirs evoke realities misunderstood by the dominant culture: *Black Like Me* reveals the experience of a segregated minority as whites refused to see it—though obviously not at the depth African Americans live it—and *Scattered Shadows* illuminates the interior world of darkness as the sighted could not perceive it. Griffin's views were considered controversial, even radical for their time. But truthfulness always is.

Part I of *Scattered Shadows* charts the gradual deterioration of light perception caused by a 1945 war injury, until Griffin was totally blind at age twenty-seven. In 1946, he made a retreat at the Abbey of Solesmes to study Gregorian Chant with the Benedictines, an experience he always called a "high point" in life—and it was also a crucial turning point.

Part II details the adaptations the sightless must make in a sighted world and Griffin's experiment with raising livestock "by feel" to prove that the blind could become independent beyond presumed limits. During that decade he also embarked upon interior journeys: a spiritual quest that the mystics have called "the dark night of the soul" and a parallel creative process of composing novels based on musical forms inspired by Gregorian Chant and masterpieces of the classical tradition.

The setting for his first novel, *The Devil Rides Outside,* was an austere monastery and a nearby provincial village in northern France, based on the abbey and village of Solesmes, where the smug agnosticism of a young American musicologist is shaken by the simple humility of the monks, the magnificence of the medieval chants and the spiritual clarity of his guide—the fictional Father Clément, modeled on his actual mentor, Friar Marie-Bruno.

The unnamed first-person narrator endures his dark night of the soul, which does *not* lead to conversion, as the author's eventually did, when Griffin was baptized as a Roman Catholic on July 13, 1951. In 1952, his 600-page novel written in the immediacy of the present tense was the first title from a Texas publisher. It became a surprise best-seller, a 1954 paperback censored as pornographic in Michigan, and finally a test case adjudicated in 1957 by the U.S. Supreme Court.

Griffin said that the novel "wrote me into the Church," for it was composed at an ecstatic pitch in seven weeks, but also by an arduous method. Each night he spoke French into a wire recorder and the next day typed the words in English, translating as he went along. The music he knew informed and actually formed his work. Applying Beethoven's late String Quartet opus 131 to the first novel, he pushed characters on stage as the themes entered, literally transforming the forms of music into prose.

His 1956 novel, *Nuni*, was also in first-person present tense and based on musical forms; a second allegory of modernity encountering a distant past—not St. Benedict's *Primitive Rule* but the law of the jungle. He set the novel on a remote island in the South Pacific where he had lived in 1944. The narrator, Professor John Harper, is symbolic of modernity-as-useless to one stripped of civilized trappings. *Nuni* ("world" in the native idiom) uses the antiphonal structure of Gregorian Chant, developing a single theme with variations on a sacred text—not the *Psalms* but Harper's varied refrain on "driven along paths not of our own choosing"—echoing through streams of consciousness.

While the first novel builds a bridge toward a religious conversion, the second maps paths of physical pain, emotional loss, and spiritual crisis—Harper's and Griffin's. In 1954, the blind author, paralyzed and confined to a wheelchair, was doubting not the faith but the worthiness of his work intended as praise. Before completing *Nuni*, he had lost all visual memory. Thus, his difficult creative challenge was to make readers *see* a world he could not, as if a sighted author had created it. This accounts for its intense sensorium of hearing, smelling, tasting, and touching, but also for the abstract nature of its lush description. Harper's gradual loss of memories metaphorically parallels the author's loss of visual images.

As he wrote novels, Griffin kept journaling—over twelve hundred single-spaced typed pages while blind—and began making notes for *Scattered Shadows*, first mentioned in entries from 1954. He explains that his title was based on a Latin text for Holy Saturday, which says that the "light of Christ dissipates the shadows of men's minds."

The memoir opens with the "Adventure-Prone" Prologue, recounting a 1938 trip to attend an opera in Paris. Realizing that he could not afford the ticket *and* a room for that night, the eighteen-year-old student decides to risk it. After the performance, when forced to sleep on a stone floor under a stairway, he becomes "totally absorbed in my misery." But slowly he detaches from it, intuiting a fresh perspective beyond self-interest. "All things took on new values," he writes, understanding that the place itself began "giving up its secrets . . . because instead of *immersing it in myself, I was immersing myself in it.*"

To immerse experience within oneself meant, from Griffin's viewpoint, to internalize it, to distort its intrinsic shape to fit one's preconceptions and prejudices. In art, this would be the humility of the creative process falsified by one's pride of self-expression. Instead of reducing an ideal to ego, he attempted to dissolve ego to serve an ideal. In the spiritual realm, he believed that the perfect examples were the anonymous monks who had composed the masterpieces of Gregorian Chant as humble praise to God. This attitude of immersing oneself in aspects greater than self was his primary theme, and variations are played out in the memoir in relation to blindness and sight, joy and pain, music and silence, languages and cultures, the creative process and love of humanity and the Divine.

II

But these journeys without maps began a quarter century before the memoir's opening. John Howard Griffin was born on June 16, 1920, in Dallas, Texas, which was then strictly segregated. His father, Jack, from Georgia roots, was a wholesale grocer; his mother, Lena, of Pennsylvania Dutch stock, had studied to be a concert pianist and gave piano lessons. His parents raised four children, but only he had learned what his mother knew about music. At fourteen, he read of pianist Moritz Rosenthal, an eminent musician with degrees in medicine and philosophy; Griffin had found a role model, who "opened me up to a far more fascinating horizon." At fifteen, frustrated by the regressive public school system, he spotted an ad for a boys school in France and wrote a letter pleading for admittance.

He was admitted to the Lycée Descartes in Tours and, in 1935, sailed to France in search of "a classical education." After graduating, he was on scholarship at the University of Poitiers school of medicine in Tours and later became an assistant to Dr. Pierre Fromenty, director of the Asylum of Tours. Among the doctor's psychiatric techniques was to expose the most alienated patients to Gregorian Chant, which had a curative effect on them. This influenced the American intern. Also in this period, he was studying music with Father Pierre Froger, organist at Tours Cathedral, with whom he coauthored a technical work on music. But with the outbreak of the war, his advanced pursuits ended. Dr. Fromenty was conscripted into the military, and Griffin was left in charge of the asylum.

Soon he joined friends and other students in the French underground resistance, smuggling Jewish children in the asylum ambulance—disguised as patients in straitjackets—out of Tours to other teams in the countryside who transported them safely to England. But their plan was discovered during the occupation of Tours in 1940, and Griffin's name appeared on the Gestapo's death list. He was smuggled out and returned to America. Having witnessed the tragic effects of the Holocaust, refined to hideous perfection by the Nazis, he never forgot the horror.

In 1941, he enlisted in the Air Force and was shipped to the Pacific front. Griffin spent 1943 living in a native village on a remote island in the Solomon chain, assigned to study the indigenous culture, translate the dialect of the inhabitants, and gather strategic information on Japanese positions from the native allies. At first, he viewed them as "primitives"—as *Other*. But after he was unable to navigate jungle trails without a five-year-old boy to guide him, it became obvious "that within the context of that culture, I was clearly the inferior—an adult man who could not have survived without the guidance of a child," he admitted. In 1945, he was reassigned to the landing base on Morotai when a Japanese invasion plan was intercepted. The sections on the war in the Pacific begin *Scattered Shadows,* and we learn that Griffin drew the short straw for a dangerous mission. During a harrowing night of bombing, he was severely injured and began gradually going blind over the next eighteen months. He had fought the war on both sides of the world—a rare experience—but he never claimed his stripes, medals, or disability checks, and he became a pacifist thereafter.

In the summer of 1946, he returned to France to study composition with Nadia Boulanger, the century's greatest teacher, whose students included Leonard Bernstein, Aaron Copland, and Walter Piston. Griffin realized he would not be among these fellow American composers, since his work had been judged technically correct—but not art. Soon after, he received permission to do research at Solesmes, eventually becoming an authority on Gregorian Chant. By spring 1947, the light went dark and, at age twenty-seven, he was totally blind.

Scattered Shadows

He went home to live with his parents in the Texas countryside. After enduring a frustrating adjustment, he took courses in animal husbandry and began to breed pure-bred livestock, winning ribbons in local stock shows. Although intensely interested in all of this, he came to accept that being a farmer was not his true vocation.

Meanwhile, he retreated every night to the barn, where his father had fashioned a study in the feed room. In a space as primitive as a monastic cell—roughly "three long steps each way," as he described it—he studied taped lessons from contemporary thinkers around the world. The healing qualities of study and music, meditation and prayer in the silence of that interior solitude gradually transformed him. His solitude was not divisive but unifying, not an escape into stoic isolation or indulgent fantasy but an abandonment of self-interest for "a selfless self-awareness." In 1953, he married his mother's most gifted piano pupil, Elizabeth Ann, the seventeen-year-old daughter of Clyde Holland, his close friend. (Wed in a Catholic ceremony, they had a twenty-seven-year-marriage in which they raised four children. Griffin died from complications of diabetes in 1980.)

Part III of *Scattered Shadows* begins on January 9, 1957, when Griffin perceived red glints of light that stunned him. For the first time he saw the faces of his loved ones. Regaining sight would be as exhausting an ordeal as losing it, and there was no certainty whether sight would improve or whether that blinding vision would go dark again. Slowly sight improved. Thrilled by this gift, Griffin observed all with new innocence, astonished that commonplace things appeared as objects in magnificent paintings.

Griffin had accepted blindness as a matter of Divine will that he be plunged into darkness for a purpose, and he believed that the recovery of his sight was a revelation of spiritual healing, a vision of mystical light. Unlike most sightless people, his dark night had a beginning, a middle, *and* an end—as well as a glorious new beginning.

III

Black Like Me and *Scattered Shadows* are somewhat naked memoirs, both drawing from Griffin's *Journals,* which are even more raw. The journal format became his natural literary form—first, because it was simple and the only way he knew to write in the beginning. Perhaps his best works are journals, including *Black Like Me, The Hermitage Journals* (kept in the early seventies while he was researching a biography of Thomas Merton); and *Scattered Shadows* (half of Part II, all of Part III). *The Devil Rides Outside* and *Nuni* are also journals, although Professor Harper keeps an internal diary without dates, falling from clock time into a timeless past.

The *Journals* (1950-1980) were his source for transforming experience into insight. He kept them "because it puts on paper what would enter into the realm of forgetfulness, and I am thrifty enough to know that I can come back to these, and in these thousands of pages, find something that I could never reproduce later—find some thought, some expression, some reaction that lives and breathes." He thought André Gide's journals "too carefully written for effect," but discovered in Franz Kafka's diaries a truthfulness that was "total reality and therefore total inconsistency."

While Griffin composed Part I, most of Part II, and "What It Means to See" in Part III for publication, one-third of *Scattered Shadows* has been drawn from other published pieces and journal entries. The strict journal format opens with "A Different Species" (1954). Subsequent sections were developed from selected passages, which represent neither the sprawling nature of the *Journals* nor what Griffin might have chosen to write and polish had the work not been interrupted by racial crises in the sixties.

During the time of this memoir, from 1945 to 1957, Griffin was between the ages of twenty-five and thirty-seven. The composed sections, written when Griffin was in his forties, reflect a mature style— "The Blind Man of Tours" for example. While he was naive when he met the blind man, he was an accomplished stylist when he wrote of him. The same cannot be said for some sections drawn from his journals when, as a beginning writer and religious convert, he had opinions on everything. For the most part they were solid views, but not always expressed with clarity or humility. These represent an earlier time—he began writing at twenty-nine—when he was isolated from the cultural mainstream, mentored by the previous generation (Friar Marie-Bruno, Pierre Reverdy, Robert Casadesus, Abraham Rattner), and impassioned by ancient monastic ideals and the lives of the saints.

Essential as the spiritual was for Griffin, equally important were his family life and the ethical responsibility to speak out against injustice. "In truth," he writes, "I practice and find my spiritual home in another time . . . back into the old houses of the soul—of St. John of the Cross and St. Benedict. This would appear to be a contradiction, and I suppose it is. The contradiction of yearning to withdraw from public life into silence, solitude and obscurity—this yearning that has torn at me many years; and yet my life and work, precisely because it was long ago given without reservation to God, is in the world, in activity. Somehow these contradictions are resolved within me, because there, at least, they are not contradictions."

Griffin connected these seeming opposites at the level of Being. The body was not debased to purify the soul; the mind refused to trivialize matters of the heart. He was called a "Renaissance man" by those impressed by his talents in music, photography, and writing, and by the disciplines he studied. But the term obscures the surface of his deeper spiritual orientation, grounded in the medieval ideal of obedience and humility in offering all to the Divine. The Renaissance was the "invention" of the Ego in the West, and its focus was on the secular, historical time, and progress—exactly the opposite of Griffin's focus on the religious, eternity and process, with a preference for cultivating a "selfless self-awareness."

Griffin's radical incarnation in *Black Like Me* links his name to the incendiary issue of racial segregation in the twentieth century's context. His critique of racism was heard in the passionate yet nonviolent tones of Gandhi and Martin Luther King, who had based their views on ancient natural law and the Christ ideal of *res sacra*—insisting on the sacredness of life and the necessity of equal justice for all.

Even so, we might venture to perceive him as a "modern medievalist" blessed with a modern alchemical imagination: after all, he wrote novels shaped by music; produced photographic images of transformation; and turned the *I* into the *Other* in *Black Like Me*.

Scattered Shadows was his long dark night of the soul, painfully endured because of his abiding faith, but rewarded by the illumination of a glorious light. John Howard Griffin lost his eyesight but never lost the transcendent vision.

– Prologue –

Adventure-Prone

The greatest background education for a writer—and too often the most neglected—is experience. By this I do not mean a wild dashing about from place to place or having love affair after love affair. I mean the ability to make experience out of everything that happens to you.

Experience for the writer is in many ways an attitude of mind. It is the ability to feel adventure in the smallest things in life, a walk in the rain if you like. It is this sense of adventure which many young writers lack, and yet I am sure it can be developed. Perhaps I can explain this best by telling you about what happened to me when I was eighteen years old.

I was a student living in a tiny attic room in Tours, France. It was a winter afternoon and I was huddled before a small stove reading about Kirsten Flagstad's upcoming Paris performance in *Tristan and Isolde*. It was to be a single gala appearance, and a friend had told me that this was something I should not miss. I counted out my scant savings and began to figure. If I went third class and bought the cheapest ticket, I would have enough to go but not enough to buy a meal or get a room.

Going to Paris would mean a night under a bridge or in a doorway and a day without food. I had never done anything like this. I was far from adventurous then. I was a studious scientist and the whole idea horrified me. But I knew that if I didn't go, I might regret it all my life.

I decided to go, and that simple decision had far-reaching effects. That one night in Paris transformed me into being a more "adventure-prone" person—and that experience probably was directly responsible for my becoming a writer a decade later.

There are few other vocations that list such a high percentage of those who are adventure-prone. Almost all writers—from Dante to Molière to Hemingway—are capable of tremendous intellectual adventure. They give the impression of living grandly, even when isolated in a lonely room over a work desk. We think of them as people *to whom things happen.*

An adventure-prone person is not simply someone assaulted by a set of adventurous circumstances. Rather, he or she is one who perceives the possibility for adventure where others do not. It appears to be a matter of conditioning, a conscious technique that can be acquired.

Actual physical adventure has relatively little to do with it. This is proved by the cloistered nuns who sometimes lead most fascinating and vivid lives. On the other hand, we have the classic example of the big game hunter in Africa, sitting on his folding chair, swizzling his rum and wondering where in hell all the excitement is.

In an effort to understand what makes an experience high adventure for one person while the same experience merely jades and bores another, let's return to that night in Paris to see what happened to that teenager.

After the opera, which was magnificent, I faced a cold, drizzly night in a strange city with nothing in my pocket except a return ticket to Tours. I was hungry and cold and had no idea where to turn.

I began walking and looking for some place to shelter me from the weather. When I was about to give up, I saw a chestnut vendor folding up his roasting-stand for the night. I went up to him and asked where a man "without a *sou*" could sleep. He told me of *Cour de Rohan*, a thirteenth-century sector across the river from Notre Dame. He explained that the old quarter was poor, that the doors were never closed, and that I could probably sleep under the stairwell without being disturbed.

He gave me a sack of hot chestnuts to warm my hands and we walked together to the narrow passageway leading into the district of the poor. I gazed down the cobblestoned passage toward a yellowish, misty street lamp at the other end. "Enter any of the doors," said the kindly man, and then he departed.

I tried a couple of the doors which were so low I had to stoop to look in. At the third door, I realized they would all smell the same, and so I entered and felt for the stairway. I walked around behind it and forced myself to stretch out on the grimy flagstone floor.

For a time, I was acutely aware of my discomfort, of the hardness and filth of the floor, of the chill that crept in under my clothes. I was lonely, desolate, and somewhat frightened. I was totally absorbed in my misery.

But slowly, another feeling aroused me from my self-preoccupation. It occurred to me that all of this was interesting. I began to detach myself from my discomfort, realizing that this was an experience worth having—or rather, one that would someday be worth having *had*.

I asked myself how many men had ever slept under the stairway of a thirteenth-century house? To sleep in a comfortable bed was fine, but if you looked at it in a certain way, this was fine, too. I would forget the many nights spent in comfort and safety, but I knew that I would never forget this night. It was worth experiencing, worth giving myself up to.

All things took on new values.

The floor became, instead of something hard and tormenting, stones that had been laid there centuries before with pride by some craftsman. It became a thing that had known the weight of saints and sinners long dead. It became itself, revealing its secrets to me. Why?

Because instead of immersing it in myself, I was *immersing myself in it*.

All I had done was change my attitude.

I was still miserable, but it had become unimportant. I had ceased to be a person judging everything on the basis of pleasure or comfort. I had gone out of myself to the value of things in themselves, and I have never since been able to step back consistently into mere self-interest.

This is the crucial difference, I believe, between the person whose life is monotonous and the one who is adventure-prone. It is also a crucial point in the richness and originality of a writer's work.

In 1945—after having left war-torn France, and then serving in the Army Air Force in the Pacific theater, where I suffered head wounds—I began gradually losing eyesight. What I thought had been my "education" in medicine was rendered useless. I faced an entirely new life, a totally unexpected one.

Blindness was a revelation because it exposed the enormous ability we have to be distracted by the things of the world, and the fundamental deficiencies of a strictly academic education. Being sightless demanded that I learn from experience in the most primal, clarifying manner. At age twenty-seven, I was totally blind, and a few years later I began to write.

The writing allowed me to make experience from what had happened. It was not that I made factual use of experience—not at all—but that I made use of the insights that have come through experience.

In the writing itself I discovered a process of understanding. I began to keep a journal—of a different sort than I had as a student in France—one that would be brutally honest. And I started writing fiction. After I had drafted several novels and countless short stories during a decade of blindness, I embarked upon the autobiographical

Scattered Shadows. It was to be an account of losing sight and the inward reality of blindness, with no expectation that it would also be a book about sight-recovery.

When I regained eyesight in 1957, I returned to the rough typescript, relieved that I had developed those then-vivid early memories which soon faded in the excitement of new vision. Just as important, I had recorded those daily events and seemingly insignificant details of experiencing sightlessness in more than twelve hundred journal pages. These were pages that I might never have been courageous enough to reread, because it would have meant involving a sighted person to read them back to me or into a tape recorder.

I know that *Scattered Shadows* could never have been written had I not kept my journals faithfully during those years of sightlessness. I also believe that I would not have become a writer at all, had I not discovered this sense of being adventure-prone, while sleeping under the stairway of a thirteenth-century house on that cold, rainy night in Paris.

I

Shadows

— Enemy Invasion —

By 1945, we had lost so many men and had been bombed so often that we had long ago learned to refuse any thoughts about death. Death did not exist for us except as a cold fact to be recognized and quickly dismissed. We had long ceased to mourn the deaths of our companions.

In life, a warm and often devoted friendship existed between us. In death, nothing. They were there at the table one day, and then we saw them no more and that was all.

Most of us in the 424th Bomb Squadron's radar section were in our third year overseas. Although our unit had been bombed often, this was the first time we were under a black alert. Now we were threatened with invasion from the enemy. We stood, perhaps a dozen of us, in the radar tent on Morotai Island and drew straws. Pops Fendler drew first, and then Mills. Each got a long straw. I was third in line and got the short one. Corporal Fred Kaplan cast me a glance of sympathy, tossed the remaining straws into the coral dust at our feet, and cursed.

The section captain told me I would go on duty at six this evening.

"Do you know what to do?" he asked.

"Not entirely."

He glanced up at the tent roof where rot holes let in thin rays of sunlight. "Intelligence has intercepted the Jap's orders. They're supposed to take the airstrip, kill the tower operators, and then proceed here to the radar tent, kill whoever is on duty, and take all our technical data before it can be destroyed. You'll have your gasoline ready to burn the place up. And you'll have the jeep outside to make a run for it. If they follow orders, they'll hit the tower first and you'll have some warning."

21

I wondered. The Japanese would surely not be so stupid as to attack the tower first and give me warning. They would undoubtedly strike both places at the same time.

"I'll be in touch with you by phone from headquarters," the captain said. "Don't set off the gasoline unless you actually see one of them or unless I tell you to."

"Couldn't I just grenade the place?"

"No, the papers might not be destroyed. You pour gasoline over the files and see that they get burned."

The others waited, silent. Finally Kaplan asked the question. "Is there any law against telling us what's going on?"

"Two Japanese suicide units landed on our side of the bay last night. We expect an invasion—sometime tonight probably."

"Well, what the hell's everybody leaving for?" Kaplan asked. "It looks like they ought to be sending in more men instead of taking them out."

"We expect a massive bombardment to soften us up before the ground troops come in," said the captain. "Headquarters has ordered evacuation of all dispensable planes and personnel."

"Are they going to evacuate any of us?" Kaplan asked.

"Have you had instructions to pack?"

"No, sir."

The captain shrugged and turned away. Pops Fendler honked the jeep horn and called us to go to lunch. Six of us piled into the jeep while the others took the pick-up. We drove down the airstrip under a glaring sun, past open bunkers where B-24s made ready to take off. Palms with fronds whitened by coral dust from propeller backwash flashed by.

We entered the jungle on a ten-mile road that had been cut from the airfield to the camp. After rain, it was a slush, but today we bounded over the sun-baked mud, deeply rutted. At regular take-off intervals, the B-24s rumbled over us, so near they almost touched the treetops. As each appeared, Kaplan, in the back seat raised his arms and implored: "Wait—take me with you."

The camp area had been evacuated when we reached our tents. Morotai had quickly become a ghost island. Rumors spread that the Japanese had massed a force of 47,000 men across the bay, while our total remaining American and Australian forces were about one-tenth of that.

In the mess hall, the rows of empty tables and the lack of noise emphasized our isolation. We sat in small groups. From the open sides of the large, tin-roofed shed, we looked across the gray-green waters of Morotai Bay to the motionless jungles of the opposite shore, which was held by the Japanese.

Someone turned the kitchen radio up to full volume and shouted for us to listen. Tokyo Rose's familiar voice floated through the shed, its sensuality amplified by a squawking harshness. "I really feel sad about all my boyfriends on Morotai. I like you boys. You know that. I'm thinking about you today while you eat that tasteless dehydrated food. I could just cry when I think this is going to be your last meal on earth. Even a condemned convict gets a tasty last meal. But boys, try not to be bitter. I know it's hard. After all, you're out here eating this trash while back home your family and friends are probably enjoying some fresh corn on the cob, dripping with real butter, and maybe a bottle of ice cold beer. Wouldn't a nice can of iced cold beer taste good right now?"

Kaplan's sentimental black eyes filled with tears. Midday heat pressed like fever against our cheeks. We felt the desperation of sweat in our hair, on our eyelids, and dribbling down our buttocks. Our dehydrated potatoes and embalmed meat repelled us. Rose's other silliness made no impression on us, but our bellies made us painfully vulnerable to her description of food and drink. Nothing could have awakened a deeper ache than the mention of cold beer.

"I hope you boys have a mail call today," she went on. "For most of you, it'll be the last time you hear from your wives and sweethearts. I wonder how many of them have dates with stateside soldiers tonight? After all, it's part of their duty to keep up those boys' morale. But it does seem a shame in a way. Here you are out fighting for them and—"

"Bitch . . . bitch!" Mills shouted, struggling to his feet and glaring at us. He repeated the word "bitch" furiously as he turned and ran out.

Kaplan picked up Mills's mess kit, dumped its contents into a garbage drum, and dipped it in a barrel of boiling water.

Then Pops Fendler joined Kaplan and me in the walk toward our tent.

"I can't figure that little Mills out," Fendler said expansively. "God, I hate to see a man that's got no guts. What the hell's eating him? He hasn't even had a bath in a week."

"He's just had it, that's all. All he can take," Kaplan said.

"He's so scared that wife of his is screwing around," Fendler snorted.

Kaplan looked at the older man's thick features with contempt.

We climbed the hill to our tent. Inside, Kaplan and I hung our mess kits on the tent's center pole and sat down on our cots.

Fendler undressed and tied a towel around his thick waist. He flexed his shoulders in a gesture retained from youthful days as a professional boxer. The whiteness of his well-preserved body contrasted to the tan of his pugged and aged face. Gray body hair on his chest and belly matted in his sweat.

Mills stuck his head through the tent opening. "How about a game?"

"Sure. Come on in," I said, astonished by his cheerfulness.

"You must have had a letter from your wife, kid," Fendler said as Mills entered carrying his cribbage board.

"You bet," Mills answered. He slapped the older man's bare shoulders and then rubbed Fendler's sweat from his palms against his tee shirt.

Fendler's eyes closed in irritation at the familiarity. He walked to the door on wood-soled shower shoes.

"Where you going, buddy?" Mills asked.

"Now where would I be going dressed like this?" Fendler said in a supercilious tone he often affected. He clumped out and we heard him mutter, "What a crazy goddamn question. Christ."

Mills straddled my cot and faced me across the cribbage board.

"What's he so pissed off about?" he asked.

I watched him scratch an inflamed mosquito welt at the neckline of his soiled T-shirt. Ammonia odors of old sweat and fresh urine emanated from him. His khaki pants bore the almost-dry pattern where he had wet himself in anguish. His gaze fixed on my face, questioningly. Mills apparently had not realized. I hastily looked beside my cot for the deck of limp blue Bicycle cards.

While Mills dealt the cards on my green wool army blanket, I stared out the tent door. Coral shimmered blindingly under the sun. When I looked back to the tent's interior, a black-light aureole surrounded all objects. Silence deepened by the wash of the surf hung over the camp.

Mills soon had a large lead but he was tensing. "I hope you make it all right tonight and they don't get to the radar tent," he said. Muscles twitched in his cheeks and ragged fingernails dug into the mosquito welt.

Kaplan looked up from the letter he was writing. I saw concern in his black eyes. We had both seen men break under the strain and we did not want it to happen to Mills.

Lavender soap fragrance entered the tent with Fendler. "Just heard Tokyo at the H.Q. shack," he laughed. "You kids better start saying your prayers. It looks like the real thing this time. Better go write that pretty wife of yours a letter, kid," he said to Mills.

"Why don't you shut up?" Kaplan said.

"What's the matter, buddy, you getting nervous?" Fendler teased.

Mills dragged himself from the cot. "I guess I'd better go."

"Okay," I said. "See you later. They won't hit the camp. It's the runway they're after."

"Ha! It's the whole stinking island," Fendler snorted. Then he noticed the stain on Mills's trousers. "Well, for godsakes. . . ."

Mills walked hurriedly away.

Fendler shook his head slowly. "Did you see his pants? I believe that poor cluck's so scared he's pissed in his pants."

"No, one of those damned Jarvis tubes backed up on him," Kaplan said, inventing the excuse to silence Fendler; referring to a type of urinal made of a pipe inserted in the ground with a funnel at the upper end. These hygienic contrivances, technically dubbed Jarvis Pee Tubes, were invented by our Major Jarvis and constituted his greatest fame in the Pacific area. When heavily used, they overflowed back on the user. This imperfection had never been corrected despite the major's dedicated attempts to improve his product.

Kaplan returned to his letter while I stretched out on my cot and lit a cigarette. If Fendler felt nervous, he did not show it. He was whistling softly to himself while clouding the tent with lavender talc that he loudly patted with a huge puff under his arms, over his chest and between his legs. We welcomed it after the stench of Mills had left.

The sky clouded over. I walked through the floating white talc to the door and looked out. Beyond the white reefs a colorless ocean stretched to the horizon. The coral no longer glared.

"Well," Fendler said, "I guess I'd better go buck up the kids."

I turned to see him dressed in fresh khakis, his gray hair carefully combed into deep waves from a center part. "See you later," he said, edging past me. I watched him walk away. He assumed his "tiger walk"—smooth and somewhat crouched, again a carryover from his fighting days, whistling and snapping the fingers of both hands.

"What's going to happen if Mills blows tonight?" Kaplan asked. Though he spoke quietly, his voice carried clear in the silence. I realized planes no longer flew overhead. The evacuation had been completed.

"God knows," I said. "He ought to be in a hospital right now."

A streak of lightning flashed down from low clouds into the ocean.

Two giant white cockatoos flew out from the top of a tall tree and circled against the black sky before settling again into the branches.

"I guess I'd better go take a shower," I said. I stepped back into the tent's gloom to undress.

"Yeah, it looks like a storm," Kaplan said. Then, brightening, "God Griff, I hope it does come." He lifted his skinny arms heavenward and in a mock rabbinical tone cried: "O God, send us torrents of rain and wind and thunder and lightning and inundate this island, O God—"

"What the hell's eating you?" I interrupted.

"Man, man I want it to rain and storm so the enemy calls off his nasty, nasty plans."

"Well, then don't let me interrupt you," I laughed.

Not a leaf stirred in the trees when I walked down the hill to the open-air showers at the water's edge. The few men left in camp showed no interest in the threat of invasion. As I passed their tents, I saw that some were writing letters, others were cleaning carbines, but most lay listlessly on their cots.

I reached the showers. The floor was a platform of perforated metal runway strips built over the reef at the bay's edge. Square metal drums on overhead struts fed water to the shower heads.

Looking out over the gray expanse of bay, I felt alone in a world where all was silence, all was peace, and I took a long time bathing. My home, my family, my past hung remote in memory. I concentrated on my family in Texas and our home. Was the living room here or there? What kind of furniture did we have? Evoked scenes came to mind— faded, static, like old photographs.

The years in the tropics had dimmed everything. Was there really such a thing as an easy chair? Did men still shave with hot water and enclose their bathing within the privacy of bathroom walls? What was the taste of fresh milk or eggs? How did it feel to wear a suit, to experience winter, to live where women could be seen in homes or streets. All of that floated unreal and mysterious. The reality lay here in a world of jungles, tents, khakis, jeeps, carbines, and planes.

I stood alone under the cold shower water. The jungle and the ocean stretched serenely about me. I felt content. I sensed the solitude of the deserted island, the potency of a quiet sea and motionless trees and overcast sky—the passionate calm of nature trembling at the edge of violence, holding back, hushed.

I dried with the towel, wrapped it around my waist, and walked to the mess hall for a thermos of coffee. The mess sergeant filled it, remarking how dead everything was in camp. Above the wash of the surf, I heard soft music from his radio in the kitchen. Jo Stafford sang "I'll Walk Alone" for the seven millionth time.

"I understand you drew the short straw for tonight," the sergeant said. "I sure hope you don't win any medals out there."

When I arrived at the tent, Fendler was seated on his cot drinking Dewar's Scotch from the bottle. He stared at me, his face slack and covered with sweat-filled wrinkles that glistened in the sallow light.

"Where's Kap?" I asked.

"Over at the chapel. All of them's gone over."

I took my helmet to use as a bowl and went outside to shave. Fendler followed me.

"What's going on?" I asked.

"Having some sort of special service—a little last-minute plea to God, I guess. Sonsabitches," he sighed.

"When did they call this festival?"

"That Australian chaplain made the rounds a while ago and invited everyone," he said.

I filled my helmet with water from a canvas lister bag that hung from a nearby tree.

Thunder crackled directly overhead. A deep greenish gloom settled over the area, giving the sand beneath our feet the look of snow. Men's voices drifted to us from the thatch-roofed chapel some distance away. "Onward Christian soldiers," they sang, "marching as to war . . . "

Fendler swigged at his bottle again. "God damn," he said softly. "There ain't nothing creepier than hymns to me. Don't they sound piti-ful singing like that?" His washed-out blue eyes struggled to focus. "Do you believe in God, Griff?"

"You're damn right," I said. "Especially tonight."

"You hypocrite bastard," he laughed. "No, I do too, only hell . . . "

"Why don't you go to the festival then?"

"I'll tell you the truth. You put Jesus over there by that tree," he pointed drunkenly. "And you put a good-looking woman, or hell even a lousy-looking one, or some booze or a steak by that other tree . . . and you know which way you'd go, and I'd go, and all of them over there singing sweet songs to Jesus would go? Ain't a one of us wouldn't leave Jesus standing by His tree and go for that other. But you let a little dan-ger come and they go flying right into the Savior's arms and acting, by God, like that's where they wanted to be all the time. Well, I'll tell you, when the day comes that I voluntarily go over to that Jesus tree, that's the day when I won't feel like an ass-head for going to church."

Sweat poured from his face. Trees rose like towering specters in the somber light, dwarfing us in our isolation.

"Do you want a snort, Griff? God, that damned pitiful singing!"

"Better not. If anything happened out there tonight and they smelled whiskey on me, I'd never get off the work pile."

"I guess so at that." He lowered his gray eyebrows in a frown of con-centration. "You got it once before, didn't you? Were you boozing that night you got your ass smashed on Los Negros?"

"No, but I might've been better off if I had been." Like many others, I had caught some shrapnel during one of the Japanese air raids.

I dumped my shaving water and went inside to dress. He followed me, stretched out on his cot, corpse-like, hands on chest, holding not a lily but a bottle of Scotch. As I dressed in the stifling obscurity, I heard the men singing in the distance: "Stand up, stand up for Jesus . . . "

For an instant, I was vividly back in time, a youngster in St. John's Episcopal Church in Fort Worth, Texas. It was Sunday, almost any Sunday in July. Windows were open and fans hummed. Dressed in the red cassock and white surplice of an altar boy, I stood near the lectern and posted the hymn schedule for the eleven o'clock service. Processional 538 it was, and everyone knew to sing "Stand Up For Jesus."

The church and the people and the smells of long-ago Sundays in the city faded to the jungle with its reek of rotting nature.

"I guess I'd better get going," I said. "Tell the captain, will you?"

"Yeah, sure. You got anything to read?"

"I think I'll take my whole library."

Squatting before the cot, I reached under to pull out the books I had brought overseas. I had abandoned clothing and army equipment to stuff one duffel bag with books and musical scores. These represented almost my only connection with the world of the past.

I stacked them beside me: The little cheap volumes of Molière and Racine we had used in literature classes at the Lycée Descartes in Tours, France, during adolescence; *Rhythmique Gregorienne*, Dom Mocquereau's classic studies of Gregorian Chant; pocket scores of piano concerti in Mozart and Beethoven; and a small notebook of musical scoring—Organ Interludes for the Mass that I had composed in the village church organ loft at Kahuka in Hawaii. A small stack, it represented almost all of my worldly possessions. The pages were stained and rotting from overexposure to tropical dampness.

As I drove down the road from camp, the men in the chapel continued their doleful hymning. I drove fast until I could no longer hear them.

— The Beethoven Quartet —

At the radar shack, I arranged my carbine, books, and coffee on the desk and placed a five-gallon drum of gasoline on the radar files where I could knock it over and toss a match to it if the need arose. I forced myself to forget that I was alone, ten miles from camp, and that the only other humans on this vast and deserted strip guarded the tower far from view on the other side of the island.

When night fell, I ate some tinned rations and went outside to start the electric generator. Nothing moved. No light shone anywhere on the horizon. I returned inside and switched on the lights and the radio. To occupy the void, I dusted the desk and the files, emptied tin cans of cigarette butts, straightened the blanket on the cot, and listened to music, a light concert on the BBC Overseas program. When it palled, I turned the dial aimlessly until I came to a station from which I was greeted by sounds that affected me the way I would be if I met some beloved friend after a long absence.

The Beethoven String Quartet opus 132, one of the sublimest of all human utterances, poured from the speaker's black vents. In a setting of night and solitude and tension, Beethoven came into the tent with music that spoke intimately to the soul. The slow movement absorbed all my attention. Though I knew every note, I listened spellbound once again, as it restored in all its simplicity and grandeur the fresh vision of compassion, gratitude, and great tenderness—that vision against which men harden themselves in war until imperceptibly it is overcrusted.

With my head on the desk, I felt the dim memory return. Defensive crusts softened and gradually dissolved within, leaving me defenseless.

In its slow unfoldment, its strange Lydian harmonies, its shafts of light leading the soul into worlds where all was order, it entered the brain and heart and nervous system and totally altered them from what they had been. It created response to the profoundest mysteries, leading to spheres beyond joy or sorrow where the soul is struck with wonder and longing before a fulfillment too immense to be contained.

The war, the black alert, man murdering man—all of these things that had before been commonplace suddenly were incredible, monstrous. With the trauma of callousness dissolved, astonishment overwhelmed between what ought to be and what was.

I raised my head. The music transfigured vision. Above the khaki line of my outstretched arm, objects on the table appeared in the sharpest clarity—a package of cigarettes, the red and blue thermos, the stack of books, the loaded carbine. The gun fascinated my gaze. It lay like a lump of obscenity in clashing dissonance to the music's evocations.

I wondered if a man, tempered to his fullest humanity by this divinely mysterious order of sounds, could actually pick up that gun and kill another man.

I wondered if one of the "enemy" appeared in the doorway, and paused long enough to listen to this music, could either of us commit the tremendous act of killing?

In this musical dialogue with God, Beethoven restored too clearly the universal order of things. Hearing this, feeling it, how could a man cause another's heart to stop, erase his future eatings and love-makings and sorrows and joys, cause his love for wife or children or parents— and theirs for him—to undergo death's modulation?

The music entered its sublimest phase, a part now of my being, more me than myself. With the upsearching viola theme at the end of the *adagio*, a phrase from Pascal filtered through memory: "Why do you kill me? What? Do you not live on the other side of the water?" It turned the music coppery. Flurries of wind flapped the tent roof and I turned my chair to see lightning flare silently over the jungles. I reached to increase the volume of the music when the phone rang.

"Hey," Kaplan's voice fought through a crackle, "has it started raining out there yet?"

"No. Not yet. How are things at camp?"

"Mills busted up about an hour ago. Said he knew the world was coming to an end at midnight. He was going to kill himself. He was wild. I had to report him. They took him off to the hospital."

"Hell, I thought he might make it when he got that letter from his wife," I said. "That means he'll have a Section Eight on his record."

"I couldn't just leave him to kill himself," Kaplan said.

Above the Beethoven, I heard the first large drips of rain slam against the canvas roof. "Of course you couldn't. How's Fendler?" I asked.

"Pie-eyed. You say it's not raining there?"

"It's starting now."

"It's pouring here," he said jubilantly. "They won't come out on a night like this. Don't you know they're getting their asses soaked out there in the brush?"

"You don't think rain is going to stop suicide troops, do you?" I asked. "Have you organized any kind of defense at camp?"

"No, hell, nobody's doing anything. But listen, they can't bomb us while it's raining like this. I don't think the ground troops would strike without letting the bombers soften us up first. Look, I'll call you later if anything happens here," Kaplan said and signed off.

The Beethoven continued into the final movement as I replaced the receiver. I glanced toward the door to see a glistening screen of rain that blocked my view beyond. It seemed that the rain provided ideal cover for the Japanese to strike. They could be at the doorway before being seen.

I switched off the lights and sat on the cot with the carbine across my lap. With the conclusion of the Beethoven, a feeling of abandonment and regret spread through me. Beethoven had withdrawn, leaving me alone after he had dissolved all the callousness—including that callousness to fear that sometimes passes for bravery—and left me strangely defenseless against the night. Fright lay heavily on my stomach, with a foreboding of violence and a certainty of death.

For an instant, I saw Beethoven in the robes of a parish priest, come to prepare a condemned man's soul to meet death. At least they had not sent some dead-souled mumbler, but a saint, a master of souls. I tried to shake the image, but I could not rid myself of the idea that Beethoven's quartet had been the last sacrament.

Leaning toward the table, I searched the radio for other music, for anything that would rid me of the fixation. Nothing. In the dial light, I glanced yellow highlights on the tinned ration. I opened the can of ham and scrambled egg and ate it—not from hunger but from the consolation of a purely animal function, reassured by the simple act of eating.

As my eyes adjusted to the darkness outside, I could see some distance through the rain. If anyone approached, I would not be taken completely unaware. The rain slackened a few minutes past midnight. I felt immediately safer and walked to the door to look around. Just then the phone rang. I turned back and fumbled in the dark for the receiver.

"Are you all right out there?" the captain's voice blasted at me.

"Sure. Why?"

"Well, what the hell's going on?"

"Nothing that I know of."

"Have you been listening to Tokyo?" he asked in an easier voice.

"No, sir."

"Well, they've just broadcast that they've taken the strip and killed everyone there and they're now ready to take the rest of the island."

"Well, I'll be damned . . . "

"Has there been any shooting out there?" the captain asked.

"Not a shot."

"Those bastards. They said there were five thousand dead on the runway. I knew that was a lie but figured they might be up to something."

Then sirens and horns began to blare all over the island, signaling an air-raid alert.

"Looks like they're starting. You'd better head for cover, Griffin."

"What about leaving this place unguarded?"

"This is just to soften us up before sending in ground troops. You take cover now. If they come in, try to make it back to the tent and set it on fire." With that, he signed off. I was about to hang up when I heard the switchboard operator say, "Good luck, Griff."

The alert sirens lapsed abruptly into silence. I stepped to the door. Not a bird squawked in the rain-soaked night. I listened to the unrhythmic drip of water from the tent roof. Coral glowed white on all sides, lighted by bluish spotlight beams that coned upward at angles in search of enemy planes. The light beams reflected in puddles of water alongside stars that shone through rifts in the clouds.

Then the high, uneven rumble of airplane motors emerged from the silence. Hearing the "Washing Machine Charlies," as we called the Japanese bombers, I wondered about Mills in his hospital bed, hearing that dreaded sound. The motors droned louder, many of them.

Then I began to trot down the slope away from the radar tent toward a trench shelter we had long ago dug.

A massive pattern bombing began at the far end of the strip. I judged they were dropping one hundred pounds of bombs every twenty-five yards.

A spotlight caught one of them and other spots raked across the sky to converge on it from all angles and follow its flight. Anti-aircraft guns boomed and red splotches exploded high in the air around the bomber. The tiny fleck of silver did not swerve from its course.

As the bombers approached, I coldly concentrated on their height and the angle of the bombs' descent. Beneath me, as though detached from the upper body, my legs moved like pistons carrying me rapidly over the coral. A shell shrieked downward and I threw myself to the ground.

Covering my head with my hands, I heard my voice boom back from the wet coral against my face—*Mater misericordiae*. While I cringed against the falling bomb, I felt astonishment that these words had burst into consciousness.

The shell exploded nearby and shrapnel whizzed unseen around my body. Relief and exhaustion overwhelmed the senses. The soaked ground chilled through my shirt and coral granules gritted between my teeth. I wanted to lie still and rest, to ignore some gigantic urgency in the atmosphere. Then a new wave of motors, ack-ack explosions, and shell screeches swept toward me. I hurried to my feet to run ahead of it.

The black edge of a ravine we used for an ammunitions dump brought me to a halt. I realized I had missed our bomb shelter by a hundred yards or more. I turned to go around the ravine, listening always to the planes and the pattern of explosions. Then I headed on at the exact angle.

If it dropped its bombs they would pulverize me. I heard the high starting screech and felt intestines convulse. For an instant, I stood paralyzed, listening to the bombs hurtle toward me. Without any voluntary movement of my own, I felt my body hurl itself over the cliff and crash into the ravine.

Two days later when I regained consciousness, I lay naked in a bed. Sensations spiraled through a long tunnel of numbness. My brain roused to life without radiance, to odors of sunlight and iodine.

I skittered at the edges of awareness, wanting to disappear back into myself. Through a haze I saw white bedclothes and white figures move about. I closed it out and burrowed deeply into the numbness, the blackness, the silence.

Then there were patches of nights and dawns and patches of phrases. "Concussion . . . damage to the sub-arachnoid area of the brain . . ." And patches of faces . . .

A doctor with his thumb on my eyelid, lifting, "You see, he's still in deep trauma," as though I didn't exist. Faces hovered, fading from blurs.

"Damn, you were lucky. One of the bombs landed twelve feet on one side of you and the other landed seventeen feet on the other."

"That's luck?" I questioned.

Kaplan laughed and remarked about a sense of humor that made me furious with him. "Lucky they were using hundred-pounders," he said. "Anything bigger and you'd have been gone."

"How come they didn't take us?" I asked.

"God knows. They bombed the hell out of the strip, got the radar tent, but didn't follow it up.

The deep inside fog remained between me and myself. Who were my sisters? Yes, I knew I had sisters but what were their names? It lay in me like a shameful secret, something I must never divulge.

"Griffin?"

I opened my eyes. "Kaplan?"

"Yeah. Do you want anything?

"Yes . . . "

"What do you want, buddy. You just name it . . . "

"The Beethoven . . . "

"Griff, goddammit, don't talk like that or they'll never let you out of here," Kaplan pleaded.

I felt caged, cramped within head and body, certain the Beethoven would release me. The fog thickened and thinned but the sunlight remained too brilliant. Only later did I realize that something had happened to my vision.

I received mail that I could not read, but I pretended to read. I felt I must not let them know. I had been in the army too long. I had enough points to get back to the States, if I could ever get medically cleared. But I knew if they found anything else wrong, they would keep me in army hospitals perhaps forever. I began to play the role against them. I perfected the role in all its details, with an obsessive patience and cunning—the role of the fully recovered man.

Finally, the day came. I stood in a little room with the doctors and laughed and bid them all good-bye. But one of them hedged.

"He should not be released," the chief doctor told the others. "Look at his eyes. He's still in a traumatic state."

"Please," I said, suddenly without any defenses. "I'll go to the best doctors once I get home. Don't keep me here. I've been in the Pacific over three years. It's my turn to get out. If you don't let me go now, I'll be here forever. It's the heat and the fact I didn't sleep last night that makes me look like this. I promise you, I'm really well enough to go."

They understood. They wavered, but finally one of the doctors said, "I guess it will be okay," as though he did not believe it at all.

"We'll release you," the chief doctor said, "but you must get to your doctor immediately after mustering out."

"I promise I will," I said pleadingly.

"Okay, then you're dismissed, soldier," the chief said.

I thanked him profusely.

"Good luck," they all chimed in as I left their office.

— 20/200 —

Few images penetrated the numbness I felt during the long boat trip across the Pacific back to the States. Awareness was there, hovering in the background except for moments when it pulsed forward in a sharp perception of the ship's crowded hold, where we slept in tiers of hammocks. There was also the sight of the ocean from the ship's rail—an endless surging of blue water and white spume—and again an intense starlit night when someone played polkas with dazzling skill on the accordion. All of the images were permeated with an undercurrent of jubilance that the war was over and we were going home.

A band met us when the ship docked after thirty-one days at sea. Girls waved white handkerchiefs. Some man in civilian clothes made a speech that howled at us from the loudspeakers. Even an hour's delay in getting out of the army irritated us. But if we viewed these patriotic shenanigans sourly, we would not have wanted our arrival ignored.

I had been in the army more than four years, in the Pacific area three years and three months. I was not out yet, but I was close now. I feared they might never release me if my condition were discovered. We'd heard of others returning stateside for release, only to be hospitalized again.

Shadows

To be hospitalized in the army was to be still in the army, to be a ward, to be under obedience, to be unfree. And after all the years of taking orders, we were avid for the freedom to decide things for ourselves, to act on our own decisions. Five minutes longer would be too long.

We disembarked late that afternoon and were immediately transported to an island near San Francisco. Another island. We were still not free to walk into a town.

They served us a festive dinner in the mess hall—our first whole milk and first steaks in years. We ate and drank, comparing these tastes to our memories of prewar foods. But our systems, so long unaccustomed to fresh nourishment, reacted as though it were poison.

We walked as near as possible to the guarded shore at dusk, looking across the water to the mainland. Entertainment was provided, but few of us went. In a time of such drastic change, we did not celebrate. We sought to absorb it as quietly as possible. We strolled like shadows in the twilight until, one by one, as the pains hit, those shadows would suddenly hasten their steps and move directly to the latrines.

The following morning we began mustering out. Long lines of clerks interviewed us and prepared our discharge papers. The young corporal who interviewed me spoke through a cigarette in his mouth and typed with spectacular rapidity.

"Any injuries?"

"None . . . "

The word came out, almost inaudible to me, so unconvincing I was sure he would not believe me.

I waited for him to check the stack for my medical record. I heard his fingers clack four times on the keys as he stared straight ahead through the smoke of his mouthed cigarette.

"How many months overseas?"

"Thirty-nine."

"Okay, next," he shouted and I got into another line.

In the shuffle we were separated from men with whom we had lived for years—without a good-bye. Each group went from building to building.

I thought I was through with the important matters and my attention hazed to what happened, until we were marched into a room. The words came through dimly at first and then focused quickly into fright. We were being told to strip naked, line up, and prepare for a final examination.

Doctors hurried in and I was relieved to see that this would be only a superficial examination. They stethoscoped us, probed into our genitals to check for hernia, and made other rapid tests. Within moments that mass of naked humanity was declared free from hernia, heart disease, and venereal infection. We moved out to make room for the following batch of weary soldiers.

Next we were sent for eye tests. I struggled to read the charts as the technician held a cardboard over each eye. Without comment, he marked his findings on my papers and handed them to me. Outside, I asked a soldier to read the results of the eye test. He told me I had 20/200 vision.

"That's not possible," I said.

"That's what it says here," he answered.

I was stupefied. I felt I could see reasonably well and yet 20/200 meant that I could see at 20 feet what a person with normal vision could see at 200 feet. I was legally blind.

We continued through a series of interminable lines. Standing in the sunlight, I saw a tall, heavily decorated black sergeant who was being berated by the young white corporal who had charge of getting our group into the proper lines.

"You may be a damned hero overseas, but you're nothing but a nigger here—and don't you forget it."

I approached the gathering group.

The sergeant, his body in a violent tremble, whispered: "I've been four years fighting for this mother-fucking country. I'm damned if I'm coming back to this shit."

"You're back to it all right," the corporal shouted back.

An older white soldier edged toward the black sergeant, who was losing all control of his nerves. The crowd, made up of overseas veterans converged around the two men. If the sergeant, now that he was home, were to strike a white corporal, he might never get out of the brig. But the corporal appeared to be pushing him into such action.

Even those of us who were southerners could not stomach this abuse of a man who had fought overseas in a segregated unit for his country. We knew very well that the black troops had held the perimeters between us and the Japanese, and this was an injustice we found difficult to swallow, no matter how prejudiced we might have been.

The older soldier elbowed past the sergeant and spoke to the corporal in a toneless voice. "If you don't want your ass beat into the ground," he said, "you'd better shut that big mouth of yours right now."

"I'm in charge here," the corporal said loudly. "Your sergeant stripes don't mean a thing to me. All of you are under my orders."

Shadows

The older soldier stood face to face with the corporal. "Listen, you screwed up little USO soldier, you lay off him, and right now, or you're going to walk through life without an ass."

The rest of us nodded agreement.

The corporal shut up.

The sergeant stood there shaking his head and saying in a thin voice: "I can't stand this shit. I know I can't stand coming back to this."

We drifted away from him, leaving him alone, wondering what would become of such a man. The world was not overpopulated with little white corporals, but there were still too many.

Shortly before noon, my turn came at the pay window. I was paid and handed official discharge papers.

"Where do I go?" I asked.

"Out that gate, buddy, and then anywhere your heart desires," said an M.P. with a grand flourish of his hand.

It felt strange not needing a pass to go through a gate. I picked up my blue denim duffel bag and walked out of the military compound. About ten feet beyond, at the curb, the autumn sun warmed my back and the sensation of intense relief flowed into me.

On December 15, 1945, after years of obeying orders, I was free to go in whatever direction I chose. I took a taxi to the airport and, after waiting six hours, I took the first plane going to Texas. Because there were no more flights to the Dallas-Fort Worth area until the next morning, I boarded a plane departing for San Antonio.

I walked for a long time aimlessly through the streets of San Antonio, savoring the marvel of freedom. Only my uniform kept the illusion from being complete. I walked into a clothing store and looked around. A very dignified man, middle-aged, approached and asked if he could help me.

"I want a suit, a topcoat, a tie, a shirt, a pair of socks, and even some underwear," I said.

"You're going to shed the whole works, are you, son?"

"The whole works."

"You're not the first," he said in a voice that sounded sad, implying that it was not that great to be a civilian once again. He asked me when I wanted to pick up the suit.

"I won't buy it unless I can wait for the alteration. I want it now."

"We'll do our best," he said.

He fitted the suit first and had the tailor make the markings.

In the dressing room, I put on new underwear, bundled my uniform and shoes into a package and waited for the suit to be delivered. I spent the time going through the barracks bag. I had retained only the objects I prized and had carried halfway around the world.

In the afternoon, after leaving most of my possessions in the dressing room at the clothing store, I took a plane to Fort Worth and telephoned my parents from the airport. I awaited them in front of the airport, aware that they had suffered agonies during the Morotai black alert, as well as my subsequent recuperation. I braced for the meeting, but when their car drove up the ramp, I began losing control in the emotion of seeing them again after such a long absence.

My mother opened the car door and kept repeating: "Why you look fine . . . just fine." She stood back after kissing me. I kissed my dad and felt his embrace as he said: "You sure do." My mother's fingertips touched my face and she began to weep.

"I'm sorry, honey, I promised myself not to cry. But I can't help it."

We drove home, making the unimportant conversation that masks the meaning of the emotions.

"It's a nice car," I told my dad.

"Yeah, it runs pretty good," he replied.

I felt dazed, without feeling, yet happiness and peace filtered through the terrible deadness.

At home, my twin sisters rushed from the house to embrace me. They seemed extraordinarily grown now, but I was distressed to find myself blanking out on their names.

My parents had hoarded rations and bought the finest steaks they could find. They served an opulent homecoming dinner. The strangeness of being back in a family, in the presence of women, soon gave way to dim familiarity—a remembrance of how things once were and should be in a family. Surrounded by their discretion and kindness, my stupor dissolved to enthusiasm.

I sat in an overstuffed chair for the first time in years and listened intently. Looking around the room, I felt stiff in new clothes, for they seemed as comfortable as the casual clothes they wore.

I discovered that people could speak all evening without uttering any four-letter words. And I discovered also that, with no real strain, I could carry on a conversation without those same words.

Only then did I realize that I was fully and finally out of the jungles; that I was in a world of concrete and stone, schools and parks, prosperity and comfort; and most overwhelming of all, a world where women once again existed, and there were children romping on well-kept lawns.

We retired late, but I could not sleep because the bed was actually too comfortable and the strangeness of being in a room with a floor and rugs and windows and furniture fascinated me—and to be there alone, to have privacy, not to hear snores and breathing and nightmares of others.

I got up and turned on the light to see it all once again.

My sisters saw the light under the door and crept in to join me. The three of us smoked cigarettes and talked about their husbands, both away in service. An overwhelming sense of well-being surrounded us as we talked and laughed deep into the night.

The eye specialist I consulted in Fort Worth sent me to be examined by a neurosurgeon. After tests and an examination, he advised me to give up the idea of continuing my medical studies.

Before the war, I had been a student research assistant to Dr. Pierre Fromenty at the asylum in Tours, France. The mental hospital worked in conjunction with the medical school at the University of Poitiers, also in Tours. I was doing coursework at the university toward earning a degree in psychiatry. Assisting Dr. Fromenty in the development of sound therapy led to specialized studies in music as it relates to the physics of sound. I concentrated on medieval music, particularly Gregorian Chant, because of its proven curative effects upon even the most alienated patients.

I studied on my own while in the service, constantly reading medical texts and musical scores, as well as playing keyboard instruments and developing new compositions whenever I got a pass to Hawaii or the Philippines.

The neurosurgeon's suggestion that I could not continue medical studies—and that I should sit back and wait simply because I was to be blind—was impossible to accept.

The doctor had not meant to be blunt. He tried to explain by saying: "There's still a great deal about the brain that we don't yet know."

I thanked him for his candor.

He sent me back to the eye specialist, who fitted me with thick lenses, deeply tinted to keep the light bearable. Even with these, the correction was not sufficient for normal reading.

I acquired a powerful magnifying glass—round, small in diameter, with a short wooden handle. I kept the glass hidden to avoid the questions and the concern it would evoke.

Since the vision was already too poor to consider finishing medical studies, I decided to shift all my energies to music. Music had been my first love before I became impassioned with the sciences. My experience with Dr. Fromenty had brought music back to the center of life.

Scattered Shadows

Return visits to the eye specialist confirmed a rapid deterioration of sight. The doctor warned that I could not count on usable vision for much longer, perhaps only a year. That was all I needed to know.

The next day I made an overseas phone call to register for classes as a composition student at the great Fontainebleau Conservatory in France.

I would study with legendary teachers like Nadia Boulanger and Jean Batalla. And I would also renew an earlier friendship with the famous pianists Robert Casadesus and wife Gaby and their gifted children, who were continuing a long tradition as the first family of French music.

⏤ Return to France ⏤

In the summer of 1946, I returned to France to spend the remaining months of my sighted life. There, in the magnificent surroundings of the Palace of Fontainebleau, nourished by music, the act of seeing became its own intimate and personal drama. And it became very nearly sublime.

I led one life as a conservatory student and another, hidden life as a man looking avidly on things with the peculiar light of knowing he sees them for the last time. I told no one. I felt that losing my sight was a thing I had to do alone.

My attempts to hide my condition were not always successful. Toward the end of summer, the celebrated baritone Pierre Bernac had arrived in Fontainebleau to give a recital with Gaby Casadesus.

Early one afternoon, I was with Bernac and Gaby in the empty concert room of the palace, where they prepared to rehearse for the concert later that evening. Seeing my reluctance to leave them, Gaby asked Bernac if he minded my staying.

"Of course not," he said. "He can turn the pages for you."

Standing behind Gaby Casadesus at the piano, I saw the music as a white page with blurred gray notes. She played the accompaniment while Bernac sang to rows of empty seats.

The first page ended with a descending scale, which I saw as a streak. I managed to turn it correctly. However, on the second page, I could make out nothing, and I knew I would never be able to bluff my way through.

I kept my gaze fixed on Gaby's head, thinking she might nod at the point where the page should be turned.

They halted in mid-phrase.

Bernac sighed with disgust, the disgust of a master musician who wondered how an advanced music student could fail to follow such a simple score.

I apologized, muttering, "The light is so poor in here. I'm terribly sorry." They passed it off gently. Perhaps a glance was exchanged.

Gaby reproached herself. "It's my fault. I should have memorized the top few measures of each page."

I knew that Gaby had suspected I could not see for some time now. I wondered, in view of the abrupt change in Bernac's manner, if he did not now understand also. He offered me a chair on the empty stage and the two continued without my help.

I had no doubt Bernac had guessed the truth when he began to sing Gounod's *Berceuse*. He turned directly to me and, at the point where the mother tells the child to close its eyes, Bernac leaned over me and sang in a whisper, pleadingly, infusing the words with direct meaning that the three of us understood in an almost unbearable evocation. Then Bernac's voice moved away from me as he continued.

No mention of it was made afterward.

When they had finished rehearsing, I crossed the street to the Hotel d'Albe. Climbing the narrow wood steps to the third floor, I asked myself why I had not told them. But the answer was clear.

I feared myself—feared that I would not be able to cope with the temptation to play the tragic figure, to become the noble sufferer accepting the world's pity. My silence was the only guarantee against falling into that trap.

I opened the door to my room. Lighted by one dormer window and sparsely furnished with a bed, a writing table, and a washstand, it gave out its welcome hints of poverty and warmth. The desk and bed were stacked with scores of Bach, Mozart, Chopin, Stravinsky, Hindemith, and with cheap twenty-franc volumes of paperback classics. With the aid of the magnifying glass, I immersed myself in the works of Heraclitus, Epictetus, and Aurelius.

They refreshed the dim certainties within, assuring me that I had a will that was free and therefore a right to understand that tragedy lay not in any condition, as Epictetus had said, but merely in humanity's concepts of that condition. I knew that my fiercest struggles would not be against losing sight, but against the assaults of public opinion about blindness that would judge my condition tragic.

I knew that there were truths in this experience that I had not found, and that I must discover them or risk being sucked into the vortex of society's castrating pity. These truths were certainly not to be found in the platitudes: "You must not be bitter. You must take this like a man." They meant nothing. My fear and hatred of blindness lay in the dread of its forcing me to adopt a mask—the "brave blind man" mask—that might edify others even while it corroded me with its falsity.

I read and analyzed music through my glass. The jubilant mystery of Mozart—that "second innocence"—preoccupied me. This had meant not the innocence of ignorance but the innocence of knowledge.

I sought to analyze it from the black notes on white paper of the Mozart score, to catch this supreme secret of which Mozart's art was the embodiment, for it contained the answer to the way I searched for— not musically but in my humanity.

But when the headaches started, I paced the floor and smoked too many cigarettes and raged with some focusless love. I could make no sense of any of it. Then I looked out the window on a view into the flower-filled courtyard below. I looked down on the heads and shoulders of conservatory students who sat on benches doing their lessons in harmony and counterpoint. And I marveled at the sight of hair and flesh and the evidence of intelligence as they worked. A floor below to my left, I saw Bernac and Robert Casadesus look out the window of Bernac's room. All of it registered. All of it was new. Sunlight glistened from Casadesus's balding crown. Lichen grew up the stone wall, touching Bernac's unheeding fingers on the windowsill.

It was enough. I saw these things as few others would be privileged to see them and, indeed, as I had never seen them before—with a sense of astonishment. I stored them, engraved them, not in my mind but in some deeper place of the passions. I became aware of the guilt of jaded eyes. Now I was given a few months in which to make up for the times when I had walked along streets and not deigned to look, when I had turned away from good hearts because they were hidden behind unattractive physical features.

Faced with nothing, very little becomes everything.

The sight of a pin, a hair, a leaf, a glass of water—these filled my being with trembling excitement.

The plants in the courtyard, the cobblestones, the lampposts, the faces of strangers—I no longer took them in and bound them up in me. Instead I went out to them, focused on them, immersed myself in them—they retained their values, their own identities and essences.

My room became lonely at twilight. Dusk brought me face to face with the inevitable questions. How did a man without sight find love? Was it possible in the human realm to love what one could not see? Was not love a thing of glances and gestures? These questions haunted me in their murkiness when I tried to solve them alone. I needed to converse with a sightless person. How could any sighted person know these answers or even speculate intelligently about them?

But the strange light of fascination shone through the murkiness. It was like the light I had seen in kitchens when I walked past homes in the evening. How often I had dreamed of the time when I would belong in such a kitchen, enclosed there from the nakedness of dusk with my wife and children, while another walked outside and noticed the glow and perhaps dreamed of the time when he would belong in his own kitchen.

The room chilled rapidly after sunset. I took off my clothes and bathed, trembling in the half-light of the open window. Using a sponge and the pitcher of unheated water from the washstand, I soaped and rinsed and dried. The activity and fresh clothes destroyed my somberness.

It was time to go to Bernac's recital and then to dinner with friends. The light of dedication and its examples—like that other light in the distant kitchen—surrounded me with its illumination. At dinner after the concert, I looked at Robert Casadesus's hands, the hands of a master never ashamed to practice the simplest passage for hours. I looked into the faces of Gaby and Bernac and Nadia Boulanger, seeing faces that were long ago unmasked and clarified by work and sacrifice and devotion. I thought of their years of preparation in lonely rooms before they had showed the world the finished product of art's past mastery.

After dinner, we walked to a sidewalk café near the palace, where we sat under an awning, drinking the unripe beer they served in postwar France. From an overhead speaker, Edwin Fischer's performance of the Beethoven *Emperor Concerto* sang out into the darkness of cobblestone streets. The bitter fragrance of Robert's pipe tobacco scented the chill night air. Students, exalted by Bernac's concert and the beer, talked too loudly about Schoenberg and Stravinsky, while Beethoven surrounded us in the yellow lamplight.

Casadesus glowered at them and mumbled about "the little respect they have for music." He leaned across the table, touching my hand with his pipe stem. "Why do you stay here and listen to these conversations?"

"God knows," I said.

"You should be out finding yourself a wife. You should marry now. At your age, you should spend all your time making love . . . "

Gaby interrupted her husband. "But since when do you stick your nose into other people's business like that?"

Robert puffed his pipe benignly. Then he leaned toward me and said: "It is better to make love than to discuss theory, my friend. You learn more about art and truth that way. I don't understand why you remain here. If I were you, I'd go back to—"

"Why do you stay here?" I asked.

"Because I'm old. It's my duty. I'm now an *educator*," he sneered at the word. "But you are young. I don't understand why you stay on here."

"Because he wants to hear the Beethoven, perhaps," Gaby retorted. "To hear it in peace and without your interference . . . "

"Perhaps," Robert said and shrugged.

When the final cadence of the Beethoven sounded, there was a loud upswing of applause, and then the announcer broke through to say that the program would continue after a brief intermission.

Bernac rose, stretched, and said: "I think I'll go turn in." He turned to me and asked: "Would you like to walk back to the hotel with me?"

I stood and, after saying good night to everyone, Bernac and I walked toward the hotel, his hand on my elbow, guiding me.

"You won't find what you're looking for here, you know," he said in a casual tone. "That's what Robert was trying to tell you."

"I know you're right," I said.

"You find what you're looking for alone—never in a crowd. You won't get it from Robert or Gaby or Nadia or me. We can give you a hint, show you how to work hard and not to despise loneliness, but nothing much more. Each of us had to do it alone. It would have been commonplace, even worthless, if we hadn't."

We walked in silence until we entered the hotel courtyard. Bernac turned and said: "May I ask you something?"

"Of course."

"Your eyesight . . . why do you keep it a secret?"

"You just said you had to do it alone. If I told everyone, I'd be in the midst of the crowd."

"I see. Will it get worse?"

"Yes."

"Soon?"

"Yes—it goes fast now." His hand dropped away from my elbow as though the touch suddenly burned him.

When we had reached the door of his room, he said "Good night," and then hastily asked: "Oh, can you make it to your room all right?"

"I'm fine," I assured him. "Good night, and thank you for the talk."

Mail lay under the door when I entered my room. I picked it up and carried it to the table. With the magnifying glass, I studied the top letter. It was from Friar Marie-Bruno Hussar, written on the stationery of the Dominican monastery, the Convent of St. Jacques in Paris. He was the older brother of my closest friend in Tours, Jean Hussar, with whom I had worked in the French Underground. After I had escaped from the

Nazis in France and returned to the States, Jean was killed fighting with the free French against the Germans.

The friar wrote that he had received extraordinary permission from his superior, allowing me to visit, and that I was expected there early next month. "Your stay here will be a good transition between Fontainebleau and the studies you will make at the Abbey of Solesmes," he wrote. At the end, he added: "My poor friend, why are you so determined to be brave? Bravery of this sort is nothing but a role you play. You must work toward finding a way that will not require you to play roles . . . "

Insomnia. I sat on the edge of the bed in pajamas and drank a glass of red wine. In the pale amber light of a single globe, I listened intently to the silences of the hotel. Sleep was a waste. I put it off, wanting it but fighting against it. I felt I should later begrudge every moment passed in darkness that could have been passed in light. But the wine drugged my heart and sleep pressed heavily. I turned off the light at the wall switch and walked barefoot across the wooden floor to the bed.

I was almost asleep when footsteps rumbled on the stairs. The hope that someone might be coming to visit brought me fully awake. But if a friend should come and see no light under the door he would go away. I hurried to the wall and flipped on the switch. With my ear against the door, I listened to muffled voices.

"I hope this will be all right for tonight. Tomorrow I can put you in a much nicer room downstairs." I visualized the proprietor, a fat middle-aged man with his habitual smile.

"I'm sure it'll be fine," a woman said, her voice full and mature. A man mumbled agreement. A key grated in the lock. I heard the door bump against the thin wall that separated our rooms.

"Here are the towels. I think you'll find the bed comfortable. The water closet is directly across the hall. Good night, and may you rest well."

I turned off the light and listened to the proprietor shuffle downstairs.

"Are you tired?" the man asked from the adjoining room.

"No . . . " the woman answered tentatively.

I listened to footsteps, to the sounds of unpacking, to the silence, realizing that this was the way I would know all things in the future.

They seldom spoke. I judged them to be a couple long married who no longer needed many words to communicate. The ease of their silence was extended through the wall. In darkness, seated on the floor with my back to their wall, I followed their movements.

Keys and coins jingled and I knew the man was removing his pants.

The woman coughed and almost immediately sniffed. Shod footsteps became the padding of bare feet. Water gurgled into a glass. A moment later the glass thumped back into the saucer.

Bare footsteps moved to the door. "All right?" the man asked.

"All right," she said, creaking the bed as she crawled into it.

I heard a click. His footsteps moved toward the bed cautiously now, his cadence altered by darkness.

They settled into bed and I envisioned them lying side by side under the same covers. Did they lie on their backs, I wondered, or face to face? It did not matter. What mattered was that they were together, sharing the warmth.

Cold air through the open window chilled me, but I was reluctant to move. The invisible scene, with its overtones of confidence and intimacy, stirred my deepest hungers. A middle-aged couple went to bed, as they did all over the world in all times.

But at that moment they revealed something essential to the heart. My longing was fixed on this subtle sensation of drifting off to sleep in dim awareness that a part of myself slept beside me.

— Friar Marie-Bruno —

Scaling green paint showed worm-pocked wood on the door of the Convent of St. Jacques. I hesitated before ringing the bell, watching my taxi ascend the narrow street past a jumble of stores, cafés, fruit stands and cheap apartments that stretched upward into distant haze under a cold noonday September sun. In the other direction, I looked down the street's steep incline, past the convent's ugly red brick walls with their chalked obscenities, to the intersection of St. Jacques Boulevard, where men walked in and out of a green metal public urinal. This view was streaked by cars rushing past trees on each side of the grand promenade.

The idea of leaving this sunlit and bustling quarter of Paris for the shadowed poverty of the cloister repelled me. I waited, afraid suddenly to venture into this place of silence where men devoted themselves to God.

Without pulling the bell chain, I tried the knob. The door opened to the odor of boiling cabbages and onions, faintly overladen with the fragrance of cold incense from the chapel door to my right. I closed the door again, rang the bell, and stepped back beside my suitcases. After a long wait, the door opened.

"Is it really you?" Marie-Bruno asked quietly. He was smaller than I had remembered, and his hair, clipped in the Dominican tonsure as a circle around his head, changed his appearance. The eyes, clear and large in his skeletal face, dominated his figure. It was impossible to escape them and, as they peered into me, I felt what I had felt with few people in my life—the instant certainty that here was a man who had been burned with all the pain and love that men can know, and from whom nothing needed to be hidden.

He insisted on carrying my two heavy bags up to the third floor and into my cell. I followed the rustle of his white robes through the shadows of the corridors toward the cell I would occupy.

In the cell, we sat for a moment, talking of his brother, Jean Hussar, a friend of my school days in Tours who had worked with me in smuggling German and Austrian Jews to safety at the beginning of the war. I had met Marie-Bruno before his entry into the religious life, when, as André Hussar, a scientist, graduate of the famed Ecole Polytechnique in Paris, had visited Jean in Tours. Even then, his reputation for sanctity had made me ill at ease until the moment when we had faced each other and his kindness had melted my discomfort.

Now, more than six years later, his face was thinner and more deeply seamed. It was as though a great simplification had clarified his features and expression, stripping him of all self-consciousness. His eyes spoke his awe, his astonishment with some mystery I could not fathom.

In the heavily patched robe and black boot-shoes, he was the picture of voluntary poverty. I realized I had entered a world where all standards were altered from those I knew. All the things that were important in the world—position, ambition, accomplishment, success, esteem—meant nothing within these rooms. If I were a derelict in rags, he would view me with the same expression. I found this frustrating. I was poorest precisely in the qualities he would value most.

A short time later, I was relieved when he left me alone in the cell. I sat on the cot and allowed time for the new surroundings to become familiar. The plank floor, mealy from countless scrubbings, reflected soft light from the single window. I flicked on the bed lamp to test the weak globe. It appeared to add no light. I got up and walked to the washstand with its white bowl and pitcher of water, filled and waiting for use; beside the bowl on a plastic dish was a piece of soap already much used.

The only window looked across the high convent wall to an apartment house, as ugly as man and chrome could make it. Clothes hung at some of the windows on improvised lines to dry in the sun. At one window, a woman in a negligee sat motionless with her head against the glass. In the adjoining apartment, daylight crossed the figure of a man, probably a night worker, asleep on a bed. Only a few inches of wall separated him from the woman next door. From this third-story window, I glimpsed them in a way they could never glimpse one another. Silence ruled in the Dominican house, but horns blared and traffic rumbled on the boulevard below. Shouting children and street vendors added to the din.

I wondered how a man could have any spiritual life, any sense of elevation in such a dismal place. I remained in an irritating confusion of sentiments, realizing that to Marie-Bruno and his brothers the comfort or discomfort, the beauty or ugliness of surroundings made no difference.

After unpacking, I poured water from the pitcher into the bowl and washed my hands with the lye soap. Then I carried the bowl to empty it in the small toilet cubicle at the end of the corridor. A young man in white robes nodded without interrupting his mopping of the hall.

Inside the cubicle, I closed the door with my foot and poured the water into the toilet. On a nail driven into the wall, I noted a sheaf of cheap paper with mimeographing on one side, cut into squares, that served as toilet tissue, which was almost unobtainable in postwar France. I bent down to study the printing but could not decipher it, so I lifted the top sheet from the nail and carried it into the cell, where I examined it with my magnifying glass. It appeared to be intended for novices to study. I read:

It is the gift of self that liberates. This gift is immensely difficult to accomplish because man's nature has a thousand artifices with which to delude him. These may give him the delusion that he loves God, that he is generous and he has reached the sublimest spheres of spirituality, when in reality there remains the infatuation of the self. This is so subtle, so enveloping, so intangible that we can only liberate ourselves with the help of the Holy Spirit. It reduces itself to the fact that we must become Christ through the intimate union of our wills to His.

The text continued on the back of the paper. I turned it over to read:

If we can say to God, from the depths of our souls, without the slightest mental reservation: "Not my will, Father, but thine," we can be sure that we are true. Once this conformity of the human will to the Divine Will has been reached, then God communicates His Being to that soul and transforms it into Himself, because He sees nothing in the soul that He does not see in Himself, since the soul has labored to strip itself of all things that are not God.

As I had felt estranged from the scene of the middle-aged couple retiring at the hotel in Fountainebleau—an outsider who observed that and longed for it—so I felt just as estranged here. I looked on, aware that somewhere in the building's wretched entrails these truths—so strange to me—were their reality.

But it was too new. It repelled and frightened me. I sensed the drama of men's souls struggling to make themselves perfectly conformable to the workings of God within them. And this seemed an occupation out of our time, out of our concepts of balance and proportion. It repelled, but it stabbed painfully inward for recognition.

To escape the solitary cell, its stained walls and forbidding crucifix, I wandered downstairs into the chapel. A center partition separated the portion where the monks chanted their offices from the side where the people of the quarter attended.

No one spoke. When I passed them in the corridors, they lowered their tonsured heads in a bow and smiled toward the floor. They were young, mostly in their middle twenties, vigorous in their movements. Their eyes were all alike—painfully alive and clear, painfully reflecting some mysterious joy. But I saw none of the smoldering traces of fanaticism that sometimes tend to distort the eyes of the religious.

I took lunch in a small side room that adjoined the refectory. Through an open door, I saw monks and novices seated before their plates as though sculpted there. The high chanting voice of a reader accompanied the eating of our meal, which consisted of steamed veal, cabbages and potatoes. Other than the occasional sound of silverware touching plates and the reader's monotonous voice, the meal was taken in silence.

After lunch, I returned to the cell. The skies turned black and it began to rain during the mid-afternoon. Chill penetrated as the downpour splattered against the window of the cell. I lay on the cot, then pulled a blanket over me, and slept.

When a shout outside awakened me in late afternoon, I went to the window and looked down into the street. A man in a black raincoat and rainhat pushed a fruit cart with metal-rimmed wheels over the cobblestones, calling out his wares.

I hurried down into the street and bought a magnificent peach. "Do you live in the quarter?" I asked, wanting to hear a human voice.

"Of course," he replied, as though my question were idiotic.

I walked under the trees along the promenade as the sun attempted to break through thinning clouds. Birds on lower branches fluttered away, showering down raindrops from the disturbed leaves. The clean-washed air carried the heavy fragrance of roasting coffee from spice shops nearby.

I finished my peach and tossed the seed into the gutter's rivulet before crossing over to a neighborhood café. The room was empty except for one client, an elderly man who eyed me above his newspaper. A waiter took my order for a glass of Dubonnet, bowed slightly and left. I saw the dullness of eyes. I knew they had not changed, but that I was comparing them now to the eyes in the Dominican house. I glanced at the mirror behind the bar. My heavily tinted glasses masked my own eyes.

The atmosphere of poverty in the quarter and the ugliness of the brick buildings, combined with dark skies and the harder rain that now began, filled me with an almost desperate desire to get away, to escape to those brighter sectors of Paris, even though I knew there was no escape. How often as a student working with Dr. Fromenty at the asylum had we struggled to get patients to accept and face the consequences of their actions, to draw strength by plunging directly into the core of difficulties. I knew it was the only way, and I told myself I must return to the empty cell and swallow the medicine prescribed by wisdom.

My desires to escape into pleasure, into the bright places of sensuality vanished. They centered on the cell and drew me back with such force that I was astonished.

When I returned, soaked with rain, I found books stacked on the table. I hurriedly stripped off the wet clothes and dried with a towel that hung beside the washstand. Bewilderment returned. I had tasted this life only a few hours and had been repelled by it. But now on my reentry, the cell welcomed me in its coldness and hinted satisfactions. As I was reaching into my suitcase for dry clothes, there was a knock, discreet and questioning, at the door.

"Yes," I called out. The door opened, closed. "Come in," I said.

It opened, Marie-Bruno entered and deliberately turned his back. Puzzled for a moment, I realized he was uncomfortable in the cell with me unclothed in this way. "I'm sorry," I said, hastening into clothes. "I was in the army so long that I've forgotten about propriety."

"That's all right," he reassured me, not turning his head from the wall. "I just wanted to see if you were all right. If you need anything here, you must simply ask for it, without any hesitation."

"Thank you. I'm dressed now if you want to stop studying the wall."

Shadows

He turned to me. "I had hoped to spend more time with you at first, but we have been kept busy all day cleaning up the leaks. This place needs new roofing. In fact it needs everything. Even the walls leak."

Rain muffled noises and blotted out the dusk views. Electric lights from the apartment windows shone as diffuse yellow splotches in the gray welter of rain. Time slowed at twilight as I waited for the bell.

A strange felicity between body and spirit pervaded the atmosphere, and I began to savor unashamedly the simple acts of combing my hair and tying shoelaces.

Each of these acts became worthy of full attention.

In the soft light, the walls cast off resonances of past occupants who had known these same spaces in contentment or anguish; men unknown to me and yet who were like me. The sagging cot had known their bodies, supported them in moments of darkness and light, of temptation and doubt, as they began hearing the dim chanting voices reverberate down corridors of the soul. And, too, it had witnessed some in their moments of acceptance and peace and lightness of spirit.

The bell sent its silver tinkle through the halls. I felt my way down the dark stairs, guided by the rumble of beginning prayers. In the chapel, illumined by the glow of candles, men and women knelt. A red sanctuary lamp, suspended on a chain from the ceiling, flickered brightly.

I knelt in a pew at the back and listened, aware that the world moved outside in all its loving and hating activities, while in here people withdrew into the hush for a time before plunging back into the streets.

The stale fragrance of incense mingled with odors of rubber galoshes, damp hair, and stenched clothing. I saw only older people, each hunched and withdrawn into a bundle. The rhythm of murmured prayers carried me like the waves of a sea, feelingless, unthinking, profoundly relieved to drift, unknown there in the obscurity.

Those days passed in a gray sameness of rain views. I entered their monastic routine and found there, despite the constant discomfort and unrelieved ugliness of surroundings, the undercurrent of adventure that lies invisible beneath the tranquil surface of the religious life—to arrive at a state of perfect docility to God's working within.

Here was no hint of pietism, but rather the clarity of cold water that washed away the residues.

Each day consisted of prayer, study, and physical labor, although as a guest I did no work, except to clean the cell. We began with the bell to rise at six in the morning, when we washed our faces and straightened our beds, then dressed and attended the first office of *Prime* at six-thirty.

This was followed by private Masses. An hour later we recited *Terce* and attended Mass. Around eight, after an hour of prayer, we went to the refectory for our breakfast of coarse brown bread and coffee. The morning passed in study, spiritual conferences, cleaning chores, and meditation.

At fifteen minutes after noon we recited the offices of *Sexte* and *None*. After these short offices, we returned to the refectory for our noon meal, taken in silence. Then, just before two, we said the long, beautiful office of *Vespers*, followed by a brief recreational period. The afternoons were taken up with study, more spiritual conferences, and work until nearly seven, when we recited the rosary, followed by *Compline* and a time of silent prayer. We took supper around eight in the evening and at nine we recited the offices of *Matins* and *Lauds*, offices that overflowed with praise. Thus each day ended on this tone of jubilation.

I soon perceived that my stay would not be a matter of instruction. No one would seek to guide me in anything. I was left alone to absorb what I could from the atmosphere, from the rhythms of monastic life, and from the liturgy. All needs were cared for.

Each day someone put fresh water in the pitcher on the washstand. Each day someone came into the cell, which I cleaned inexpertly, and put the finishing touches on it. But all of this was done anonymously. I noticed I was given supplementary food—a piece of meat would appear on my plate when the others had none.

During the periods of physical labor, I was permitted to keep up piano practice on the small upright in the recreation room. I practiced Bach and Mozart, and though these monks were mostly connoisseurs and I played poorly, they thanked me for sending music through the corridors.

My deepest bewilderment—and edification—lay in finding that all my preconceptions of monastic formation were utterly false. I had imagined that men seeking union with God languished in a state of mystical trauma, soaring above the baser aspects of daily living. But here men lived in intimacy with the rich polyphony of philosophy and theology rather than with some lyrical emotionalism. The odors of cabbages and mop water no longer jarred against the fragrance of incense, but were complementary.

At certain hours we filed into a room for the spiritual conferences. Some took notes as we listened, seated behind long tables. The director faced us, speaking in a matter-of-fact voice of the truths wherein God was the central term. I had to twist my brain to accommodate it. He was not just saying the right words, he believed what he was saying.

God was not being interpreted according to our lights, prejudices and comforts. We were being shown that we must adjust our lights and prejudices and comforts to the truth of God.

It made me uneasy because it threatened the superficial liberty and objectivity I thought I possessed. I began to feel the terrible shock of realization I had never before faced. Although I had been brought up in a virtuous home and had been given careful religious training, after leaving home as a teenager for France, slowly I had begun to feel religion was mere religiosity, and that it must be protected from close scrutiny for fear that other truths would reveal it to be a total fraud.

But here the director said it clearly. "You must not be afraid of any authentic truth. Some men fear this and try to reason toward the Faith. If the Faith is the One Truth, then no truth discovered in science or nature can be in ultimate contradiction to it; if the Faith is the One Truth, then nothing authentically deduced from the Faith can be in ultimate contradiction to truths discovered in science or nature." None of them appeared to doubt this strangely bold proposition, based on the thought of St. Thomas Aquinas, a Dominican who had been a student of St. Albert the Great in this very novitiate.

I knew that the saints had existed, but always considered them to be special beings—men and women set apart from the rest of us, uninvolved in all the greed and lust and gluttony of ordinary men. In my experience, however, we professed a religion because it was the thing to do, a convention harming no one that brought social and spiritual benefits. But in truth, it took second place to almost any contrary desire a man might have. It left him room for both goodness and the degraded actions dear to him. Religion for the rest of us had been a compromise tacitly agreed upon. We had perfected the techniques of sensual pleasure, of avarice and ambition, and of self-seeking during the week. Then on Sundays we spoke prayers without concern for what the words really meant.

The difference between these men and us was that they actually did believe, they concerned themselves with what the words of the prayers and liturgy and Gospels actually meant. They sought no compromise between their aspirations and what the world calls "lower appetites"— and thus did not despise these appetites. Religion was a matter not of truncating humanity but of perfecting it.

I saw them intimately and I saw they were men like me. I lived with them, saw them bleary-eyed at dawn, smelled them sweating after labors, and yet sanctity lay there within them, anchored in the realities of living.

My idea had always been that personal integrity demanded that a man have all his doubts satisfied, all his questions answered before he could honestly and totally embrace any faith. Their idea was the contrary—that they must freely embrace the faith before the light of understanding could fully begin to be given them.

I had demanded that the vastness of God's truth come to inhabit the smallness of my mind before I would commit myself. They believed that the experience of the faith was in part the teacher. Faith in search of understanding, the medieval motto, was also theirs. In such an atmosphere of openness, my attitude shamed me with its reek of arrogance. Then all too soon my visit drew to a close.

The last evening, Marie-Bruno came to tell me good-bye. I wanted to tell him of my confusion, but I could not bring myself to express it. And I sensed that anything I might say would sound false and that he would detect it instantly. He sat in a straight-backed chair next to the bed. Immediately, he directed the conversation mercifully into the one field where I was at home. We talked of music. As the light faded outside, I turned on the lamp, which cast an amber highlight on his face and tonsured head. He looked like an ancient engraving of a monk come to life, speaking, smiling. This brought a moment of ease and I could then tell him.

"I hated it when I first came here, and now I hate to leave. What you have makes sense, inside these walls. It seems tremendously important here and now, but once I leave, I know I can't hold it. I wish I could believe, make the leap, say yes and mean it with all my heart."

Marie-Bruno's eyes livened with sympathy, and I realized that he must have seen many others arrive, fall under the spell, and then fear to lose it by leaving. He did not speak, but listened carefully.

"I know that I am wrong not to accept what is," I added, "just because my mind insists on demanding proofs that will never be given."

"It's a thing you have to solve within yourself," he said. "It is true that some knowledge must precede love, since you cannot love a thing that you do not know. But you need only enough knowledge to let you know it, because a greater knowledge comes from the experience of loving."

He then spoke of André Gide's novel *The Pastoral Symphony*, about the pastor's attempts to help a blind girl understand what the word green signifies. "The difficulty of understanding the color green without the experience of sight must be similar to that of understanding God's truth without the experience of faith." I listened carefully to the logic of his analogies as he discoursed. "The experience itself teaches. It is not unlike human love. Can a man, no matter how much he studies the physical or psychological aspects of love, really know what it is without having been in love? Love instructs, and the simplest soul deeply in love knows more about it than the greatest 'specialist' who has never been in love."

I reasoned that love in the supernatural realm, even though I felt its enormous attraction, demanded an abdication of self that was beyond my powers. Once committed, your decisions could no longer be expedient or comfortable ones; actions could no longer depend on conduct that was convenient. Rather, they all depended on the immutable laws of God.

The irony of my speculations struck me. There I sat in a cell, opposite a man of God, thinking myself at least sincere. But in the background, I knew my body planned to remedy the effects of isolation, the tasteless food and the cold that had sharpened my desire to return to the world of women, excellent food, and warmth. I recalled what Pops Fendler had said that drunken day on Morotai; and I knew that my body would not walk to that tree where Christ stood, but would hurry to the tree where the woman waited. As Fendler's tough, pugged face superimposed itself over the emaciated face of Marie-Bruno, I could see clearly how weak the boxer and I were beside the strength of this monk's frailty.

The silence grew burdensome. A light rain struck at the window. The monk rose to leave. I walked with him to the door, saying that the visit had been a matter of unflagging fascination. "It appeals to me," I blundered on. "What you have found here. It's even deeper than appeal."

He hesitated, waiting for me to continue. I could not doubt from his eyes that he saw through me. I felt my face flush. I spoke the truth and yet it had all the nuances of the most fatuous lie. "But I'm afraid of it," I confessed. "I know my belly too well."

He looked up into my face, his brown eyes sharpening, and spoke: "You don't seriously think your belly is different from any other man's, do you? Dear God, I believe you do. The religious life, more than any other, demands the destruction of such delusions. No man has ever progressed very far in it without feeling this same terrible unworthiness, without seeing clearer than ever before the depths of vileness into which his nature has too often led him, and could so easily lead him again."

I said nothing. What could I say?

"You speak as though the *Great Yes* need only be said once and then everything is somehow arranged. God's grace comes, but so too the full power of temptations to resist it. The *Yes* has to be repeated again and again. And it never gets much easier to do. Look at you, you are the picture of discontent. That, at least, is good."

"How?"

Scattered Shadows

"You are ashamed. You have had carnal stirrings in a holy place. Oh, it always happens. We're not maiden aunts here. We know the patterns, because we have had to face them, and we will always have to face them. You are discontent now because your pride is hurt."

I nodded, knowing he had read my doubts.

"But there is another discontent in all this," he said. "It is a sort of divine discontent which has not so much to do with you as with what life appears to offer you. This discontent can grow. It may become so painful it will drive you to love, and that is what is good about it. You do have a free will, you know, some choice in the matter. You can *choose* to love. You deny it now, but you will see."

The bell for Benediction sounded thinly up the stairwell.

I waited for him to continue, tense against the vague disappointment he might be trying to convert me.

The monk stepped into the corridor, turned to me and said: "I hope it goes all right for you. I hope God spares you."

I listened to his heavy boot-shoes clump slowly on the wooden floor of the corridor, then down the stairs, until the distance silenced them.

— The Blind Man of Tours —

For the next few weeks I visited the home of dear friends I had known before the war reached Tours, where I had lived as a lycée student. The Duthoos were an important industrial family in the region, and their son and a schoolmate, Jacques Duthoo, was a gifted painter who divided his time between business and art. He was a second-generation cubist who knew Braque, Picasso, and many other painters, including the New York expressionist Abraham Rattner, who had spent twenty years as an exile in France. It was through Jacques that I had first met Rattner, as well as the Casadesus family, Nadia Boulanger, Francis Poulenc, and other great musicians during my student days at the Lycée Descartes in Tours.

Before I had left Paris, I was beginning to experience blurring vision, and severe headaches came more frequently. Because the Duthoos were people of great kindness, my presence was painful to them. Each time I ran into furniture, I raged with embarrassment and they stood silently by. I made them miserable, despite their protests of delight to have me.

I wanted almost desperately to find a place where I could make the transition into blindness in solitude. I wrote Marie-Bruno, explaining the situation and asking for permission to return there. I felt a great substructure of weakness and believed that the monastic routine would provide the strength and calm to make it bearable, even though I had no intentions of becoming a Catholic.

Meanwhile, I spent days away from the Duthoo mansion, revisiting old haunts where I had spent such happy years. Tours was a city of parks and fountains and many bridges over the rivers, a city steeped in history. Every cobblestone gave up its echo of the past, recalling kings and some of her saints, recalling Ronsard and Balzac and Rabelais. Each morning, under a radiant autumn sun, I strolled along the stone ramparts on the banks of the Loire River, gazing endlessly at the river and at the little island where Ronsard had died—all of it now a haze.

Every afternoon, I bought a sack of chestnuts, as much to feel their warmth and to talk with the vendor as for the pleasure of eating them. The vendor and I became friendly in the casual way of people who meet frequently. I enjoyed his talk and also the cheerful, sweetish odor of the chestnuts that surrounded his portable charcoal oven. He was from nearby Chinon, "where Rabelais came from," he said with pride.

It occurred to me that I had never seen a blind man in Tours, a city of some sixty thousand inhabitants. I asked him about this one afternoon.

"There are some, Monsieur. Pitiful things. One of them lives in my neighborhood, over near *les Halles*."

"What's his name?"

"Who knows? They call him *l'Aveugle*. That's all I've ever heard."

"How long has he been without sight?"

"Always, I think. I've lived in the quarter thirty-five years now."

"He's a vendor?"

"A beggar, really. He begs postcards, books, any kind of trash. Then he hawks it on the streets."

I left him and walked through the old quarter beneath balconies of houses dating from the thirteenth century that almost touched overhead across the narrow cobblestone streets. All was small and worn and squalid. The area smelled of old stones and spices and urine. From above I heard a Haydn sonata being practiced on a tinny piano. Narrow streets converged on a large open square where executions had once been held, a marketplace dating from the Middle Ages. At this hour of the day it was crowded with workers returning to their homes.

I went into a dingy café and shouldered my way through the apéritif drinkers toward the bar. The barman said that *l'Aveugle*, who would be the only blind man in the quarter, had a room in a corner house three doors down. I drank a glass of sour red wine and walked out into the sudden chill of the square. The sun hung like a cold blue orb above the bakery shop, filtered of color by the haze of smoke from cooking fires.

The entrance to the house was so low that I had to stoop. Inside, I slowly raised my head to a somber foyer a yard square, with a door on each side and stairsteps ahead. I tried the door on the right. It opened into a black hole of a foul-smelling toilet. I knocked on the door to the left and it opened a crack.

"Pardon, Madame, I am looking for *l'Aveugle*."

"Mount the stairs, then, Monsieur. Last door on the right."

I felt my way along the dark hall of the landing. At the final door, I heard the sound of a news broadcast from a radio—strange sound in a city where radios were not common and in a quarter where they would be expensive luxuries. I tapped on the door. Footsteps shuffled within and stopped on the other side of the door.

"Who is there, please?" I heard an aged voice, soft and cultivated; not the sour tones the chestnut vendor had led me to expect.

"You don't know me. But I should like to talk with you."

"I'm ready to retire. Do you want to buy something?"

"Yes, please."

"You are alone?"

"Yes . . . "

"One moment, please."

His footsteps moved slowly away from the door. After a time he called me across the room. "You may come in now."

I opened the door, prepared to hate what I saw, expecting a view of poverty and blind disorder. Instead, light from the window revealed an immaculate and cheerful room. Even the stale odors of the hall were obliterated by the fragrance of lavender water.

An elderly and stooped man, with white hair and thin aristocratic features, finished tying the belt of an expensive red-and-black striped silk robe over his white brocade pajamas. His skeletal feet were encased in red leather house-slippers of an expensive cut. I thought I had got into the wrong room, then he spoke: "Talk, please, so I know where you are."

"Yes sir. I'm right here."

"You must excuse me. I retire early."

"Please . . . I shouldn't have come so late."

"What do you wish to buy?"

"Perhaps a book . . . "

"I'll show you what I have," he said gently. I watched him kneel and drag a box from under his bed. "Sit down if you wish. There's a chair by the window." I took the chair and glanced out to dusk on a small and cluttered courtyard behind the house. Across the way, lights were being turned on in other rooms and shutters were being closed. On the table beside me, the radio's light gleamed, downstreaking the oilcloth with yellow. I had obviously interrupted his supper. Partially eaten on a plate lay slices of buttered bread and salami. A tall bottle of unlabeled red wine stood beside a half-filled glass.

The old man stacked books on his bed. His clothes, neatly folded over another chair near his armoire, contrasted oddly to his splendid night apparel. They were the ragged, filthy clothes of a pariah.

"Should I close your shutters?" I asked. "It's getting dark."

"Yes, if you will," he said, carrying an armload of books to the table.

As I closed the shutters to a view of twilight on rubble, I wondered how I should ever get back to the Duthoos.

"There, you may find something interesting. Are you a scholar?"

"A student. Yes sir."

"You talk like an educated man," he said.

"So do you, sir."

"I learn it all from the radio," he sighed. "In the evenings, for years, I have come home and listened to the radio until time to sleep. I'm a slave to that machine," he laughed. "Without it I'd have gone mad long ago."

I asked permission to turn on the light.

"Of course. I forget others must have electricity when it goes dark," he apologized. "There's a new bulb there. I always turn on the light when I close the blinds."

"You have some sight then?"

"No, it's just that I cannot bear the idea of sitting in the darkness. Though I have never seen it, I like the idea of light."

I lifted a large book to the drop-light and examined its title.

"Would you be kind enough to read the titles to me. I never really know what I have."

I deciphered the large printing. "*Pages Choisies* of Pierre Louÿs."

"Really?"

"Yes. Here's *Balthazar* by Anatole France. And here's Maeterlinck's *La Grande Porte*." As I read through the stack, I became aware of the old man's mood of intense pleasure. I saw the scene as though detached from it—the two of us sat at his table in a circle of lamplight on a cold autumn's evening. He leaned forward, an expression of concentration on his wrinkled face, his blue eyes alive, but without focus.

My attention was jerked back to the volume in my hand, an obvious piece of pornography. I flipped through to glimpse hazed drawings of sex orgies, and then set it aside. He heard the page-flipping and the rustle as I placed the book down. "What was that one?"

I told him and watched his face tighten with anger. "They give me these things. I have no way of knowing what they are, you understand. They think it amusing to give me these things. Twice I've been selling scabrous postcards without knowing. All right if some man wants to buy them. But I'm afraid to show my supply to women or children, afraid they'll see something like that and judge me a hawker of filth."

"Couldn't you get someone to go through them for you?"

"Who? I am alone. I have no one in the world." He hesitated a moment. "Can I tell you something, Monsieur?"

"Of course."

"You're the first person who's ever read these titles to me. You can't imagine what it means. Twelve years ago a letter came for me. I carried it for days, not even knowing who it was from. I could have asked someone in the street to read it, but you get timid about such things. Finally, do you know what? I took it to St. Martin's and asked one of the priests to read it for me. I'm a freethinker not a Catholic, but I took it there. He read it for me. It was a tax notice. Since then, until tonight, no one has read a word to me. I get everything from the radio, Monsieur."

His frail body trembled with an emotion that astonished me. "It is cold. I'm sorry I have no fire," he said shakily.

"Shall I go on?"

"Please."

"*Hölderlin* by Stephan Zweig."

"Who was Hölderlin?"

"A German poet. I don't know his work."

"Would it be asking too much . . . yes, of course it would," he sighed.

"What?"

"If you would read me just one line . . . a sentence anywhere."

Without my reading glass I could not hope to decipher the body text. "The light is too poor, I'm afraid," I said, feeling my own voice become unsteady. "I could come back tomorrow and read to you."

He nodded his head as though he accepted the disappointment but did not believe me. I struggled with a page, holding it almost against my eye, but the lines were fuzzy gray streaks. I heard the questions within me: My God, is this the way it is? Is it so bad that a man goes to pieces at the emotion of having a few book titles read to him? Must he beg for a sentence, any sentence, from a book?

"There are other scabrous books here. Shall I separate them?"

"Please, if you would."

I arranged separate stacks and placed his hand on the stack nearest him. "These are the books you'd not want to show to women or children."

"It is foul of them to give me these things," he said with dignity and hatred. "They think it's amusing."

I chose a book I thought he would probably not sell to anyone else: *Les problèmes non résolus de la science*, by Haslett, and asked the price.

"Thirty-five francs," he said cautiously.

I counted the money into his beggar's hand, which protruded from the sleeves of his princely robe.

"Will you have a glass of wine with me?" he asked.

I accepted and watched him pour. He held his finger over the lip of the glass and judged fullness by pouring until the wine touched his fingertip. He did not clink glasses at the toast, as would most, but offered it like an aristocrat, in a raised gesture, saying: "To your good health."

"To yours," I answered, raising the glass in salute. I wondered why I had done it since he could not see the gesture. I felt for a moment that it was a wasted gesture, but then was pleased I had done it. I had honored him and that alone was important.

He gazed toward me, his eyes a blare. "What brought you here, I wonder?" His voice sounded hoarse, deep in his throat, as though full of dread. In the background, slick jazz bounced against the stone walls.

"I really don't know, Monsieur," I said.

"You didn't come for a book though, did you?"

"No sir."

"Did you come to see a blind man?" He asked and leaned forward, his face covering my entire field of vision, consuming me.

"Yes sir . . . "

The jazz raked across us.

"Why?" his voice exploded, as though he dreaded the answer.

I wished for silence. The room needed silence. But we were bombarded by the cheap upsurge of saxophones and clarinets.

"Because I had hoped to learn something from you."

"From me?" he said in sneering disbelief. "What, for example?"

"How you do things. How you live. What it's like . . . "

He drew back as though I had slapped him. "Good night, Monsieur," he said quietly, with dignity, dismissing me with finality.

"You don't understand," I said. "It wasn't morbid curiosity."

"What then? A sociological study? How a blind beggar—"

"No . . . no, not that . . . Believe me."

His voice sharpened with resentment. "Why should you want to know what it's like to be like me?"

"Because that's the way I'll soon be," I answered with equal sharpness, throwing it into his face.

He blanched and the flesh crumpled around his mouth. No matter what reassurances he might give, I knew the truth of his reaction at that moment on his face. He was visibly, severely stunned.

"I know nothing about it, nothing at all," I said. "I've never even talked with anyone who's had such an experience. I thought I could get an idea of what it was like, of what I will have to face . . . "

His voice cut in, rasping: "How old are you?" he shouted.

"Twenty-six."

"A child. God damn. A child. Are you married?"

"No sir."

Music from the radio filled the room: "He was a beautiful sailor boy/ Who brought into port my fullest joy," the woman sang savagely.

The cold penetrated our clothing. Both of us trembled uncontrollably.

"You have a family?" he asked more gently.

"In America, yes."

"Will you have more wine? We can talk."

"I'm keeping you awake. And it's getting so cold."

He rose to his feet and stood motionless for a long time, supporting himself with one hand on the table. "Have you had supper?" he asked without opening his eyes.

"No sir."

"Ah," he smiled and slapped his hands together to create a different atmosphere. "Then I tell you. Let's eat. I have blankets. We can wrap up. Come, we will enjoy ourselves, eh? We will talk all night if you wish. It's not really so bad, you know. When one thinks of it, it's not really so bad. You see, I have nice things—a nice room, a radio. I'm king here."

The discomfort dropped from between us. We were two people safe in a closed room, separated from the rest of the world by the night. We had something in common, so deeply felt that it destroyed all barriers.

"I tell you, I have good clothes in that armoire. Someday I may have a friend, someone like you perhaps. And he'll take me to a nice restaurant for dinner. I mean one of the really fine places."

"I'd be glad to take you."

"Would you?" He cackled with pleasure, as a father at some gesture from his child. "I'd pay for it, of course."

He grimaced and reached for the radio, but drew his hand back. "Do you like this music?"

"God no. I've been wanting to change it myself."

"Good. Tell me if I come to something you like. And there are blankets in the armoire, if you'd not mind getting them. You are at home here." He spun the dial and stopped on a woman's chorus from England. They sang a bouncy, madrigal-like arrangement of a religious song.

"It's nice, eh?" he said. "Do you understand the words?"

"Yes sir. 'Hold Jesus, dear Jesus, in your arms like a lamb.'"

"*Merde,*" he whispered. "It sounded like it might be something." He turned the dial again. "There, that's good, I know." A jubilant passage from a Handel violin sonata turned the aural atmosphere festive.

I placed one of the blankets around his stooped shoulders. Touching the table edge, he drew his chair around to the correct angle facing it and began slicing slabs of bread and salami. Wrapped in the other blanket, I sat across the table and observed his expert handling of the knife.

We felt at ease talking about blindness now. The pleasure of listening to the music, of eating and drinking in one another's company overrode the somberness of our subject.

"I can teach you," he laughed. "I'll make you the most accomplished beggar on the continent and show you how to avoid the awful mistakes I've made. There's nothing else we can do in a provincial town. No jobs, not even the humblest. But begging is fine as long as you don't believe in what you're doing. You must live two lives, keeping your self-respect even when you act as though you had lost it completely."

The idea of becoming the old man's protégé excited my imagination.

"You are intelligent. You would learn quickly. And there is much to learn—an entire new way of living. The worst is the loneliness and the ungodly stupidity of sighted people. A blind man needs a great friendship, even more than he needs a woman. I've never had a friend, but you must have. The loneliness is too terrible otherwise. When I was much younger, I thought of taking a wife—one of those women who pledge themselves to marry only the maimed or disabled. But at the last moment I couldn't. Do you understand what I'm trying to say?"

"Yes sir, I think so."

"Self-respect becomes the only important thing—it saves your life, really. I could not marry a woman I did not win right, who wouldn't be reserved for me like a pension check just because I was blind. Can you imagine what that would do to a man? To know that a woman slept with you not because she loved you but because she loved God! What a horror. Do you understand?"

"Yes sir."

"If you give in on one point like that, you're defeated. They have won."

"Who's that?"

"They—those out there—the sighted ones. They want you to act in a certain way. They want you to be taken care of and stay out of sight, not remind them of blindness or some guilt. They castrate you of self-respect thinking they help you. Sometimes I hate them in their arrogance and superiority. But it's stupid to hate them. And sometimes a saint's voice breathes in your ear for just a moment—out of the clutter of sound—and then the love for humanity comes back. You will experience this. It is a great mystery to me. I am not a man of faith. I hate their pious unction.

"But when you are blind, people will reveal themselves to you, knowing you can never identify them. They will show themselves to you as they never would another. Most are ordinary, dull. But you come quickly to see that some are saints and some are satanic." He sipped the wine and continued. "For instance, I have heard elderly women and men—I could smell their dentures—with the odor of incense from Mass fresh on their clothes, whisper to me things that only Satan could utter."

His patrician face hovered before me, his eyes closed, the long wrinkles of his cheeks deeply shadowed in lamplight. "And again, others smelling the same, have shown me hints of the most extraordinary grace . . . souls like the sunlight."

Then his voice assumed a detached, impersonal tone. "What do you know about women? Do you go to whores? I only ask this because when you are blind everything changes. Everything is crushed or becomes highly exaggerated. It takes a certain hardness inside you, a callousness, to go to the whores. What will you do about sex?"

"I don't know," I said. "I've wondered about that myself."

"That's the great trap," he said. "You see me? I am a puritan of the worst sort. I'm a ruined human being because I am puritanical to the marrow. We blind people often become deeply sick in this way. But you can avoid this awful wreckage if you know about it in advance and can guard against it. We can't evade the sexual impasse like the sighted can. It is such a burning point with us that it turns us puritanical. I believe it's the worst of our handicap—not the sexual part that caused it, but the fact that in defense we end up viewing even the healthful aspects of sex as vile. We become terrible prudes all in knowing it is a sickness, but unable to help ourselves. I know that now, but I didn't realize it until it was too late. Now I'm too old to change." He paused and emptied the glass of wine. "I know better in my mind," he said, "but I can't persuade my body and my heart. I freeze with loathing for everything that brings sex to my attention."

He pushed the bottle over the oilcloth toward me. I took it and filled our glasses. He located his glass and sipped the wine. "When I was younger," he continued, "I had a great craving for love. A person with sight can see in a glance that someone has affection for him. He sees a thousand indications of it and even has a sort of union with everyone he sees. With us, all of that's gone. We know them only by their voices. It is not enough. The voice doesn't really tell much. It comes out of the air. When it is tired, it sounds exactly the same as when it is sick or angry or disgusted. We unite by touch. And you can't go around touching people the way the sighted can go around looking at them. If no one ever touches you, you crave even a handshake, the feel of something human. With a friend you can have that and even that is enough. But without it, you crave, you crave . . . " His voice trailed off, and then he said: "You think I exaggerate? No, it is a very great thing to a blind man. You thought nothing of putting the blanket around my shoulders. To me it was—*Dieu*, how could I begin to tell you . . . "

He realized only then that he had not offered butter for the sandwich. He hastily brought it out of a small upright cupboard with gauze-covered doors beside his chair. I noted his accuracy in reaching for it.

"I judge everything from the location of the radio," he explained.

"How do you mean?"

"I know just how many centimeters to the right of that sound I keep my butter. You will learn these things. Indeed they are the least of it. It is the affections that present the problems. Do you know my name?"

"No sir . . . "

"I've lived in this quarter almost fifty years. Not a soul knows my name. Not that I would keep it a secret. God no, I should like to hear my name called. They never think to ask. You see, I am not an individual—not Pierre or François or Charles like the rest of them. What do I hear when I walk down the street? '*Bonjour, Monsieur l'Aveugle.*' I have no name—only a condition. I am known, but not for who I am, only for what I am, the blind man."

I sipped the wine, intently listening to insights I'd never considered.

"I tell you these things not to complain, but to show you what you must do. You must become more a man than blind. You must overpower the condition with some individuality and you must find some way not to kill your love. People don't understand about this. What are you, sitting there? To me you are nothing, really. But if I touch your hand, you become something. Isn't there something terribly wrong about that?"

"I don't understand exactly what you mean," I said.

He drank from his glass, more rapidly this time. Then he raised his thin hands to massage across his forehead, hiding his face.

Just then the radio announcer said that Marguerite Long would be the piano soloist in Mozart's Concerto number twenty-three. Almost immediately the opening measures of this ravishing music poured out into the room.

With his face still covered, the old man spoke. "I'll tell you something terrible, because you'll feel these things, too. When I was young like you, this craving for affection got so bad I even tried to go to prostitutes. Do you know why? Not because of sex, really, but because there, at least, I would be touched. I'd get so desperate I'd buy the whole thing just to get the touches of affection. You can buy orgasm, but not those affectionate touches that give it meaning. So you buy only a deeper wretchedness. I searched for some true warmth when they put their arms around me, but I never once found it. Their embraces were no more real than if I'd laid in a mannequin's arms. I hated them for it. Each time, I felt sick because there was never that special touch or that soft expression in their voices. Each time I swore I would never go back. And always I did. Always I hoped," he said, still holding his head.

"Finally, I realized I would never have the peace of affection unless the gods sent me either a real wife or a real friend. I started hating what is profoundly good, because it hurt deeply. I was virile, but I blocked sex out of my life long ago, because I could never find a way to nourish it with affections. By itself, without affection, it is worse than nothing. I killed it like one kills a well-loved animal who will otherwise torture you by starving to death before your eyes. But one can't really kill it, you know." His voice trailed off, as though he could find no further words to express the immensity of it.

I felt his despair, mingling with the long and moving phrases of the Mozart and with the rich aroma of the salami.

"It's strange I can talk about this at all," he said, dropping his hands and smiling uncertainly. "I tell you these things because you must not be cheated the way I feel I have been cheated. No, that's not really it. It's because you are here, and there's warmth in you. For these few moments, it's almost as though you were the friend I've never had. I can talk to you about these things without the feeling of nausea, because there is safety in here between us. Do you understand that?"

"I think so," I said and drank again, finishing my fourth or fifth glass.

"Did you have enough to eat?"

When I assured him I had, he stood slowly, balanced the blanket over his shoulders, and began stacking the dishes. He wrapped the bread in a piece of cotton toweling, lifted my glass, felt that it was nearly empty, and replenished it with astonishing adeptness.

The Mozart absorbed our attention as it entered the slow movement, piano and orchestra in a dialogue of contemplative tenderness. He stood with one hand on the table, the blanket around his shoulders, his head slightly raised, staring toward the ceiling. His hand on the table began to shake as though he were struck with palsy.

"Could I ask you something?"

"Of course."

"You are the first person who's ever visited me, who's ever been easy with me. There may never be another." He hesitated.

"What is it?" I asked.

"I'm afraid to ask. It might offend you."

"I doubt it," I laughed.

His voice rattled deep in his throat. "Would you let me feel how your face is?" His tone of intense dread and longing touched me deeply.

"Certainly," I said.

"It's not repugnant to you?"

"Not in the slightest."

I removed my glasses and lifted his hand to my face. His fingertips were like ice to my flesh, timid and trembling.

"Is it all right?" he asked.

"It is fine. Do not be concerned."

With this reassurance, his touch became more certain as he explored the contours of my face. I smelled the faint odor of lavender soap and the stronger aroma of salami on his fingers. "This is very moving to me," he said, his face sharpened to total absorption.

"Is your hair blond?"

"Brown."

"Your eyes?"

"Greenish, I think."

"They are deep sunk."

"Yes sir."

His fingers, hard as sticks, moved over my head to the nape of the neck again and again, trembling less. His features became calm. Then his hands drifted reluctantly away and rested on the table.

"I could teach you to be a good beggar," he said.

"Thank you."

"You could live here with me, perhaps?"

"I honestly wish I could. But I'm leaving Tours soon. After I lose my sight, I'll have to return to America to attend schools for the blind."

"I see . . . "

"In fact, I'm afraid I have to be going now. I'm visiting friends here. Only I'm not sure how I'll get back. I can't see well enough to get around after dark."

"Then stay here. We could talk all night if you wanted to."

"My hosts will surely become alarmed if I don't return," I explained.

"Well, if you feel you must go, I can take you there. I know the town well. Where do they live?"

"*Rue Jules Simon*, number twenty-three."

"An elegant part of town," he said in disappointment. "You are a rich man?" he asked. I felt overtones of humiliation that he had dared suggest that a rich man become his pupil or be his friend.

"No, I'm sure I'm much poorer than you are," I reassured him.

He talked rapidly while he changed into his ragged day clothes.

"I hope you realize what this has meant to me. I have had a visitor. We have dined and drunk together at my table. Do you know that during all my years here—nearly half a century—I've never before had someone for supper? Do you know that I never before touched a grown person's face? And I shall never again. I know that. It's too much to hope that another will come here as you did, and then stay for a time as you did. You, my friend, are the one big event that has ever happened to me. I know you won't believe it. But it's true. Come, I'll take you home now."

With his left hand clutching at my arm above the elbow, he guided me down the hall with the accompaniment of light tapping from his heavy cane. "Fine now," he whispered. "A few more steps and we are at the stairs. There. Step down. Careful."

Outside, the chill and cold stench clamped over us, but we walked slowly, far more slowly than necessary. We strolled past houses from which no light showed. We talked softly, as friends with no barriers, speaking to express the pleasure we felt in one another's company.

"Here we are, young man," he said at last. He squared me gently so that I felt the high metal grill gate that led into the Duthoo courtyard against my back.

"How did you ever know to stop exactly at this spot?" I asked.

"All the virtuosi are not in the concert halls," he laughed. "I know that twenty-three is the Duthoo mansion. And I know that it is set back from the street with a garden in front, whereas those on either side are set on the street, with gardens in back. So when I hear the cane tap a hollow sound, I know we are where we should be . . . "

I realized I had forgotten my book, but said nothing about it. He would probably never know, and he might be able to sell it again.

"Can you see anything at all?" he asked.

"Not in this darkness."

"You are like me now," he said tentatively.

His hand descended my arm and came to rest in my hand. It was time to say good-bye. Neither of us could think of anything to say. No easy words came. I felt tension in his touch. His breathing became agitated.

"What is it?" I asked uneasily.

His fingers contracted like thick wires around my hand.

"I hate it for you," he groaned. "We don't think it's so bad when it happens to us. We get used to it. But then when it happens to somebody else, we realize how horrible it is. There's no way to explain." His voice ground out the words in despair.

He released me suddenly and his cane tapped wildly away.

For a moment I thought of going after him. But at that speed, and without his skills, I knew I could never catch him.

I leaned against the grill, felt frost on the iron bite into the back of my head and listened to his cane dim into silence. A sullen pressure ached in my throat and I hoped I should not have to talk with anyone before I got to my room.

Mounting the dark stairs as quietly as possible, it occurred to me that he never did tell me his name, and that he did not know mine.

— The Fake Pearl —

The sliver of amber light under the door signaled the location of the guest room on the second landing of the Duthoo mansion. Someone had been there, left on a lamp, turned up the heat, and spread back the bed. Three letters lay on the pillow. Before examining them, I removed my clothes and got into pajamas. I found my magnifying glass and examined them. The one from my parents in America was cheerful and brimming with confidence. Then I thought of *l'Aveugle* without a family to protect him from the raging loneliness that afflicted him.

The next letter, from Marie-Bruno, was printed in large script, far different from his usual miniature handwriting. It informed me that he had been unsuccessful in getting permission for my return to Paris for a prolonged stay, since the rule allowed only for brief visits by retreatants.

His letter continued: "Now the calm tone of your letter allows me to dare to speak to you of the manner in which you might accept this loss of sight. You are being given an opportunity to offer a great sacrifice to

God, and thereby to grow in spirit. If you can accept this and abandon yourself to God's infinite dynamism, in a short time you will surely enjoy peace and the knowledge of how to find God in this darkness."

I sat on the bed and read that passage again, until ashamed reactions to certain expressions like "a great sacrifice to God" were finally quelled and the words "what rot" no longer reverberated at the back of my brain.

"It is not easy," wrote the monk. "It might even be impossible without the grace of God. The secret is in this, that we cannot make progress if we try to follow our own inclinations; but we must seek God's will, even where it most conflicts with our desires. This in a very great love, in a great docility, until our every thought, our every action and reaction even, is attuned not to ourselves but to the God within us."

I recognized with some regret that for someone else these would be words of infinite wisdom. But I could no more fix my attention lovingly on God than I could on the wallpaper of the room. Even the thought filled me with intimate embarrassment. God meant nothing to me, to my great sorrow. He was an idea, the comfort of my youth, a myth worthy of respect, nothing more.

The third letter was from the guestmaster at the Benedictine Abbey of Solesmes, offering a vacant cell for a visit and that the Father Abbot would be happy to receive me. Even more exciting, I would be allowed to do research in the *Paléographie Musicale*, where the original manuscripts of Gregorian Chant were archived. My years of dreaming of someday studying in this great citadel of learning were undramatically realized in these few lines.

I went to bed, filled with uncertainty, and lay there in half-dreams in which *l'Aveugle* pulsed in and out of view. Solesmes was yet another move. Should I really go? Would it not be wiser, at least kinder, to stay here and learn from the old man, offer him the consolations of friendship?

But no, I had made myself a promise years ago, always to take the new step. That alone decided it. I would leave, abandon all I knew here in this well-loved city and travel to the unknown. As my body gathered warmth beneath the covers, Solesmes absorbed all my concentration. I heard in imagination its great silence, the bells, the chants drifting down endless corridors of the cloister.

The next morning I told Jacques Duthoo that I would soon leave for Solesmes. Father Pierre Froger, the organist of Tours Cathedral, sat in the salon having coffee with us. During my student days, I had studied harmony and counterpoint with him after Dr. Fromenty had advised that I continue musical training to complement the medical studies. With Father Froger, a musicologist as well as a gifted musician, we had coauthored a technical study entitled *Interpretation of the Ornaments of the Music for Keyboard Instruments of the 17th and 18th Centuries*, which had been published privately in 1939.

When Father Froger heard about my upcoming visit to Solesmes, he immediately offered to accompany me. "My brother is a monk there," he said. "I go there as often as I can. I will stay two or three days and help you get settled." Jacques Duthoo, who had not seen Solesmes since the war, suggested he drive us there, and the matter was soon settled.

The next day I took a last walk along the tree-lined ramparts of the Loire River. Thoughts of *l'Aveugle* preoccupied me, but I decided against seeing him again. We had said everything last night. Another visit would be painful for both of us.

After a mild, clear early afternoon, the sky began to fill with black thunderheads and chill sifted into the breeze. I turned back toward the mansion, guided by the towering gothic spires of Cathedral St. Gatien. Then the first heavy drops of rain smacked against the cobblestones as I arrived in the cathedral square. Trees and buildings were dwarfed to miniatures by the nearness and massiveness of the cathedral. Lightning flickered, pinpointing the façade in greenish light against the black skies.

I hurried inside to escape the downpour and waited for my eyes to accustom themselves to the somberness of the interior. Long queues formed at each of the little upright coffins they used for confessional booths. Men, women, and children, the wealthy and the poor, were all there for Saturday evening confession. I gazed at them through the dim light and wondered. Their world and their home life, their ethics and their way of looking at things—all of it lay behind the fog of mystery. Were they at all like me? Did they harbor the beast in their bellies? If so, how could they pour out such filth into the unseen ear of the confessor?

A few prayed in the central portion of the church, tiny figures dwarfed by the vast heights of the vaulted ceiling. My hungers stirred painfully for what they had found, but my mind congealed against it. In the gloom, lighted here and there by clusters of red and blue votive lamps, the intensity of prayers pervaded the atmosphere. I felt alone and under an almost magnetic compulsion to enter the black-curtained confessional box. I rejected the idea but it returned insistently. After all, the priest would never know who I was and I should never know who he was. I would be hidden behind the curtain and the grill, in the dark, speaking to a person vowed never to divulge what he heard. I approached the shortest line and stood waiting, advancing as each penitent entered the curtained room.

Then a statement from Gide came to mind.

Referring to a group of nuns, he had observed how they cherished the pearl of their faith, never realizing it was a false pearl. He had added that as long as they did not realize it was a false pearl, perhaps it had the same value to them as a real one.

I turned and walked away from the confessional, past statues of saints mounted on giant pedestals that loomed above me, past a young woman whose face was blank with prayer. I felt my body hanging about me as an encumbrance. My feet, cold and sweating in shoes, walked on toward the door, removing me from contact with the false pearl.

I strode toward the normalcy of cobblestone pavements and the noise of the world outside. But where could I go? I saw the world as nothing but an endless dusk leading down a thousand alleys that I knew ended nowhere. They ended nowhere unless one had a kitchen, a family, a bed, and the brains and hearts of others to share.

The idea of returning to the Duthoos and sitting at a glittering dining table repelled me. I should not be there. They were a family complete in themselves. The picture of them without me was the natural picture.

My footsteps slowed. I turned back from the square and returned to the cathedral. I sidled into an empty pew and knelt. A veiled woman lighted votive candles at a side altar. I watched her and heard the words rise up in me: "You poor woman. Do you think that's going to change a thing?" The vision crystallized. The widow deep in her veils not lighting candles, but naked under me, her face still swathed in black gauze, her legs locked around my waist in a frenzy.

A cough reverberated in the obscurity, jerking me out of the vision. Drawing my coat more tightly around me, I shuddered. Odors of age and stone and humanity combined to create a stench that stifled the spirit. I looked on the backs of kneelers who worshiped the pearl. Each stone of this immense structure had been laid centuries ago with devotion to the same pearl. Generations had worn the stone floors down with footsteps.

They had mumbled the same prayers, confessed the same sins, wasted how much energy and how many hopes on the false pearl? I sat for a time in the rustling silence. A heavy fatigue began to make my feet recede to some far distance, when the thought quietly settled in me.

How did Gide know? True, I shared his belief, that the pearl was false. But how could we know? Did we, ourselves, possess the true one? If true, then why were we so tormented?

Marie-Bruno had said that the experience of faith teaches, that it opens the door. Never having opened that door, how could we know the truth or falsity of the pearl that lay beyond? And not having possessed this pearl, how could we know what it might teach?

The picture of myself was suddenly thrown coldly in my face. I saw a young man going blind, it is true, but clinging to all that was pathetic in it, mourning because of a faith denied him. He played the classic role after all, even while sincerely thinking that he struggled against it. He cast his last lingering glances at the world, vacillating endlessly for fear of compromising this sense of his precious intellectual integrity. Yet all the while he was sinking deeper into the falsity where his concepts of intellectual integrity mired him. I felt blistered by self-contempt and embarrassed to catch myself in such falsity of which I was not even aware. But now, the self-indulged pathos shone clear and cheap in all its trappings of tragedy and sacrifice.

I got up and stomped out of the cathedral, relieved to have seen this image of myself, even in such a brutal way. Filled with an upsurge of energy, I sloshed through the downpour to a tobacco shop and bought a package of strong black cigarillos.

I hurried to the Duthoo mansion and sneered at my room which had been the locale of so much sadness. Stripping off my soaked clothing, I dried with a towel and plopped down in a chair. Rain gusted against the window—not the sad rain of the past weeks but the harboring rain of my youth, evoking warmth and accenting elements of safe shelter and the taste of butter cookies near the hearth.

I switched on the radio and listened for a moment while an elderly British poetess chewed the crystal of her verses. Cutting her off in the middle of a squawk, I turned the dial. The needle paused at Radio-Paris where a massive-voiced soprano bellowed. " . . . tergiversation . . . " the British poetess enunciated as I passed her station again. Then I landed on a full-bodied performance of Bach's second *Brandenburg Concerto,* which seemed to bounce into the curtained window corner where I sat.

I sank back in the chair, overwhelmed by the vigor and sanity of this music, as I would have been by some unexpected gift. It filled me with a jubilance that returned my entrails to health and brought tears of relief to my eyes. I lighted one of the strong cigarillos and savored the mingling of its aroma with the Bach.

So I would be blind. So the dim whiteness of curtained windows

73

would become nothing to sight. With such music and such smells, I could state it bluntly and laugh at it. So I would be blind. So what? By all rights, I should have been dead, buried somewhere in the Pacific. This was a new life, freely given. I could do with it whatever I wanted.

When the Bach ended, I switched off the radio and listened to the rain-filled silence, watching my nakedness fade to invisible shadow with the approach of night. From downstairs I heard the children's muffled voices and smelled a lamb roast.

Dinner was festive that night. I drank much wine and ate with good appetite and joked with the children.

It was a time of change, influenced by the Bach, the cathedral, and the rain. I felt contempt for sadness. That was all right in the ordinary run of living. A man had to try to get a little of everything in his one life, and feel cheated if he were denied any of it.

But with me, it was different. If I should consider that I was killed back there, dead and gone, then my life was done and I no longer had to look for my little of everything or to feel sad when I did not find it and cram it into my living. The years to come had been given me to live an experience which I was free to color any way I chose. These free hours were added gratuitously to the end of life. I was no longer bound to the ordinary reactions of men who lived their first and only lives.

However it might go, I should have no regrets. If I should be reduced to begging in the street, then I should enjoy the feel of pavement beneath my feet and the odors of asphalt and automobile exhausts. Good and bad fortune were equally attractive when viewed in such a context. Hunger was as interesting as satiety. A life without sight was as interesting as a life with sight. Who was to say different? Society? The bulk of humanity?

They were living their first lives, cautiously aware that someday they would die. They had everything to lose. They could not take the risks. But I had been through death, had my insides burned out by it twice.

I was living a second life, freed of those cautious awarenesses.

I had nothing to lose. I could take all the risks.

— The Abbey of Solesmes —

While packing, I recalled an errand I had promised to perform for the painter Abraham Rattner, who had asked me to take packages of clothing to friends in France. Among the bundles, most of which had been delivered in Paris, was one for the poet Pierre Reverdy, who lived in Solesmes. Reverdy's had been the only name on Rattner's list that was familiar. It was a name to excite and intimidate anyone who had studied in France, for it was one of the great names of French literature.

I had pinned to the top of his bundle the thumbnail sketch Rattner had written me. I carried it up to the room and read once again in Abe's enormous handwriting: "Pierre Reverdy—the purest of French poets. Not a self-pusher. Refuses to encourage publication of his work. One of the pioneer cubist group, along with Max Jacob, Braque, Apollinaire and Picasso. Fiery temperament; discourses beautifully. Tender, considerate, gentle, warm—also violent. Take him toothbrush, toothpaste, two large-sized shirts, two suits, underwear, three pairs of socks."

During my school days in Tours before the war, the great painters and poets were our heroes. The regimen of the lycée was almost monastic in its strictness. We were not allowed to leave the enclosed grounds, rarely heard a radio, and almost never saw a newspaper. In those days, we as students had read books and studied paintings for recreation, and our discussions were an awakening of thought, art, and sexuality. The Latin and Greek classics, Molière, Racine, Balzac—these were our background, and our most heated enthusiasms brought forth the names of Braque, Vlaminck, Chagall, Matisse, and Derain in painting, and those of Rimbaud, Apollinaire, Claudel, and Reverdy in literature.

To meet Reverdy, the modern French poet I most admired, would be as personally daunting as working with the music masters at the Abbey of Saint Pierre of Solesmes, the motherhouse of Gregorian Chant.

Jacques Duthoo's automobile motored us to the monastery and we arrived there about nine-thirty in the morning of a clear, cold day. We stepped through the gates into a world of the Middle Ages, an austere world of black-robed monks. The change was sudden, physical, tangible. Quietness settled over us as we stood in the courtyard and stared up at the sunlit façade of the towering stone structure. The birds had gone for the winter, and the rush of the wide Sarthe River, invisible below the monastery walls, added depth to the silence. Away from the highways and railroads, the massive Benedictine Abbey rose in solitary splendor from the river. Surrounding it was a miniature village, also medieval in appearance, with two hundred inhabitants, most of them farm workers.

A large, balding monk strode across the courtyard, smiling broadly. After Father Froger introduced us to his brother, he asked if we had time to put our bags in our cells before Mass. "Yes," the monk said. "Mr. Griffin, you will occupy a cell there over the chapel." He pointed to a second-story door. The stone steps, worn low in the center and without a guard rail, led up to the entrance.

They accompanied me up the perilous stairs to the cell, a small sun-lit room furnished with a cot, a washstand, a writing table, and a straight-backed chair. The single window looked out on the trees in the courtyard.

The monk handed me a hand-lettered card from the night table. "This card has full instructions and the daily schedule," he said. "Do you think you'll be all right here?"

"Fine," I said.

"Be careful of those outside steps when it rains. Immediately after *Compline*, we begin the Great Silence. From then until *Matins* in the morning, no conversation shall be allowed unless it is an emergency." He stepped to the window and pointed down toward a long, squat structure surrounded by hedges. "Down there are the water closets." Leaves from the tree stirred in a light breeze, moving shadows over the monk's hand on the window sill. "But you are requested not to leave this cell after *Compline*. You'll find a chamber pot in the night stand if you should need it at night. And let me see. The nearest water for shaving and washing is downstairs to the left of the door, which is a faucet in the courtyard. But your pitcher here will be filled every morning. If you feel you can, you might clean your cell each morning."

A bell clanged close by and the monk left immediately to take his place in the choir. "No hurry for us," Father Froger said, knocking his pipe ashes out against the window sill. "Let's stroll about a bit."

Though the air chilled, the sun warmed through our clothes as we walked to the end of the gardens and fruit orchards. I noticed a friar stooping before a barred cage.

"What are those over there," I asked, "hog pens?"

"Yes, they are virtually self-sufficient here," he explained. "Behind these walls they have a complete community—gardens, livestock, shoe shop, laundry, bakery—everything. He pointed toward the main building. "Up there, where you see that row of large windows, you'll find one of the world's great libraries. They have either the originals or copies of every known Gregorian Chant manuscript in existence."

We sidestepped a large puddle of water. "I don't suppose you could find such a gathering of scholars anywhere else in the world," he went on. "Certainly not living under these conditions of poverty, chastity, and obedience. They are true monks. When they enter here, they also take a vow of stability. That means they can never ask to be transferred, never go to another monastery. They know they will live out their lives here behind these walls, die here, and be buried here."

"Such a beautiful place," I said.

"Yes, beautiful, but wait until you know it better. Life here is hard and primitive. They are never warm enough in winter. You will see how simple the food is. Never again will they taste a fine roast chicken or a slab of cold lamb gigot with mayonnaise, or even French fries. And the silence . . . "

"The silence?" I asked, listening to the sounds of stock animals.

"It's the silence that gets me," he said with a grimace. "After three days here, I always feel like shouting."

Muffled through stone walls, organ music then drifted to us. Not at all like dolorous funeral-parlor music, but clean and robust sounds that sang in the autumn air. When Father Froger pulled the heavy door open, the music poured out from the chapel. We walked directly under the organ loft, where we could feel the pedal notes reverberate on the stone floor beneath our feet.

We knelt in a pew midway to the front of the empty chapel. Odors of cold incense lay strong in the high vaulted nave. Far to the front, bathed in the sun's slanting rays, the altar glowed with its white linens, its golden tabernacle, its lighted tapers.

Black-robed monks began to enter by twos into the sanctuary from a side door. They ambled in, approached the altar and made profound obeisance, then took their places in the long rows of ornately carved benches at each side. Movements were made in slow cadence to the accompaniment of splendid organ music, until the one hundred and twenty monks were in their places.

A final bright chord echoed forward through the chapel. As the sound died, the *Introit* began with a soft upswing of monks' voices. Many voices in perfect unison breathed life into melody, spreading in an ocean of sound without sharpness. The chant floated in long undulating lines as a feather might float on the waves of a sea.

This was my reason for being here. This moment culminated years of study when I had sat in tents in the Pacific or in lonely rooms around the world, poring over this music. Now, imagined sounds became real. I listened to tender, awe-stricken chants of adoration and petition, buried myself in the timeless splendor of the Mass. Nerves detached and settled into peace. I knew that I was living one of the high points of my life.

After Mass, the spell of this music lingered with a lightness, a hush that made it impossible for us to speak when we walked from the chapel.

I took advantage of the free time before lunch to return to the cell and to unpack. The odor of fresh straw from the mattress, which apparently had been newly stuffed, greeted me when I opened the door. I glanced at its lumpy surface, its worn blanket, and remembered the good bed of the previous night with its thick mattress and crisp linens. I preferred this poor bed—a cot, actually. And I preferred this cell, so sunlit and yet so cold, hidden here in a labyrinth of stone, surrounded by silent monks.

Unpacking the Reverdy bundle, I carried it down to the gatehouse and asked the monk on duty to certify Rattner's directions to the poet's house. Abe had written that it was located "only a hundred yards down the lane in front of the gatehouse entrance. It's the last house on the right, an old *grange* he converted into his living quarters when the Germans occupied his house next door." The directions were correct, I was told. I hurried down the lane, lined with a jumble of tile-roofed stone houses. A high stone wall surrounded the Reverdy property.

I rang the bell and waited before the solid plank door in the wall. After a long time, I heard the house door open and close. Then footsteps approached across the yard toward the wall. I shifted the bundle to my left hand, so I could shake the poet's hand with my right. Nervousness surged in me at the thought of meeting one of the legendary figures of French literature.

"Yes?" a woman said without opening the door. "Who's there?"

"Is this the Reverdy home?" I called out, aiming my voice at the top of the wall a few feet above my head.

"He's not here."

"Is this Madame Reverdy?"

"Yes, what do you want, please?"

"I bring a package of clothing for Monsieur Reverdy from his friend, Abraham Rattner in America," I shouted in French.

"Oh," she said uncertainly. "He won't be back for some time."

"May I leave the package?"

After another long hesitation, she opened the door a crack. I looked into an attractive middle-aged woman's face, into her clear brown eyes.

"May I carry the bundle in?" I asked.

"I guess it would be all right," she said uneasily.

"If you prefer I didn't . . . but it's a large package, as you can see."

Opening the door wider, she admitted me and closed it again quickly. Then she tightened a brown shawl about her shoulders and led the way.

The wall enclosed an orchard, a small garden, and the stone *grange* that was now their home. The *grange* had been made into one large room with two small sleeping alcoves and a kitchen to the side. One wide window looked out onto the garden and orchard. A wood stove had been installed in the brick fireplace. The opposite wall was solid with bookshelves. On chalk-white walls hung two bright and serene

Braques, a large Leger, and Picasso's portraits of Reverdy and St. Thérèse of Lisieux.

When I complimented Madame Reverdy on the paintings, she shrugged and said: "They're pieces done by friends." When she did not invite me to sit, I deposited the bundle on a sofa.

"We don't receive guests here," she said apologetically. "Pierre sees all of his friends in Paris. He receives no one except the gardener from the monastery. He leads two lives: One as a farmer here in Solesmes, where those who know his real identity guard the secret; and the other in Paris, among his friends. Only special friends are ever allowed behind these walls. The rest have to see him in Paris."

"I understand. I certainly didn't mean to intrude."

She asked for my address, saying Pierre would want to thank me for the bundle. I explained that I was at the Abbey for an indefinite stay.

Her defenses softened instantly. "Oh, well, then he can thank you in person when he comes back. He's in a hospital in Paris."

When I expressed concern, she said: "Again Rattner was involved. He sent Pierre a beautiful new overcoat several months ago. Pierre wore it to Paris and there, in the foyer of his hotel, a friend introduced him to a communist. The communist sneered at his new coat and called him a capitalist. So Pierre swung at him." With a sober face, she illustrated a short uppercut that tossed her shawl wildly. "He hit the communist in the jaw, so hard it broke a bone in Pierre's arm. He came back here. He's so stubborn, you know. Well, the arm got worse, but he wouldn't allow me to call a doctor."

"I'm so sorry. Did he suffer much?"

"Oh, frightfully. You'd have to know Pierre to know how he suffered," she said with a faint smile. "It alarmed me, but I could not get him to do a thing. Then, thank God, Picasso came in and took charge. He made all the arrangements with doctors in Paris and got Pierre a private room at the hospital. Then he told Pierre he would hire thugs to carry him there bodily if he didn't go quietly. They operated on him four days ago. Heaven knows how long he will be there." I promised not to reveal to the villagers who their neighbor was and bid Madame Reverdy good-bye.

When I entered the monastery gatehouse, the clangor of small, high-pitched bells greeted me. I walked toward the refectory, where a small monk with white hair nodded me toward him. In one hand he held a silver urn, and over the black sleeve of his robe hung a white linen towel. A much younger monk stood beside him holding a silver basin. The elderly monk introduced himself as the Father Abbot, explaining in a soft voice St. Benedict's rule that the Abbot wash the feet of every guest. Because of the cold, he said, he would wash my hands instead.

"Hold out your hands, please," gesturing that I should turn my palms up. He poured warm water over them while the younger monk held the basin beneath to catch the drippings. Afterward, the Abbot dried my hands as though handling precious jewels, with a reverence that embarrassed me. The young assistant took the urn, the used towel and the basin, bowed low and disappeared into the shadows with them.

"You are American?" the Abbot asked in English, looking up at me.

"Yes, Father."

"Big," he said affably, spreading out his frail arms as though he were encircling an invisible barrel.

"Yes sir . . . "

He raised a wrinkled forefinger to his eyes and his face pursed into an expression of sympathy. "Poor eyes."

It surprised me that he should know about my condition.

Another monk approached and knelt on one knee beside us. Without taking his gaze from my face, Father Abbot made the sign of the cross in the air above the monk's head. The monk rose, bowed and went into the refectory. "Are you hungry?" he asked.

"Not very, Father."

"You must eat, eat much. Monastic food not too . . . " he searched for the word in English but then supplied it in French, "*nourrissant . . .*" He motioned me to enter the refectory at his side. As we crossed the long, vaulted room, monks at each side bowed low and held the bow until we were well past them. Father Abbot placed me at a table in the center of the room, where Father Froger stood behind a chair. Then the old man tottered to his own table at the head of the room.

With heads bowed, we recited the long benediction. At prayer's end, the Abbot struck his table with a small wooden gavel. Monks sat and tucked towel-sized napkins under their chins. I picked at a large plateful of thick mush, which appeared to be a combination of meat broths, potatoes, yellow beans, and onions cooked together and then mashed through a food mill.

We ate in silence, accompanied by the high chanting voice of a reader who sat above us on a raised lectern and intoned a text about the early nuns in Canada and their persecution by the Indians. His voice floated through the hall, enunciating as though in a trance, the details of horror in which nuns were scalped and mutilated.

After lunch, I went to the paleography room, where I watched the monk specialists stand before their tall desks and edit huge manuscript sheets of Gregorian Chant. A monk entered the room and informed me that Madame Reverdy wished to speak with me at the gatehouse.

"Can you do me a favor?" she asked the moment I appeared.

"Of course."

She asked if I would telephone friends in Paris for her. "They'll know how Pierre is getting along. I expected some word in this morning's mail, but none came. Here is fifty francs—no, I insist on paying the call. Pierre would want me to. And here are the people to call," she said, handing me a folded piece of white paper. "When you have talked with them, will you come and tell me?"

"Is there a phone here?" I asked.

"Yes, there are only two in the village. One here and one at the post office." The monk standing behind the grill nodded agreement.

"But wouldn't you prefer making the call yourself?"

"No, I'm no good with telephones." She turned toward the door as I unfolded the paper. I glanced at the name scribbled on it.

"Madame?"

She turned back at the door.

"Is this Georges Braque? Do you want me to call the painter?"

"Yes," she studied me for an instant. "What's the matter?"

"Nothing. It's just that I'm not asked every day to telephone a famous man like Braque."

"He's a very nice man," she smiled. "You have excellent French, so you won't have any trouble. Will you come tell me what he says?"

She walked out the door before I could answer.

The gatehouse keeper, a tall, pleasant man, helped me put the call through. He trembled exaggeratedly and said: "If I were telephoning Raphael himself, I could not be more excited. Just think. You'll tell your grandchildren about the day you telephoned Braque. There, the phone is ringing. Take it quick."

"Why don't you say hello first?" I asked.

"No, take it. I'm not likely to have grandchildren to tell it to. Hello? Hello? Monsieur Braque? Oh, Madame Braque. One moment please."

He shoved the phone receiver into my hand and stepped back.

Madame Braque said that Reverdy was doing well. "I posted a letter to Henriette this morning," she said. "Listen, Pierre has a phone in his room now. Why don't you call him? It would please him so much."

I copied Reverdy's telephone number and replaced the receiver.

"No Braque, eh?" the gatekeeper said.

"No Braque."

He sighed. "It's hardly worth having grandchildren just to tell them you talked with Madame Braque. I'm glad I'm a monk after all. Say," he brightened, "your friend Reverdy knows all the great ones. Why don't we profit from the occasion and call Rouault or Picasso or the Maritains?"

I told him I could not afford such calls. He glared at me and muttered his disappointment that not all Americans were rich.

I took the news to Madame Reverdy, who received it with gratitude. "I'll write Pierre and ask if we should telephone him at the hospital."

When I passed through the monastery gatehouse, the monk on duty called my name. I turned back to see his bald pate against the grill.

"Can you take a collect call from Rome?"

"Rome?"

"Yes, a Madame Michelangelo . . . "

I could not stifle my laughter. Then we talked seriously for a moment about Reverdy. He leaned forward on the counter behind the grill.

"They came here years ago to live near the Abbey. She became an oblate, but something happened to him. I don't know what. I think he was like Léon Bloy, always outraged by the cheapness and viciousness that afflict so many routine Christians."

I returned to the cell above the chapel. I sat on the cot and stared out the window, doing nothing, thinking nothing, and being perfectly content in doing and thinking nothing.

I drowsed and awoke to a more somber light. A great thirst burned my throat. I lifted the pitcher of water from the washstand and drank most of it.

As I replaced it in its white bowl, I heard someone cough in the courtyard below. I glanced out the window to see the black-cowled head of a monk. He stopped before a fruit tree, brought a limb close to his face and examined it. I looked down on a stranger, hidden beneath black cloth, elderly from the way he walked, and I wondered how it was for him. Slowly he made his rounds, examining limbs, pruning some and then casting the discarded branches into a pile beside the path.

What had happened to him that made him different from ordinary men like me? What had happened that reconciled all seeming contraries in life until mind and soul were wed in harmony? Somewhere in the past he had stepped across the void in that act of momentarily blind faith that must have been dazzling. The monk struck flame to the prunings, and the fire spread quickly over the pile, bright in the growing dusk. The pleasant odor of smoke, dampened by beginning mists, lingered in the courtyard when I went down to attend *Vespers*.

I sat in the back of the chapel and listened to the monks chant the undulating melodies, unhurried, exquisitely evocative. Time fell away.

Shadows

It was as it had been for centuries. And the food that night was the same timeless food: boiled celery, bread, and water.

I returned to the cell, surrounded by the Great Silence and the rain that blew against the window. I stared out, cupping hands beside my face against the glass. No pinpoint of light flickered out there in the valley. In the maze of corridors and cells, only my lamp burned within the cloister.

I listened with a mingling of awe and contentment, aware that although I was alone, others slept in cells nearby.

Since there was nothing else to do, I put on pajamas and went to bed.

Odors of straw and the rough muslin mattress cover rose when I settled on the cot. I reached for covers that were not there, then got up to spread my overcoat across the cot. Drifting off to sleep, cold and hungry, I was aware of the most profound happiness I had ever known.

⁓ Pierre Reverdy ⁓

The days entered into a deep rhythm, not of clocks but of tolling bells, reverberating throughout the valley, telling us when to attend the offices, when to eat, when to retire. But the jubilance of the chants, the awesome silence, the medieval tone of the monastery, grew so profound it obliterated the discomforts of the freezing cold, the dreary food, the lack of warm water or inside toilets, and even the rudeness of living without personal amenities or communication with women.

In the chapel's wintry light, I followed the chanted offices with my reading glass and missal, renewing my Latin. Often I was the only visitor in the vast room, particularly at the early morning and the night offices. Imperceptibly, the liturgy entered our being, possessing the imagination, coloring all thoughts. I began to perceive how it could transform a life.

This is how and what had happened to the monks here and those in Paris. The liturgy had become the foundation stone for their lives. They were products of the liturgical formation; it shone in their gestures, their faces, their speech, producing a strange effect each time I met and spoke with one of them. I was aware of each monk as an individual human being of flesh, appetites, and a name; at the same time I was aware of him as a living liturgy. Though individuality was liberated rather than smothered, and even though our relationships were impersonal, we knew all the nuances of one another's being insofar as we perceived the nuances of the liturgy.

If the element of mystery, the Divine Mystery, surrounded us, the secrecy between us had vanished, for our lives were transparent to all in the monastery.

I felt out of place precisely because the liturgy had *not* formed me, because my reactions were formed by and attuned to the world outside.

It would take time before I could walk silently and know that presence did not shout. I waited without anxiety for the liturgy to do its work, in its own time. Within those walls, concepts of time disappeared beneath the natural rhythms of life. These rhythms captured the heartbeat and the respiration. One floated with them, effortlessly, unthinkingly, but aware that to rush forward in time or to feel impatience would be to defile the natural order of things.

Within a few days of my last meeting with Madame Reverdy, she had a letter from her husband, instructing her to have me telephone him each day at the hospital and then carry the news to her. Standing near the entrance gate at the Abbey, she read part of the letter as though to reassure me. "You will receive him," wrote the poet, "let him warm by the fire and offer him hot tea or coffee."

I told her this was too much of an imposition.

But she waved his letter in the freezing air, as if it were a command we must not question. So it was arranged.

Each day I used the telephone at the Abbey to call him. He spoke in the warm, thick accent of the Midi. During every call, he asked me to reassure his wife that he was fine, though he did not hesitate to admit to me privately that he was dying of pain and that the hospital was staffed by devils and sadists.

"But tell her not to worry. Be certain, will you?" he pleaded. "Tell her I am well and happy. I suppose it is all right since my friends won't rescue me from this nightmare."

And when I consoled him about the pain: "The pain," he groaned. "I'm too old to suffer such pain. It is agony, my poor friend, agony. But you must not worry. Tell my wife to buy a beefsteak and cook it for you outside on the grill. You must be starving on that monastic fare. Have a good meal for once."

"But I can't deliver such a message to your wife."

"Tell her. I insist. If you don't, I'll have to write her the message, and in such agony, that would be a cruel thing to make me do."

When the weather became glacial, fuel was scarce, and we had no heat in our cells at the Abbey. I was fortunate for an hour each afternoon to sit before the Reverdy's stove and drink hot coffee, surrounded by their magnificent paintings and books. Madame Reverdy, who insisted I call her Henriette, was interested in faraway places and would ask about the islands of the Pacific or about America, or about England and Ireland, where I had been for brief periods after escaping from the Gestapo in France.

And in turn, Henriette would talk about her husband. "He was poor, but that had no importance. He could have gone into the wine business with his father in Narbonne, but he had a passionate obsession with freedom. His liberty was the only thing that counted with him. He came to Paris and took jobs as a copy editor and proofreader for publishers. But even at that, it was only substitute work, never regular. He worked mostly at night. He'd work three nights a week and earn forty francs. That was enough. When he left work, around two or three in the morning, he would go to his room and start writing by gaslight . . ."

During World War II, when the Germans occupied the Reverdy home, he became silent. He created nothing at all. And when the Germans had left, he refused to live in the house they had occupied. "No," Henriette explained, "he sold it and converted this old barn into our living quarters. He rebelled against any symbol of tyranny, anything that put a damper on his creative freedom and turned him into a slave."

And yet, ironically, I felt that Reverdy had ended up overwhelmingly aware of his slavery—his slavery to freedom itself. But I did not express this opinion to Madame Reverdy.

"Pierre dies of loneliness here," Henriette said. "His work is all from his great loneliness. It is perhaps a good thing he had to stay in the hospital. There he has friends who come to see him . . . Braque, Picasso, Borés, and the rest. But he broke with Borés again just recently," she informed me. Then she picked up a letter that she had just received from her husband and said: "Listen to this letter from Pierre."

"Borés came in while I was talking to Griffin on the phone," wrote Reverdy. "When I hung up, he had to know who it was. I told him it was an American friend. Then he said, in that sarcastic, nasty sweet way of his: 'Me, I don't care for Americans.' That was enough. I kicked him out. No, I decided then and there. I told myself I had put up with Picasso's Spanish moods all my life; and I'm too old to have another Spanish genius for a friend, no matter how much I admire his painting. I told him *merde* for good luck and never to talk to me again."

I apologized for being the cause of that rift.

"You don't know that crowd," she laughed. "By tomorrow Borés will be loving the Americans and they will have a great reconciliation. They fight and make up—always. Those Spaniards! But they are sweet people. When we were in Paris, Juan Gris would visit us in the evenings with his guitar or Braque with his concertina and we would drink strong coffee and have music. We were too poor to have anything else."

Scattered Shadows

After being warmed by the fire, the strong, hot coffee, and Henriette's companionship, I returned to the Abbey each afternoon. I spent most of the time studying beside the monks who researched the Gregorian Chant manuscripts in the paleography room.

Occasionally, I walked the four miles to Sablé to cash a check and have a cup of hot chocolate, or to take a shower in the public baths. Once, when the temperature had hung at zero for several days and the Sarthe River outside our windows was a block of ice, I felt I could not bear being without a bath. I brought a large carafe of water from the kitchen and bathed with a sponge, standing upright in the washbowl.

To my astonishment, in below zero temperatures, it was scarcely less comfortable taking the sponge bath than being clothed. I slept fully dressed, often wearing my overcoat, scarf and gloves as well. When I awoke those mornings the water in the pitcher was always frozen, and I had to rub a towel across the ice until it was damp enough to wash my face. But though the days were usually dark and the temperatures were a constant burden, the pervading impression was one of light, warmth, and peace. For days on end, I spoke to no one within the Abbey. Silence there became a value too precious to be squandered needlessly.

In mid-December of 1946, I came down with the high fevers and deep chills of malaria. When I regained consciousness, my mail lay on the table beside the cot. One of the letters was from Reverdy in Paris. "My dear friend," he wrote, "I have learned this moment by a letter from my wife that you have fallen ill at Solesmes. I am very worried. I hope they will already be subsiding when you receive this word. Here, I have at present, some cognac that I can't drink because I'm running a temperature. I wish you could have it. I'm even sorrier now not to be at Solesmes. I should have been able to take care of you. I'm about as good at nursing the sick as anyone I know, which isn't saying much."

Reverdy's letter concluded with a gentle command: "Tell my wife to make you some good coffee, very strong, and to buy a bottle of cognac. If you take aspirins, then drink the alcohol with the coffee, it should do something. And my entire library is at your disposal. As soon as you are able, give me your news." I was too sick to deliver a message to his wife and, in any case, I had had enough medical training to know that a mixture of cognac, aspirin, and coffee would not be a remedy for malaria.

A week later, Henriette sent word that Pierre would be home that following week, and they wanted me to come for lunch next Thursday. I called on her in person to accept their invitation.

"You must not pay any attention to what he says," Henriette

warned. "He is fond of you, says you have a warm heart in spite of the fact that you are intelligent in that educated way he detests. He thinks if you stop studying soon enough, you may be all right."

"He doesn't like intelligence?" I asked.

"He reveres art and only art. Pierre thinks that intelligence is damaged by too much education. He believes that too many facts nullify truth."

Before I could respond, Henriette added: "You must come in through the kitchen door. That will give him time to get up from his chair and greet you standing up."

"But he doesn't have to stand up to greet me," I protested.

"You don't know Pierre. He plans on making a great thing of this greeting," she said and shrugged her shoulders as though not entirely understanding the connection herself. "He wrote full instructions. His greeting is apparently part of his plan to divert you from your studies."

On that Thursday, I waded through snowdrifts toward their house. I don't know what I expected—an old man with burning eyes, perhaps. I had the foreboding that he would make me the scapegoat of his hatred for the intellectual stereotype, the neat mind, the fact-crammed mind. In my self-consciousness, I knew I would assume that role, fit the portrait he had of me. I told myself: "No matter what he says or does, he is a great poet, and that is all that counts." I rang the bell and waited to meet one of the heroes of my youth.

Henriette opened the gate door, smiled reassuringly but with a hint of amusement. Holding a shawl around her arms and shoulders, she led me to the kitchen door. We stumped snow from our shoes, crossed the tiled floor of the kitchen, and she opened the door of the main room.

When I walked in, a powerfully built, square-shaped man stood in the middle of the room with both arms outstretched and a smile as open as sunlight on his handsome face. "Ah-ha," he said as we shook hands.

The room was filled with a shadowless gray brilliance reflected from the snow outside. The poet was dressed in a heavy blanket-like bathrobe with a wool muffler around his neck. His dark face was hidden behind several days' growth of beard stubble, black with silver highlights. His dusty beret, worn like a skull cap, held the hair of his massive head. In one continuing gesture, he was greeting me, shoving me into a chair near the wood stove and pouring wine. He apologized for his beard.

"With this arm, I can't shave," he said, nodding toward his right arm in a sling.

"I'll shave you, if it's uncomfortable," I suggested.

"Ah, good. After lunch, eh?" He lit a cigarette and then looked at me sharply. "Did you ever shave anyone else?"

"No, but surely it couldn't be too difficult."

"Do you use the blade or the safety razor."

When I told him I used the safety razor, he decided not to risk it.

"You look bad," he said. "That fever really ravaged you, eh?"

The fevers had lingered on, and I was weak and appeared gaunt.

"I know of these things," he said. "We'll get you well. You need plenty of food, plenty of alcohol, and plenty of aspirin."

His "cure" was drastic, but there was no question who was in charge. He opened a bottle of Montbazillac, filled a drinking glass for each of us and took his seat opposite me, near the stove.

"Tell me about yourself. You roam the world studying. Why?"

Henriette, setting the table, glanced at me as though to say she had told me so, and also with a vague smile, clearly indicating that I would be perfectly within my rights to say it was none of his business.

"I don't know. What else is there to do? I have no particular talent. Until I discover one, I thought I should spend my time studying."

"I know what you mean, but in my heart I don't really understand it," he said gently. "I've had to write from the very beginning. If I hadn't, I'd have gone mad long ago. My writing is what saved my sanity."

Henriette called us to the table. But the large apéritif had gone to our heads. "Who wants to eat?" Pierre said. "We have wine and good talk." She reminded him how sick I was. He became concerned again. "Yes, we must eat," he agreed. "The talk will come later—all through the winter."

That afternoon we gave his "cure" a fair trial. He poured coffee after cognac and then handed over aspirins. The conversation became brilliant for a time and then turned fuzzy.

By early evening, I could do little more than reel back to my freezing cell at the monastery. I crawled onto the cot without removing any piece of clothing and fell into a drunken slumber. In the middle of the night, I awakened groggy and certain I was dying. The garish reflection of moonlight on snow cast a cold brilliance. The flesh of my cheeks drew tight with a stippling of chill while fever and nausea boiled within me. One desperate fact stood out: I was trapped in the Great Silence. They would want me to break it, to shout for the help I needed. They would rebuke me for not calling out. The rule was not inhuman, but I could not bring myself to break it. I rolled on my side, balled up in the blankets, freezing and burning. The shoe on one foot lay heavily on the ankle of the other. I pressed my arms hard across my stomach and concentrated on not crying out. From the corner of my eye, I saw the splotch of the crucifix hanging silently above. Dimly I tried to turn, to grasp the chamber pot, as liquids began to spew from my mouth. Consciousness faded.

Later, consciousness flickered back briefly. Someone washed my face. I sat naked in a chair under blankets, the sun streaming in the window. Two monks spread the cot. Silence. A great emptiness inside me. Back in bed. Barley soup carried in by another monk. The sweet smell of straw now tainted with old vomit and the odor of soap.

Consciousness returned fully one morning, a week later. A note from Reverdy lay on the table. He, too, had been violently ill. Apologizing, he could not understand what had gone wrong with his medical advice. He suggested it must have been bad coffee, since the "cure" had always proved effective for the fevers in his past experience.

Except for going downstairs to meals, I spent the following days lying fully clothed beneath the blankets. The snows reflected a brilliant and peaceful light into the cell. During the hours of the offices, chants from the chapel below rose to fill the cell. Otherwise, silence surrounded me.

Perhaps it was some peculiar susceptibility caused by the fevers, the weakness. Perhaps for once my physical appetites were quiet enough to allow me to think. Perhaps it was the simplicity of light on the stone walls of the cell. In any event, thoughts wandered over all the elements of my life and found it fit for the basket. I had tried many paths that led nowhere: the reflection that I could do what I wished with my life; the words of Marie-Bruno, saying I had a will and some choice in the matter; Reverdy asking why I studied aimlessly; Bloy's statement that man is chained to his flesh by a false modesty that tells him he is unworthy of the dream of sanctity; and Aquinas's vision that man attains to sanctity not by destroying his humanity but by perfecting it.

The questions formed torturously in that barren cell. Could a man of such mediocre qualities, glued to the earth, with no religious instinct left intact, set about systematically to will a complete alteration in himself? Could a man deliberately set about to make himself the slave of a God for whom he had not the slightest feeling? Could a man turn his back on the intoxications of the ego in order to open himself to other and greater intoxications? Could a man seek to become selfless? How could I, with my passion for freedom, choose to become a slave? Or was voluntary slavery the only true freedom?

We who vaunted ourselves on being free were slaves to countless masters—to social pressures, to values and standards that were rooted in the concrete and brick institutions of our age. Freely chosen slavery to God was scarcely a step down. It might be, through some mystery, the ultimate liberation.

Self-love was necessary at the outset. I could see that self-love needed to be the triggering mechanism. It was sufficient to realize, however, that somewhere along the way, it must be purged from the system—or allowed to dissipate—before further progress could be made. At a given point, every vestige of it must become so uninteresting as to disappear before what is supremely interesting.

At times, especially during the long silences of the night, I recoiled in horror from my deliberations. They were too calculated. Could anyone really assault love with quite such sledge-hammer obtuseness? But how did one go about such a thing? Could a man transfer the techniques already learned?

A phrase from Jacques Maritain's *Art and Scholasticism* intrigued me. He remarked that skill was no part of art. "The labor through which the zither player acquires nimbleness of finger does not increase his art as such nor does it engender any special art; it simply removes the physical impediment to the exercise of the art."

Could one not start from this same premise in the religious life or in the life of love—acquiring techniques not for the sake of techniques, but as a means of removing the impediments to love? If the chief impediment to the gift of love was self, self must be deemphasized.

Then what if, instead of seeking to be known or esteemed, one sought to be the least known and the least esteemed? And what if, instead of seeking to be invincible, one sought to be defenseless?

I chilled before these thoughts. Only a man with a profound vocation could enter that way, or a man with a life to toss into the ashcan. I must make the deliberate choice to learn how to do it. I must make it coldly and struggle not to take it back.

Late afternoon slanted across the snow-covered branches. A matching hush lay within me. It rarefied the atmosphere, revealing an unnoticed detail and an unknown dimension to these walls and these senses. My hand lay beside my face on the pillow. I smelled the cigarette sourness and the body stench of fingers that had not felt soap in many days.

"This must always be," I told myself. "If this ever vanishes into the other, then it will be delusion. The body must not become my enemy." I lay stunned, like a man beaten. I glimpsed the infinite gap between what I was and what I planned. But it obliterated all other values.

The things that had been my strongest desires had suddenly become blurred. What I planned drew me like a magnet, not from the brain but from a polarization of new desires centered in my heart and belly, which felt the excitement. My brain felt only the ache of incomprehension.

⟶ The Villa ⟵

The fevers recurred so frequently that in January of 1947, I had to leave the Abbey. My system could not tolerate the unrelieved cold, and I was unable to regain enough strength on the monastic diet, even though the monks often supplemented it with eggs.

Father Abbot suggested that I might rent the empty villa owned by Madame and Commandant Mahot. It was a nicely furnished house that they used only in summer and during the great religious feasts of Easter and Christmas. The Mahots made the trip from Le Mans to complete the arrangement, and they were quite open about their desire to have the house occupied. "The cold does such damage," they explained. "We have enough wood for you to build a modest fire in one room. You can live and sleep right here in the salon."

Defensively, I asked the price.

"Five American dollars a month," the Commandant suggested. Then seeing my expression of disbelief, he hastily added. "I don't think it's unreasonable for such a nice villa."

"It's unreasonably low," I said.

"Well, then, let's make it six dollars a month and we'll pay utilities."

I paid for three months in advance, before they could come to their senses. Then for a few days the Mahots set about assisting me in getting established in the villa before their return to Le Mans.

They had a large wood stove installed in the formal marble fireplace of the salon. "It is less romantic than an open fireplace," she explained, "but you'll find it heats much better and uses far less fuel."

Then she cleared the cabinet drawers in the salon for clothes storage. She pointed out that I was fortunate to have a cold water faucet in the kitchen. "Only three other houses in the entire village of Solesmes have running water. The others must carry buckets from the public pump." Then a short time later she bade me good-bye. "You are in your home now. May you enjoy it," she said cheerfully.

The villa was perched on the sidewalk, but with no door to the street. Both front and back doors opened onto a small courtyard surrounded by high stone walls. The only entrance to the street was from the courtyard by way of an iron grill gate, contrived to ring a warning bell whenever it was opened. This provided the privacy I sought.

The monks were delighted that I would have a warm room at night and more nutritious food. I was still welcome at the monastery to continue musical studies. The villa was palatial compared to the cell at the Abbey, even though I would be living exclusively in the salon. It was a large, formal room, but comfortable. A full double bed in the corner near the fireplace had been arranged to resemble a sofa, with a brown corduroy cover and pillows. Beside it, on a bedstand, stood a handsome radio.

I unpacked the box of books I had borrowed from the Abbey library, books that I hoped would guide me along a new path. I placed them in a stack on a large writing table that stood in the middle of the room. Their presence warmed me—works by Augustine and Aquinas, Teresa of Avila and John of the Cross; modern texts by Bloy, Maritain, Nicholas Berdyaev and Father Reginald Garrigou-Lagrange.

Stepping up from the salon into the kitchen, I drew water from the faucet to drink, then went outside through the double kitchen doors and walked across the snow to the opposite corner of the courtyard where the water closet stood like a miniature stone turret.

The door was hinged so that it cleared the ground by a full six inches, making it easy to open even with the thick snow on the ground. The inside, lined with raw wood and with a seat cut from wood, was immaculate. There were several packets of toilet tissue, something I had not seen in many months, since we had cut-up newspapers at the Abbey.

At dusk, I lighted a fire in the stove. I closed the doors to the salon and walked out toward the little café on the other side of the Sarthe River to have supper.

I had developed only a nodding acquaintance with the villagers. Most were older men and women who had lived in dignified poverty, scraping for an egg, a pint of milk, a piece of wood to burn. Compared to them, I was relatively affluent. If they were out in the cold, they were not on their way to have a hot meal in a café. I sat alone in a small room with coarse wooden chairs and tables.

Through the windows, beyond the delicate silhouette of poplar limbs, I could see the towering Abbey high above the river. I ate a large portion of yellow beans cooked with link sausages, buttered bread, and a bottle of good red wine, finishing with a cup of black coffee.

When I walked back across the bridge, a first star shone in a sky yet light. The valley stretched white and deserted. I thought of the monks in chapel, carrying on with the eternal rhythms of their lives. I felt strange not being there with them, strange to be alone in this cold whiteness. I thought of my family in America, in their homes in cities of neon and concrete and central heating. I wondered what they were doing.

And I wondered what I was doing here alone, so far from them in this isolated valley, immersed in silence, exposed to the night's bareness; here where life remained primitive and simple comfort was a rarity; here where a man had no distractions and must face himself. But I belonged here, for a time at least, and of that I was certain. This was what I needed, this stern and serene nourishment.

I unlocked the gate and heard the bell's high ringing, brittle on the stillness. When I opened the salon door, warmth flowed out—authentic, luxurious warmth, seeping quickly through the layers of clothing. I was able to remove the heavy coat and sweaters without shivering.

Alone in the complete privacy of this room, I tasted the return to life outside the cloister, made poignant by having become accustomed to monastic deprivation, and even having learned to love its effects. The very newness of this night filled me with delight. I had time. I did not have to retire on schedule. I could leave the salon in a way I could never leave the cell, or go wandering about, turning on lights, exploring. Or I could wash. Yes, the greatest luxury of all was to bathe without quaking, to bathe in a pan of hot water before a glowing stove.

I brought a large metal carafe of water from the kitchen and set it on top of the stove in the salon. Upstairs I found a foot basin and placed it beside the stove. When the water was heated, I took a leisurely sponge bath, drying off with what seemed like an indulgently thick bath towel.

I savored the feel of pajamas, after sleeping so long fully clothed. I lay on the bed, needing no covers, content to do unimportant things, old things now new. I played the radio loudly, enjoying a feast of concerts that first night in the villa.

Outside, the valley slept under frozen snow. I thought of the Abbey, a dark hulk at this hour, with its sleeping monks and a silent, empty cell above the chapel. For the next two months, life revolved around the Abbey during the days and the villa during the evenings.

Solesmes was a place of no color—black clothing, white snows, gray buildings. And it was a place of no noise, for there were no automobiles and the nearest railroad was beyond hearing distance. The crunch of footsteps in the frozen snow, the occasional crowing of roosters or baying of hounds, the peal of the monastery bells—these alone gave dimension to the silence.

At the monastery I attended Mass and some of the daily offices, but passed most of the time assisting the monks in the paleography room. Studying the manuscripts with the magnifying glass engraved them in consciousness; listening with a continually fresh sense of hearing echoed the chants in my soul.

At the villa, other activities absorbed my whole attention: on the one hand, the failing sight; on the other, the slow dilation of enthusiasm for philosophical and theological studies. Gradually, new perceptions began to form in this area of thought. In the coldness and isolation of cloudy, gray days, the patristic writings struck like dazzling sunlight.

I discovered a way of tracing the diminution of my sight. The different wave bands on the radio were colored blue, green, yellow, and pink. Each evening I permitted myself to study them once. It was enough. The colors faded rapidly. By early March, I could no longer distinguish one color from another, as the color bands blended into a grayish glow. Later, the magnifying glass was not powerful enough to allow me to read.

Monks at the Abbey read aloud the letters I received and passages from books that interested me. Every day a different monk volunteered. Each one read impersonally, with perfect discretion, making no comments that might be an intrusion on my privacy.

I could still write, however, by placing the white writing paper on the black tabletop. This permitted me to direct the pen in a straight lines, even though I could only see the lines I wrote as a blur.

In such an atmosphere, awareness of my failing sight never became a drama of fear or morbidity. It was interesting, yes, and that was all. The skull-cracking pains often caused me to walk the floor of the salon at night, made me dread looking at anything. The doctor gave me sedatives and I was hospitalized for a few days in Le Mans. He prescribed heavily tinted glasses against the sensitivity to light.

But even these developments were submerged beneath the great joy that sprang from growing familiarity with monasticism and from the health that radiated out like the peal of its bells. At night, the two realities often clashed: the full-vigored happiness and the full-swelled pain, and my eyes would fill with tears at both.

Yet each night, when I had made the test of peering through that gathering haze toward the radio bands, a vague panic rose in me. It was not the panic of blindness, but the panic concerning the time left to me in this place, in this happiness, before I should lose the sight completely and necessarily return to the States. To dissipate the panic, I pursued small activities, like dusting the furniture or scrubbing the floor, and these would restore felicity to its full splendor.

My contact with the monks placed these things in a sure perspective. If I had lost my sight elsewhere, I would have been absorbed in fighting the opinions of those who judged it sad, fighting it with the exhausting aggressiveness that comes from weakness.

Here, the effortless strengths came from the air, the snows, the sense of the permeation of eternity. Here, the patterns were immense. In such a framework, blindness was indeed a small matter.

It happened to me, yes, but it was a moment in time, only a fragment of the greater reality. To allow it to swell until it occupied attention at the expense of the grand design would, I saw clearly, be monstrous.

The monks saw it as I did, for I had learned to understand it through their example. We viewed it as something inevitable and accepted it as something natural—like the approach of spring.

⁓ Images of a French Poet ⁓

When I met Henriette outside the chapel one morning, she asked me why I had not visited them. I told her that I did not want to disturb his work. "But he would love to see you," she said pleadingly and invited me to have lunch with them. We walked together back to their home.

Reverdy reproached me for having deserted them. Instead of telling him the truth—that I did not want him to know of my deteriorating eyesight because he would take it too seriously—I said that I did not want to disturb his work. "It takes me a year to think of enough to write in five minutes," he said, breaking into a smile. "Besides, I do nearly all of my writing at night. I hate the night. I can't sleep. I keep a paper and pencil beside my bed, and when I have insomnia, I write. Otherwise nothing. Come any time. You are welcome always."

We had fresh coffee and then he brought out an enormous package of papers and untied the string around them. They were manuscripts of all shapes and sizes, covered with pencil scrawlings. These observations, thoughts, and fragments were later published. Since I could not have deciphered these notes even with a powerful magnifying glass, I asked that he read them aloud.

"In poetry, the only thing worth saying is that which cannot be said," he would read, making marks on the paper as he went along, talking always with a cigarette or a pipe in his mouth. "This is why we have to depend on what passes between the lines." Concerning images, Reverdy read this passage: "The image is a pure creation of the spirit; it was not born of a comparison, but of a bringing-together of two more or less separate realities."

He read another variation: "An image is not strong because of the element of the brutal or the fantastic, but because the association of ideas is distant and exact." And then another: "One creates a powerful image for the spirit, in bringing together, without comparison, two distant realities of which the *spirit alone* perceives their relationships."

But we did not always talk of poetry. I was a musicologist. I was not involved in the problems of creation, only in their results. Also, like most intensely creative people, he did it rather than discuss it.

I found it always difficult to reconcile the man whom I knew as a friend and neighbor with the works of the poet. As a man, I saw the brusque farmer or the local philosopher, shabbily dressed, ill-shaven, jovial. We would drink wine and talk about life in America, particularly concerning the Deep South, which fascinated him. His conversational language was more akin to the barracks than the ivory tower. Then, when I turned to his poetry, I would find the immaculate craftsman, the connoisseur of nuance, the expresser of the inexpressible, the user of a language of magnificent purity and vigor.

In the early spring, although it still looked and felt like winter, we went on a photographing spree and I shot many photographs of him. A week later, my left eye began to suppurate a flow of tears. When I tested it, I saw only a neutral blankness with no light perception. I went immediately to Sablé, where the doctor bandaged it merely to have an absorbent material to catch the liquid.

Two weeks after that I picked up the prints in Sablé and returned to Solesmes. I dreaded seeing Reverdy any more, because he was a man to suffer greatly the pains of his friends. But I had to go. When I took the prints to him, I immediately began talking about them.

"To hell with the photos," he said. "What's happened to your eye?"

I walked past him and sat in the nearest chair, as he hounded me with questions. I told him the truth, talking into a void, for I could not see enough of his face to distinguish any reactions. I told him the whole thing—that I was rapidly becoming blind. As I feared, it changed our relationship drastically. He went into a profound depression and took it far worse than I did.

Some days Reverdy would read to me, new works by Jean Anouilh for instance, and he would discuss them with eagerness. On one of those cold days in spring, he read from his notes on poetics: "To start reading a book is like crawling into a cold bed. We only begin to enjoy it when we have established a good temperature—ours." This was not only charming, but it expressed Reverdy's sense of independence.

When the weather permitted, he would work in the garden and we would drink wine. But always there was the great pall of sadness which nothing could dissipate. He was careful never to let me see that I was the cause of these depressions, but Henriette and I knew.

He turned to another theme—his own imperfections as a poet. If the day were too bad for outside work, he would sit at the window and call himself a *raté*—a failure. His reaction to my imminent blindness tormented him with doubts about himself. "I've always dreamed of the meteors," he said one day. "Rimbaud and Lautréamont—that's what I should have been. I'm a *raté*." At such times, he who could not console, needed to be consoled. He would become a desperate, agonizing man, speaking of his insomnia, his inability to break the chains of mediocrity.

For a long time I remained silent, feeling it was foolish, impertinent even, to cross him. One afternoon when he fell into this melancholy and we had both been fortified with a large glass of brandy, I protested and argued with him. "No . . . no . . . listen," I objected. "Is everyone wrong except you? I grew up, and so did my schoolmates, on your work, and long before I ever dreamed of meeting you. I have spent evenings in the home of a judge in Tours, listening to him read poetry, and always he ended by reading your poetry—not Rimbaud or Lautréamont, not Apollinaire or Eluard or Cocteau. No—he ended with Reverdy. You take a great deal from me when you spit on what has meant so much to me. You'd be the first to condemn a man for complaining that he was not a Reverdy. And yet you complain because you are not a Rimbaud."

I heard him snort and smelled the smoke from his pipe, but his face was obscured in shadows. He spoke then, as though he were very tired. "It's hard to believe, you know. It's very hard to believe."

"When people return to your work again and again, even long after they've memorized it, then you are not a Rimbaud *raté* but a Reverdy *réussi*—a success. You went your own way, a way only you could go. The rest of us thank God you did."

Then he murmured, talking almost to himself, but telling me a story. "Once a young man came to see me about publishing his poems in a review I was editing. I refused them. Some time later I received a letter from his wife. He'd died of tuberculosis. She told me *Les ardoises du toit* lay on his bed table, and that my poems had softened his agony."

He sighed. We drank more wine. All of my tensions had gone.

"It's very hard to believe," he kept saying. "For me, it's very hard."

I understood then the extreme privacy of such a poet, the plague of doubts and torments, and Reverdy's almost desperate need occasionally to be reassured of its value.

"I suppose it is hard for you to believe," I said, "stuck away here out of contact with people."

"I am a man of the Midi," he said. "I love the sun. I hate the cold, the darkness. I hate the night. I get up with the first light of day and go to bed before the darkness. But in that little cubbyhole where I have my bed, I can't sleep. I write during the night because of my horror of the darkness. That's why . . . well, you know something of the horror of the darkness too, I'm sure."

"Not really," I said. "It's not what you think it would be. It's not like some eternal insomnia. Anyway, your work has none of the night in it."

He murmured, as a tremble disturbed his deep intake of breath. I emptied the glass of wine and walked to the blurred window, opening it to a fresh twilight air, cool after the rains.

He walked over to lean out the window. "Can you see the pear trees?"

"Yes, a little," I said.

"If it doesn't freeze, they'll be in bloom in a couple of days. Spring comes fast here."

Our good-bye was casual.

"Come back whenever you can," he said.

"Yes, I will," I answered, walking away.

"Until soon, eh?" he called out before I reached the corner.

I waved, knowing that it would be our final visit.

During my last few days in Solesmes, a hushed atmosphere of spring hovered serenely over the village. I felt sadness for Reverdy. His reaction to my blindness brought home the truth. I knew that those I loved would suffer far more than I would suffer. I carried the responsibility not only of accepting what came, but also of comforting them. And the best way to comfort them was to nullify the stereotypes of blindness, to work for skills that would dispel sadness and make them forget my condition. And even as I realized this, I was certain it was beyond my own capacities. I saw the enormity of the task and saw that it would require help. I must be in perfect, voluntary obedience to a greater force, do out of obedience what I could not do from my own imperfect initiative. There was suddenly no alternative. If others were to be spared, I must make the act of will that turned my whole being over to a stranger.

As I passed the Abbey, I hesitated, then forced myself to blank out the hesitation and to make the act without any reflection. I pulled open the great doors of the chapel and listened for sounds that might indicate someone else's presence in the pews. I advanced to one of the back seats, burning with embarrassment. I forced the words out. The *Great Yes*. "If you exist, take what I am. I hold back nothing. Show me what you want me to do. I'll obey no matter how repulsive it is to me personally. I give you myself totally and without any reservations."

I rested, smelling the building's dust and age, and felt only deadness in my heart. Silence lay so deep I could hear the rumble of hunger in my belly. Perceptions centered in the body: my eye clammy behind the gauze; my mouth filled with the acid aftertaste of too many Gauloise cigarettes; and my buttocks creased by the hardness of the pew against which I sat.

I walked back to the villa in the softness of the early April evening. I felt no joy, no relief, nothing but a sense of terrible finality in knowing that henceforth this life was not my own.

My body struggled between two desires—its hunger for nourishment and its desire to fall into bed and sleep. For the moment, the tiredness overwhelmed me, the tiredness of years. I felt I could sleep forever.

⏤ Departure to America ⏤

The waiting was over in the spring of 1947.

I could no longer see the light on the face of the radio. The overhead globe was like candlelight seen through dense fog. It was time to have one of the monks write my family, time to return to America and to begin the training necessary to live without sight.

I walked along the cobblestone street to the Abbey, touching the wall to maintain a safe distance. Mild sun warmed my shoulders. The valley, fragrant with blossoming fruit trees, drowsed in silence. A rooster crowed somewhere far in the distance. The atmosphere was steeped in peace.

I could not find the door to the gatehouse. The gatekeeper called out, took my sleeve, and led me inside. Then I realized the temptations that would assault unconsciously—temptations to dramatize, to seek the consolations of sympathy, to hear the platitudes of condolence. "Yes," I told him, "the sight is gone. The doctor says there's nothing more to be done." I had come to know the gatekeeper, enjoying his rich sense of humor. I waited for his outpouring of sympathy.

"Oh, come now. You're not going to waste time on that, are you?"

I stood speechless. Of course he was right. And he had said this without unkindness but with a firmness that stopped me. At my request, he wrote the letter I dictated to my parents and mailed it immediately.

The problems of daily living quickly threw into my face the enormity of my attempted gift. When I tried to eat, either I speared my lip with the fork or the food dropped off in my lap. When I reached for a glass, I often knocked it over. I lost my direction in the middle of the room and had to walk until I bumped into a wall to locate myself.

My nerves jangled with each unexpected noise. I found myself cursing in solitude, trembling with impotent rage. The reality of blindness presented a thousand roadblocks altogether different from those I had attempted to foresee. I was thankful to have this initiation alone, to make the mistakes unobserved. How did a man comb his hair or find his clothes or shave? And what did he do during the hours except sit and wait for someone to come and take his arm and lead him somewhere?

These first awarenesses filled me with confusion. The monks invited me to take my meals in the refectory, but I would not eat for fear of making a spectacle of myself.

One of the oldest Benedictines, a priest whom I had not met, sent for me. We sat so close to each other that I could smell his dentures.

"You are too nervous, my son," he said in a high voice. "You must develop heroic patience. God has his own good reasons for allowing such things. You must go on faith, even though you don't understand."

I listened to this old man's good-goderies with disappointment. Yes, here in the heart of a great monastery, a man could say such things. But what did he know about blindness? What did he know about living out in the world where a man must fend for himself?

I thanked him and rose to terminate the interview.

My extended hand remained outstretched in the air, untouched. I sat back down. "You don't see either, do you?" I asked.

"Well, no," he said with an explosion of wheezing laughter. "You are very quick. How did you discover so fast?"

We fell into a lengthy conversation.

"Practice. Practice patiently," he said. "Learn to reach for a glass properly. Do it five hundred times and you'll never again knock one over. Get yourself a lightweight fork and then you can tell by the weight if you bring it to your mouth empty or if it has food on it. You are a musician. You have already learned that a passage of music you cannot play the first time comes easily into your hands after practicing it twenty or a hundred times. I still learn this way. I still am amazed all the time by how quickly things come, and I've been without my sight for many years now, maybe twenty."

I listened to his aged, almost gleeful voice and I felt hope in this. I had never to my knowledge seen this old man and yet, without sight, I felt I knew him well. I perceived in him nothing of the deep rage I had found in *l'Aveugle* at Tours.

"Your main task will be to persevere," he implored. "Remember always that word. Your main temptations will be against perseverance."

"Yes, I'm sure you're right about the temptations."

"Oh, but they won't be obvious. They come as temptations to lose patience, to murmur against the frustrations, to act superb."

I noted he unconsciously used the archaic language of St. Benedict.

"It will take time. You will learn these attitudes, but don't make the initial mistake that could cause you to give up before you have learned your techniques."

When I prepared to leave, he snapped his fingers sharply, so I could reach out to the sound and shake his hand. The gesture filled me with admiration and hope. It was a way of doing things, and I was happy to learn it. He grasped my hand in both of his.

"Watch your pride, eh?"

"I've got enough of it to watch," I said.

"Sometimes our deepest wound comes from hurt pride in this, because we think we do not have some great gift to offer God and the world. But the important thing, in God's eyes, is not what we have to give, but that we hold nothing back, that we refuse to give God even our wretchedness, our stubbornness, our littleness of soul. Sometimes those are the only things we've got, eh?"

When I remained silent, he asked if anything was the matter.

"I was just thinking how much sense those words make here, and how little sense they would make if uttered in the world I came from and must return to," I said with a laugh.

"Do you think I've told you truths?"

"I do, Father."

"Then it is not 'too-bad' for the truths but 'too-bad' for that world you're talking about, eh? Eh?"

"You're right, Father."

I hurried to the villa, astonished at my eagerness to begin the long practice now that I had some idea how to do it. He had said to do it five hundred times, pick up a glass, light a cigarette, anything. I turned on the radio, as l'Aveugle had told me, and began to locate the table, the door, the bureau from the sound until I could walk almost directly from the bed to the doors, to the table, to the drawers of clothing.

I placed a drinking glass on the table, sat before it and practiced different ways of approaching it with my hands—from above, from the side, with my hands held high or with it sliding along the table top.

I practiced the same way with an ashtray, concentrating on its location, then turning about in the chair and trying to place the ashes in it without fumbling. I had been going to the local village barber for shaves and to get my hair combed properly each morning. Now, in as profound an excitement as I had ever known, I lathered and shaved entirely by feel without the slightest difficulty. Any missed patch felt like bristle to my fingers and was easy to correct. By feel, too, I found I could make the bed and even sweep the floor, going by the sound of the radio. Alone and without any witness to my mistakes, the mistakes no longer irritated or impeded further attempts.

I visited the old monk daily and listened to his high cackles when I told him the details of my experiments.

"That's the way to do it," he would encourage. "Now, you keep at it until you don't fumble at all, until some sighted person not knowing you could not see, would not be able to deduce it from your actions. Do this until all is second nature, as natural as breathing."

"I have one problem I can't seem to handle," I confided.

"What is that?"

"All the furniture seems to have shrunk to exactly the height of the shins. I'm constantly bumping things in the center of my shins."

"Well, you need a stick. I've got two or three good ones. I'll give you one. You must keep it a little in front of you, easy, so you don't bang the furniture. The important thing is not to let it out of your hands. If you misplace it, you will spend all your time feeling around for it. Mine stays in my hand all day, and I put it beside my bed at night. That's easy. Is there anything else I can help you with?"

"I haven't found an accurate way of urinating without just taking down my pants and sitting down. I splatter everything when I try to do it standing up."

"Ah, poor lad. I should have thought of the stick earlier. Just run the stick across the toilet and place yourself squarely in front of it, so each knee touches it and aim your stream for the middle."

Now that light perception was gone, the nervousness and the pains vanished in a blessed kind of comfort. Evenings alone in the villa were filled with the activity of experimental learning, now made much easier with the cane in my hand. I practiced walking from the villa to the monastery gatehouse every day. During Holy Week, I attended all of the services and felt the particular liberation of being able to make it home in the dark alone, which I could do at least as well as a sighted person.

The day after Easter, I received a telegram from my parents. They had made arrangements for emergency passage on a Lykes Brothers boat out of Rouen, destined for New Orleans. I took first-class passage on a train from Sablé to Rouen, sitting alone in the compartment, listening to the clacking wheels carrying me away from the valley, the Abbey, the place of my deepest happiness.

At Rouen, a porter fetched my bags and grabbed my arm. He led me through the crowd, shouting loudly, "Make way for the blind man!" I shriveled with humiliation. The blind man, *l'Aveugle*. I was that now, and it burned me with the desire to regain a name, to be known as myself and not as a condition. The porter paraded me across the street to the hotel and announced with an air of importance that I was blind. Then I heard the frightful well-meaning unction of the lady who registered me.

"Can you sign your name?" she asked.

"I suppose so," I said.

"Just sign here."

"Where?" I asked.

"On that bottom line, right there."

"Dear God, if I could see the line—"

"Oh, I'm so sorry," she said in a voice near weeping.

"It's all right. Forgive me," I apologized. "If you'll just place my hand there, I'll sign."

A porter took me upstairs to the room and left me. I sat on the bed and swallowed the outrage that rose in me. He had sat me on the bed and left, not thinking to show me a thing. Was there a telephone? Could I call a porter if I needed help? How could I eat? I fumbled for the bag and opened it. All clothing felt the same to my fingers. Where was the closet, the bathroom? Where was the drinking water?

I got up and explored the room with my bare hands against the walls. A table there, a closet door, a window, the bed. Did they think I had no intestines, no bladder? Would they simply leave me here? I found no telephone. I waited to hear someone walk down the hall. When I heard footsteps, I quickly opened the door. If it were a man I could ask him to locate the restroom for me.

"Pardon," I called out to the carpet-odor of the corridor.

"Monsieur?" a woman answered.

"I'm sorry. I thought you were someone else," I said, closing the door.

Finally, I decided to venture out. I followed the narrow hall to the steps and nervously descended, feeling as though I could plunge off into space at any moment. At the bottom step, I simply struck out. Then I heard a woman's voice at my elbow, timid, uncertain.

"Can I help you somewhere, Monsieur?"

"Yes, I'd like to have dinner, please."

"Of course. Out that door and down the street three doors to the left."

"If you'd be kind enough to show me to the door," I said.

With a little moan of self-reproach, she pinched my coat sleeve at the cuff and led me to the door.

I walked with terror as traffic raced past. My foot slipped off the curb. I stepped quickly back.

"Wait here," I heard a man say, and then a woman said, "Yes, go help him." His footsteps approached in the noise.

"Could I help you, Monsieur?" he asked, close to my face—in French but with a strong accent.

"I'd appreciate it. I'm trying to find a café."

"Are you American?" he asked in English.

"Yes sir."

"I thought so. You're too big to be anything else. You've not had this trouble long, have you?"

"No sir. I'm new at it."

"Well, come along," he said easily and slipped his arm through mine. "We'll see you get a bite. My wife and I were just out for a little stroll."

He introduced his wife, Mrs. Burgess, in French; and then in English said he was British, and had stayed after World War I to marry the lady.

Briefly I told them my story. To my relief, they responded directly, simply. Both were small, their voices coming from shoulder level. They did not try to overlook my blindness or even to be diplomatic about it.

In the restaurant, they refused my offer of supper, saying they had already eaten. I ordered a sandwich for myself and wine for the three of us. They reproached me for taking only a sandwich.

"I haven't learned to eat skillfully," I explained. "I'm too clumsy to try anything but a sandwich in public."

"Well, hell," Mr. Burgess blurted out in English. "You can come take your meals at our house. Then you can have proper food. No need to be embarrassed around us."

I thanked him, but hesitated.

He explained to his wife what he had suggested and turned back to me. "Sure, it's settled. I'm retired now. I've got plenty of time. I'll fetch you in the morning and we can spend the day together. I'll take you wherever you need to go. Give us this pleasure, okay?"

After supper, they walked me back to the hotel. Mrs. Burgess remained in the hotel lobby while her husband accompanied me to the room.

"Mind if I sit down a minute?" he asked.

"Please do," I said and heard the chair squeak under his weight.

"I just wanted to say that I'm an old man, was in the army a long time, raised a family of kids. I mean I've seen a lot of things in my life. Anything you want me to help you do, you just feel free to ask, will you?"

Touched by his kindness, I thanked him, but made no specific request.

"I mean," he said, "it just must be the devil trying to do things in a strange place. I don't know what you might need in the way of help. But you shouldn't be embarrassed to ask for anything."

I realized that I knew the heart of this man, and quickly. I might not know anything of his physical appearance or movements, but I knew a great deal about him. He radiated solidity and health, an open decency that made me easy in his presence. I realized, too, that with such a man, blindness instantly lost its torturous aspects. If I blundered, then I did, and that was all—nothing to blush about, as he would probably say.

He unpacked my nightclothes and put them on the bed, guided me to the water closet and then went back and counted the steps so I could find it on my own later. He suggested that I go ahead and "shuck out" of my clothes so he could put them on hangers. He arranged everything so I could find it. "Try to sleep till I come in the morning," he said, shaking my hand. "I'll roust you around eight."

Without the distractions of sight, I found I grasped changes in the atmosphere of places, sensed something of their essences, with a clarity that was new to me. If Solesmes was calm, withdrawn, strengthening in its silences, Rouen was noisy, brassy.

But it was softened because of the Burgesses, by the smell of their old home and the profound affection they had for one another.

Then the world changed suddenly two days later when Mr. Burgess led me aboard the Lykes Line ship. Street smells changed to ship smells, odors of tar and paint and the vast, neutralizing shrimp-stench of the port. The captain, a mercifully casual man, led us to my cabin, where my new friend helped to unpack.

The cabin had two bunks, space for my trunk and suitcases, and a miniature bathroom with shower, basin, and toilet. To my great relief, I was told I should occupy the stateroom alone.

Seeing that I was settled, Mr. Burgess said it was time for him to go.

"No good-byes. I hate them. We'll always remember you," he said and quickly quashed my expression of thanks. I heard his footsteps hurry up the passageway. We knew we would never encounter one another again.

I stood in the doorway and felt a lingering warmth and an emptiness with his fading footsteps. His decency and quiet good humor had hardly cleared from the air, before it was replaced by the rich vigor of another.

Indeed, I wondered if the world which I could not see approaching were always to pass in parade like this, one type suddenly replacing another, touching and then going.

— The Doctor and Dissonance —

At a knock on the door, I shouted for them to come in.

"Monsieur?" I heard a coarse, too-loud voice declaim. "Allow me to present myself. I am Dr. Rafael Carrazo, from Guatemala. I understand you have a misfortune. I am the greatest doctor in my country, so if I can be of service to you on the voyage, have no hesitancy in calling me."

He spoke as though furious, in fluent French with a Spanish accent.

"Thank you, doctor."

"Call if you need me," he commanded and closed the door.

An hour later, he returned to shove a religious medal into my hands.

"My wife wishes you to have it," he said loudly. "She prays for you. I, too, pray for you."

This astonished me. Prayers, somehow, did not conform to the image of the man as I had deciphered him.

On this Lykes ship, which carried mostly cargo and only a dozen or so passengers, there were, thank God, no organized activities for us. We had literally nothing to do.

The doctor and I began to spend much time together. Surrounded by the isolating ocean, to the accompaniment of distant throbbing engines, we drank wine and coffee in the salon or took long walks on deck.

He revealed himself as a man of great erudition, both in classical studies and science, and yet he gave the impression of being an absolute thug. I learned that he had received all of his training in medical schools in Belgium and France, that he was the father of ten children and that he was returning home after an ambassadorial mission in France.

When we walked on the deck, he rhapsodized about the ocean, the sunsets, describing everything in outrageously purple language. He must have thought he was helping me, but overdrawn descriptions of nature, when you cannot see, become nerve-wracking. Also, it was a constant reminder of the handicap element of blindness.

I wondered if a man weren't less blind alone than in the presence of others. Did the blindness itself fluctuate? Of course not, but it gave the impression in the sense that it was an active preoccupation at some times and almost forgotten at others.

At night, within the safe confines of my bunk, I did not feel it at all. Then, I was no different from any other passenger who lay unseeing in his darkened cabin. Under the faint weight of bandages, I tried to grasp the truth of these contradistinctions.

One morning before breakfast, when the doctor had come to put fresh bandages over my eyes, I mentioned this to him.

"So you sometimes scarcely have any awareness of your blindness?"

"That's right. Last night for example."

"Let's go eat," he said, taking my arm and guiding me to a place at a table in the salon. The waiter greeted us. I heard him set out the plates, perceiving also the aromas of sausage, eggs, and toast.

With the fork, I began to explore. The softness was certainly the eggs; the more resistant form was the sausage. I ran my fingertips around the edge of the plate and located the toast.

"When do you feel it most?" he asked.

"Right now, I feel it pretty well," I laughed, while attempting to cut the sausage patty with the fork.

"You're doing fine."

"So far, I've felt it most when people describe things to me, especially when they say or imply: 'I just wish you could see such and such.' It's not the simple descriptions that bother me, like the color of a woman's hair or dress, or how the food is arranged on the plate, or the fact that dolphins fly up out of the water ahead of us. It's the long, involved—"

"Descriptions like I tend to give?" he asked.

I smiled.

"Of course, I should have known better," he explained with scientific detachment and no trace of apology.

I brought the fork to my mouth and was relieved to find it not empty. I heard a gurgle to the right of the plate and smelled coffee. I thanked the waiter in English. The doctor and I spoke freely, because as far as we knew we were the only French-speaking passengers on board.

"What you say about this apparent fluctuation in your condition is not too complicated really," the doctor said after a long silence. "There are two main classes of activity for you now. First there is activity that does not involve seeing at all, like listening to the radio or a concert or lying awake in the dark. They are consonant situations," he pointed out.

After a brief pause, the doctor's voice took on a deeper resonance. "However, if you were at a sporting event, you would be acutely aware of your lack of sight. This would be a dissonant situation."

"Yes, that makes perfect sense," I said. Since the doctor was making a psychological distinction using a musical metaphor and I was a musician who had studied medicine, what he said struck with precision.

"Each of us must find some way to balance out the psychologically dissonant situations with consonant situations that allow tensions to resolve," he continued, "or else our nervous systems collapse eventually. Now, without your sight, you still must live in a sighted world. You face many dissonant situations that people with sight are spared. Some of these will change into consonant situations as you learn to solve your problems and handle yourself better. Until you learn the skills you will need, it seems to me that you just have to avoid too many dissonant situations, or at least take time to recuperate from them by seeking consonant situations deliberately."

"Do you think I'm adjusting all right, doctor?" I asked.

"An adjustment," he said, spreading the word with his disgust, "is the changeover from interest in oneself to interest in an outside thing. If you were adjusting you wouldn't ask such a damn fool question."

I responded with a sigh and leaned back in my chair.

Then I felt his breathing draw nearer and knew he had leaned across the table toward me. "Do you know that under ideal conditions and when left entirely alone," he emphasized loudly, "the newly blinded begin adjusting within a matter of minutes?"

I started to speak, too quickly in my humiliation, and he placed his hand on mine to hush me.

Then in a lower voice he continued. "With no one around to pity them or make them feel self-conscious, they quickly shift from the shock of their condition to an interest in solving new problems. They begin to feel about for things. The danger comes when other people are around."

"You seem to know all about it, doctor," I said with some sarcasm.

"Listen, it's almost impossible to resist the temptation to use your misfortune to your own advantage. It's such a shitty trap for you to fall into. A man like you must never want people's pity, or their admiration. I hope you're above that kind of cheap self-indulgence."

I remained silent. He took his hand away.

"You have to study and work. You have to look at your problems and be interested in them only in order to solve them. You don't become adjusted until you see it for what it is, and not for what it does to you or can do for you."

I nodded and drained the last coffee from the cup.

"Let's have another cup of coffee here, and then go for a walk. Don't be embarrassed. I've done the same thing. All of us have. You understand what I'm trying to say?"

"Perfectly."

"But you don't think I'm right, do you?"

"I know you are."

"Ah, look," he said. "I'll show you. What kind of a morning is this, overcast or clear?"

"How would I know?"

"Concentrate on it," he urged. "Forget yourself. Open your senses to the things around you. At this moment you should know."

I did as he suggested and became aware of things I had ignored: the boat's gentle rocking; a faint odor of salt freshness; a warmth on my face that I could not feel on my hands. When I moved my face to the side, the warmth faded; when I turned back, the warmth returned.

"Is that sunlight on my face?" I asked.

"Yes. It comes through the porthole over your head, directly hitting your face," he said. "If you concentrate on yourself or on the impressions you want to make on me, then your senses are not free to experience all that goes on around you. This other is far more interesting, no?"

"Yes, of course it is," I said.

Under his guidance, and with this new discovery, my bewildered senses became alive to everything.

I learned that by the faintest odor, I could tell whether a person's shirt had been dried in sunlight and freshly ironed or whether it came from a laundry. By a metallic click, I knew that someone at the next table had a cigarette lighter. When someone took water, I knew if he drank from thirst, in gulps, or if he drank out of idle habit.

Isolated by the ocean, no one reminded me that I was supposed to be one of the world's unfortunates. So, I forgot it and spent time learning. The doctor followed my progress with full understanding and with the excitement of curiosity, verifying what I managed correctly and correcting me when I made an error in judgment or deduction.

One night as we sat on deck quite late, he asked suddenly: "Tell me about this night, what kind of night it is."

"It's a mild night," I said. "A balmy night."

"The rest of us see it as cloudy or clear. Without your sight, you go to the heart of it. You see in another way from us, but still you perceive the essences. Perhaps your perception means more than what we merely see."

As we neared America, the peace of shipboard life changed to extreme nervousness. I knew the full meaning of the "dissonant situation." My dread was clear. I dreaded for my parents to see me like this.

"It is a thing to be got through," the doctor said. "It will be bad at first, but soon things will straighten out."

My first real contact with America came that afternoon when someone turned on the radio: " . . . current downtown temperature in New Orleans is eighty-seven degrees," the announcer said enthusiastically, as if nothing in the world could be more thrilling.

Another sound blasted out: "Pepsi-Cola hits the spot. Twelve full ounces, that's a lot!" I sat open-mouthed for a long time, listening as men called each other "cat" and urged people to "slip me some skin." In my years of isolation in the Pacific and in France, I had heard little English, and surely nothing like this. The first contact with America was a warning that I was not really returning home, but going to a strange land quite foreign to me, a land where announcers on the radio had developed such enthusiasms that they could become equally ecstatic over a jazz recording, a Bible, or a laxative.

I remained close to the radio, thinking that without my sight I should know America henceforth by its sounds. I recalled the old blind man in Tours and his slavery to the radio. But there, he received nourishment from drama and music. Here, I heard little to assure me that I was not returning to a land gone mad with personality cults. It would not matter except for a frozen moment when I feared that I might be overwhelmed by the blindness cult of the sighted and forced into a soap-opera stereotype.

Was it possible that a nation that prided itself on individualism could change drastically in a matter of years? Perhaps most reacted to these inanities as I did. But my uneasiness persisted.

How could I resist being swept along by the pure energy of public benevolence? I was terrified without knowing precisely why. Could a man say no in America? Was a man still free to reject what society had set up as good? The true and legitimate solution for another could be the worst possible solution for me. Blindness did not level us to identical spiritual and physical needs; it did not suddenly alter personality and tastes. At the core of my concern was the memory of having given myself in obedience to an absolute. The value of that would be nullified if I took the easy way out.

Two days later, as I awoke in the cabin, something had changed. The motors no longer rumbled. We had reached New Orleans.

I dressed and went on deck. The captain relayed the message that my mother would be there when we disembarked. Then it was decided that

I should go ashore in the launch, without delay. The doctor put me in clean bandages, packed my bags and accompanied me into the launch.

I felt incredibly clumsy and raged silently against the procedure.

"I see a woman with a priest on the dock," Dr. Carrazo shouted.

"Good, that must be Father Clayton," I shouted back.

When we landed, I braced myself. It was treacherous trying to climb out of the launch boat. Two men held my arms, almost carrying me. The Lyke's agent placed my hand before me until it touched another.

"Say hello to your mother," the agent said.

The contact shattered me. What was the expression on her face? Here, I knew, was the profoundest hell of blindness. One look would have told me. I strained to break through and see.

"Hello, darling," she said in a composed voice.

I felt her desolation behind the composure and was overwhelmed with pity for what I knew must be her pain. At that moment, I loathed this blindness for what it did to those I loved. But, mercifully, things had to be done, introductions made, customs passed. I felt my mother's hand tighten in its grasp around my arm as we went through customs.

No one made the obvious remarks. From the officials with dignified politeness to the crewmen who wished me good luck, reactions were healthy and sane. There were no pats on the back, hollow encouragements or seepage of platitudes. The dreaded dissonance had passed.

In its wake, stemming from a deep sense of relief, there followed ease, pleasantness. It was safe to enjoy the homecoming. In Father Clayton's car we talked of the family, the trip, everything.

"Do you want to stay in New Orleans a couple of days?" mother asked.

"No, I want to go home as soon as possible," I said.

Father Clayton had been a family friend for many years and, as an Episcopal priest, had been my parents' spiritual guide as well. He told us he would see to the plane reservations for our trip to Fort Worth the next day. He dropped us off at the hotel and we went up to my mother's room. The conversation with her was quiet and blessedly unemotional.

"I've had several talks with Frances Smith," she said.

I had guessed she would, and I felt much of her controlled reaction was due to advice from this extraordinary young lady. After losing her sight, Frances had completed her university work with high honors. As I thought of her and the marvelous manner in which she had functioned, a sense of calm spread through me.

"How is she?" I asked.

"Fine. She certainly eased my mind. She gave me all the information we'll need to start with. You can learn Braille at the Lighthouse for the Blind right there in Fort Worth."

I cringed at the name but said nothing. Through the window I heard the distant wail of a boat horn. Far below, the noise of traffic echoed, as though the surrounding buildings were a megaphone. I was seeing again, in that strange way of the sightless—seeing the town, experiencing it, not as an image but as an evocation. The heat, the smells and sounds of the port city brought back no specific visual recollections of what I had seen there in the past. No, it was rather a dazzling painting. It might have been Algiers, but it could not have been Amsterdam. It had no form or shape and needed none.

I deduced what New Orleans was and how it differed from another city from the thousands of stimuli floating in the atmosphere. I thought of things as painters might have depicted them; not because I had ever seen such paintings, but because painters, like the blind, catch the essences of places. The effect of sunlight fascinated me. Again, not visually, but in some behind-the-eye chamber, what Matisse or Van Gogh had done with sunlight on their canvases. It was a strangely beautiful realization.

II

Blindness

⸺ A Country Place ⸺

The next morning we took a flight to Fort Worth, where we were met by my father. As he drove us home, we discussed the farm acreage they had decided to purchase. Three days later we moved to the countryside near the town of Mansfield. My parents had always wanted to live in the country, but the immediate reason was the doctor's suggestion that such a setting would be the best possible place for my privacy and freedom.

Although it was only twenty miles south of Fort Worth, I had never seen Mansfield. Our farm was two miles northeast of the downtown area. The town was inhabited by three thousand people, and its dozen or so small shops were in walking distance of the intersection of Main and Broad streets, which sported the town's only traffic signal. A narrow, winding sandy lane led from the highway and ended at the entrance of our place. Timber, watered by a spring-fed creek, covered half the land; the other half lay in open pasture. Our house stood at the edge of woods rich in wildlife. At night, we heard whippoorwills and frogs, who were our constant companions in this open space. Here we began a new life, surrounded by an impression of isolation and verdure.

For a time, though we could discuss blindness in an impersonal way, we could not bear to have it discussed or analyzed. But we realized intuitively that we had to be hard on ourselves, since I had begun systematically to learn the skills necessary to function. They understood that I had to be free to make all the mistakes and needed the privacy to experiment. Any gasps of dismay when I bungled, any unnecessary word of caution might poison the air with fear, and this would surely hamper what had to be attempted. At best, the decisions were difficult.

If I sat in the living room and decided to have a glass of water, the battle of alternatives began. I had little sense of orientation at first. The simple task of fetching a glass of water involved hazards. When I got up and walked toward the kitchen, I risked banging into a table or a door jamb. Even the slightest distraction would cause me to lose my bearings and I would end up with my nose against a wall. If I managed the task well, I still loathed the image of myself groping, hands outstretched.

How much easier for all of us if I remained seated and asked one of them to bring a glass of water! But this would be absolute suicide in principle, of course, because if it's easy to ask someone for water then it's easier to ask them for more difficult things. I had to overcome the lure of an increasing dependence on others and had to give full concentration to functioning, because decisions had to be made about the simplest actions. Always I chose the hard way and suffered through the blunders, thereby learning what could be achieved.

In the beginning, to the person who cannot see it is almost impossible to overcome the paralysis of caution. The blind person must realize the function of fear within, and he must kill it without any compunction. The reasons why some sightless persons do such amazing things is that they have, in one way or another, killed their fear. To understand this is half the battle.

There are several concrete hints.

First, he should practice walking with his weight on the back foot rather than pushing it forward on the outstretched foot. This may appear clumsy at first, but when it becomes natural it is imperceptible. Thus, when he runs into something, he will not fall or stagger.

Next, he should take a given route throughout the house, from his bedroom to the kitchen, from his bedroom to the bathroom, and so on. This should be done in privacy, completely on his own and he should practice this over and over as a pianist practices scales on the piano, gradually increasing the speed and assurance until he is absolutely at ease inside the house. Do not think that this will need to be practiced everywhere he goes. He should always train himself to walk normally at a fairly rapid speed. Once he has learned this, he will instantly memorize a room wherever he goes. After once exploring it, he will not forget it.

A very great help, either in the home or elsewhere, is to have a sound by which he can locate himself. Any aural focus will do. The blind man of Tours used his radio expertly, and I had followed his example at the villa, even before I had gone completely blind. But if the source of sound is moved, even a few inches, it can make an enormous difference. One blind friend always located the bathroom door in this manner. A clock was on the wall just to the left of it. He simply walked a few feet to the right of the clock and found the bathroom door. One day the clock was moved to the right of the bathroom door and he found himself in the kitchen!

The sightless person's sense of location develops once fear is gone. It develops freely and to such a fine extent that he will know exactly where the ash tray is in relation to the radio or the telephone. However, when a piece of furniture is moved without the sightless person knowing, he will be lost and a blank spot will develop, throwing his sense of location and the context of the room out of focus. These blank spots occur frequently.

Yet most blind people memorize house furnishings instantly and almost never forget them.

However, no strategy is entirely conscious. The deepest source of this phenomenon is natural and unconscious, depending on the stimuli of hearing, touch, smell, and something intangible about the feel of a place. Once one of these is out of focus, his sense of direction is lost and he finds himself suddenly standing in a vacuum. To correct this, he must walk until he comes to a wall or an object he can recognize, and his sense of orientation will return quickly. The constant sounds of clocks or radios greatly decrease the frequency of these blank spots. But this skill is impossible to find without practice and without overcoming fear.

It must be understood, however, that this is an exhausting thing. The sightless should not be pushed to do this, it should develop naturally. I tended to push myself, but also I learned to take frequent rest periods, when someone took my arm and walked with me outside over familiar terrain. This was relaxing, because I was able to abandon myself to the care of another for a few moments before going back on my own. No matter how proficient the blind person becomes, if he appears upset or nervous or fatigued, it is always a kindness for family or friends to walk arm in arm with him for a few moments. This is a respite and, if it is not done too frequently, it is generally a welcome thing.

In all things with the blind, tact and discretion are the prerequisites. When you walk with a blind person, tell him to step up or step down whenever necessary, but always in an impersonal tone. Do not be overly attentive or protective. This is very distasteful to the sightless. With this type of inconspicuous help, with ideas casually planted in the mind, and with care to leave the sightless absolutely alone at frequent intervals, this major task will be greatly facilitated.

I longed for the day when I would gain such skills that those around me could forget that I was without sight. My parents somehow managed to give me a sense of liberation from concern, and I was able to strike out on my own. They gave the incomparable gift—an untainted illusion of dignity and self-reliance.

Of course, they did many things to help me, but so unobtrusively that my dependence was never made obvious. They were practical, preferring to act rather than to mourn, doing significant things without fanfare. For example, my mother learned to pronounce Latin and French in order to read the theological texts and musical studies I was studying. My father cut a holly stick, which was much longer and more convenient than the old monk's cane that had been forgotten in my confusion while leaving the launch of the Lykes ship in New Orleans.

When I went to the table, my plate was always served to make eating as unembarrassing as possible. We had been told that the blind cannot cut meat, butter bread, or eat salad off a lettuce leaf. It was a common belief at the time and we accepted it without question. So when I arrived at the table, my parents had already cut the meat, buttered the bread, and diced the salad. They procured a lightweight fork. I managed to eat with less clumsiness, which can be so humiliating and discouraging. Later, we realized these stereotypes were false, and I learned to prepare my own plate, doing everything the sighted do without thought.

The most difficult task was to overcome the fear of walking naturally outside the comfortable confines of our home. I had to face the unknown obstacle that might lie directly ahead, a fallen limb or a snake—the fear that was at times a terror, like walking on a skyscraper ledge at night.

Feeling my way with the holly stick, I practiced walking directly from the house to the barn ten, twenty, fifty times a day. I practiced the scales and arpeggios of walking that route until I could handle it in a virtuoso manner, until I had attained a natural and uncautious walking speed. Always I tested myself. Would an onlooker, not knowing I could not see, suspect it from my manner of walking? When I could handle that route and that distance, I struck out for other parts of the farm.

I fell into gullies, walked into low-hanging tree limbs, got lost. It was worth the falls to kill the fear. To gain maximum freedom, my parents would frequently go into town. With the certainty no one watched, I began to develop astonishing speed, even running along pathways in the woods. I soon discovered I could locate myself by the feel of the terrain under my feet, by the sunlight on my face, by the direction of the wind.

As I learned, those about me learned also. They always made some sound when they approached, so I would not be suddenly startled by a voice at my elbow or by an unexpected touch. My parents learned to clear their throats, cough, or hum if they had reason to suspect that I did not know they were there. If I walked into the living room where one of them sat, always a movement or a sound made their presence known. Usually a question was asked or a statement about the weather was uttered, so I would know who was sitting there.

The simple act of living required intense concentration. As a result of such concentration, I was doubly startled by any sudden presence or an unexpected sound close by. Those were the most obviously dissonant situations, because they involved forces beyond my control.

Life could not merely be lived unconsciously. I had to be consciously aware of all those things that the sighted take for granted. Soon it was no longer a matter of dissonance for me to get a glass of water or do almost anything else for myself in the house. Awareness of the lack of eyesight again faded. Life in the country, isolated from all the reminders, occupied with learning and experimentation, progressed in a peaceful and happy pattern that I dreaded to interrupt. Left alone on the farm during my first months of blindness, I was so immersed in discovery that I never stopped to dwell on my condition as tragic. I felt that I was simply living in a new and different way that fascinated me.

But after a few months of relative isolation, I knew it was time to go back into the world, to meet people, to begin my studies in Braille in Fort Worth. The first trips away from the farm were made in the company of my mother to the Lighthouse for the Blind. She had read aloud some books dealing with "adjustment to handicap," and I had found most of them degrading. A good adjustment, according to those books, occurred when one recognized one's limitations and did not strive to surpass them.

My hostility to any theory based on limitation of achievement to some "average" was extreme. I told myself that if the director of the Lighthouse uttered one word about my trying too hard—indicating "aggressiveness"—I would simply never go back.

But no such thing happened. Mrs. Edith Bell, blind for many years, talked easily and held no preconceptions about adjustment limitations and encouraged me to work. We began with the Braille lessons at once. But we found such ease between us that we tended to talk a great deal more than we studied.

After the first session, she had the idea of giving me manual therapy.

"Any accomplishment, no matter how silly it might seem, is important right now," she explained. She instructed me with two long wooden crochet needles in the technique of rug making. Accustomed to absolute respect for my teachers, I did not question the wisdom of this.

I took the materials home and spent all afternoon and evening in our living room, struggling with the cumbersome needles and rag strips, but imagining the day when this beginning would culminate in an enormous and beautiful rug for the living room floor. By ten that evening, however, I was mentally mouthing every curse word I had ever heard when all I had achieved was a hard wad of knots about two inches in diameter.

The next morning when I went for my lessons, Mrs. Bell casually asked how the rug was coming.

"I threw the damned thing away," I said.

"Needles and all?" she asked.

"Needles and all."

"Well," she said, "that takes care of your manual therapy. Now, shall we get on with the Braille?"

I despaired of learning Braille, and it did not come easily. The dots meant nothing to my fingertips and I could not distinguish the patterns. But Mrs. Bell urged me to be patient and to persevere, echoing what the blind monk at Solesmes had said. She admitted that Braille had been difficult for her, too, and still she was not as expert as she should be.

I brought the Braille books home with me, gently filing my fingertips with sandpaper, and worked until I could decipher the alphabet. Once I could distinguish the dots, I learned to read, though slowly.

As I developed proficiency with cane walking, I began to make trips to Fort Worth alone. Those first solo ventures to the city took on a pattern. I would ride the bus in from Mansfield and the driver would stop to let me step off at Saint Mary's Catholic Church, which was usually empty.

When it was not, I sat in a back pew, listening for the slightest sounds that echoed in the great structure. After a while, if I heard nothing, I could be relatively sure that I was alone. Then I would walk about and feel things with my hands. The marble altar rail was cool in summer, achingly cold in winter and moist if the day were damp. I would feel free to make my way to the side altars to hold a hand above the flames of votive lamps in order to count by the warmth how many were burning. But most of the time, I would just listen to the silences, breathe in the atmosphere, and find there some renewal of peace.

Invariably, within an hour or less, a transformation took place that was tangible. Nerves that were habitually pitched high settled, and I felt as though tautness were draining away. Then the balm of contentment spread through the senses and became calm and cheerful felicity, absolutely tuned to the silence. Sometimes I tried to pray, concentrating on each word. The words remained dust-dry in my heart. I had knowledge of theology and the liturgy and had nearly memorized the *Primitive Rule* of St. Benedict. I sought to form myself to it in my actions, but always with a dryness of spirit. My religious sense remained static, even though in my blindness religion was a constant intellectual preoccupation.

Occasionally one of the Benedictine priests would enter the church and we would converse for a time about the Abbey of Solesmes. Then one day one of them said it was edifying to see me there so often. "We watch you come and go, feeling that God must be very close to you."

I restrained from laughing in his face and wondered how he could be so mistaken. For a moment, I was tempted to explain my real reasons for being in the church. I wanted to escape the stench and noise of the city and to find rest. I knew in advance what his response would be: "What better reasons are there for coming home to God's house?" I did not want to hear him say that, because it was not right or true in this instance.

In general, my trips into the city were disheartening, and the city became my hell. To most sighted people, blindness is simply the worst tragedy that can befall a man. The world tells you in a thousand ways that you are a pitiful figure. Few believe that you can be happy and interpret your own natural happiness as stoicism or bravery. To have people constantly whispering how pathetic you are becomes a grinding irritation.

On the other hand, it is just as discouraging to hear the sighted speak in awe of attributes you do not possess, or to utter their astonishment at basic adjustments. The fact that sighted people are constantly amazed at a blind person's simplest accomplishment is amusing proof that those with eyes do not always see, that the sighted have no real conception of the possibilities that exist. Every blind person knows how friends are astonished and ask how in the world he or she knew to walk directly to a chair. By a judicious use of intelligence and intuition, the sightless can learn to live in a sighted world—if the sighted will clear themselves from our path of progress.

Another reason the sighted are inclined to be amazed is that most everything connected with this kind of experimentation must evolve from a deeply personal sense of self. No person, sighted or sightless, can live without a sense of personal value. This is something that the sightless will not discuss openly with the sighted. Most blind persons neither want pity for their "misfortune" nor applause for the simplest accomplishment.

When the sightless are out in public, however, they tend to become the targets of the sighted, who are protected in their anonymity. Both men and women often revealed themselves in ways they never had when I was one of them. Tough-talking thugs showed thoughtfulness, the pious showed callousness, the learned showed stupidity. And always the drunks, who tearfully comforted me and invariably said: "There but for the grace of God go I." Unable to see them approach, of course, I could not escape them.

But I came to dread most the pious ones. They would ask if I prayed, if I were saved. At first I tried to be polite, but this kind of gratuitous pietism soon ground into the quick of my nerves. Eventually, I heard myself snap: "Hell yes, I'm saved!" to their sweet-Jesusing.

The most upsetting aspect of the sighted—and in particular the pious —was their willingness to intrude on my privacy, as though blindness were an open door for them to walk right in.

What was happening to me happens to all the sightless, just like the blind man of Tours said it would.

— The Experiment —

By the end of 1947, I realized I had accomplished all that I could in the city. Those nearly daily trips to Fort Worth, as disheartening as they might have been useful, were no longer necessary for my training at the Lighthouse for the Blind. I continued practicing Braille on my own and studying the texts of theology and philosophy, which were facilitated by my mother. I noted a strange thing. In my studies I could not bear to have her read directly to me, so she spoke everything into a wire recorder. In this way, what was deeply personal could be contemplated in privacy.

My parents and I discussed the idea of turning the country place into an actual working farm. I decided that I would learn to raise livestock in order to become independent and to earn income. We bought chickens and pure-bred hogs. We read farm bulletins together, all three of us, since I felt no such restraint studying materials about agriculture and livestock as I had with the academic works. I spent my days in the open air and sunlight, doing hard physical work and experimenting endlessly, hoping to solve all the problems of feeding, judging, and breeding stock that would allow me to work without any sighted help. Most people shook their heads in disbelief, but regional animal husbandry special-ists became interested in the experiment.

Blindness

Several professors from Oklahoma A&M and Texas A&M provided concentrated course materials, which guided me in developing techniques for feeding and selective breeding. I hoped to show that in this unlikely field a man without sight could compete with the sighted, and that the blind need not be segregated into cloistered workshops where a limited ceiling was placed on their futures.

I raised pure-bred livestock—penned stock—for several years, learning to judge by feel. This is a very good way because there are many things that escape the eye but do not escape the hands. By touch, I could pick out the flaws in an animal's bone structure that a sighted person would miss, because the sighted cannot attain the levels of sensitivity to feel that can be achieved by the sightless.

In order to prove this point, I had our stock shown by someone else so that no one could say that special attention had been given because of my blindness. I entered small local events and larger regional events, like the Southwestern Exposition and Fat Stock Show in Fort Worth. Our Poland China hogs took top prizes and ribbons, even though no sighted person had handled them. I had raised up to champions in pure-bred hogs, experimented with caged chickens and birds but with less success.

My goal was to interest the government in subsidizing the sightless in these areas, where there would be no limit to their earning a livelihood as their own bosses. The American Foundation for the Blind and the Department of Agriculture supported the ideas, because they were proven by the sightless in many cases during this period. As a result, many blind persons turned to agriculture and raising livestock. In this field they were able to compete on an absolutely equal basis with anyone.

There was another great and often overlooked advantage to living on a farm—the blind could partake in safe exercise and stay in constant touch with the stock, and something interesting was always happening on a farm! Raising stock has the added advantage of being done in a peaceful setting, and the rhythms of country life can be absorbed by all the other senses, which the blind have developed into a fine art.

Farm and ranch life offer a primal realm of experience to which the sightless can more easily adapt. The animals respond to you in direct proportion to your method and consistency in handling their needs. They will show affection and, of course, they will not prejudge the blind as people might. This life distances the sightless from the hustle of city life, the mad blaring of horns, and the paranoia of insensitive crowds. In town, the blind person's field of interests is forcibly limited. No one

121

can find great interest in walking about the house or lawn, but on a farm the possibilities are fascinating.

One of most endearing experiences that came from my experiment was the camaraderie of a certain group of sighted people who have a special gift—an instinct for treating the handicapped as normal persons. I found that stock farmers almost invariably had this gift more universally than any other group I have encountered. Their open attitude was realistic, at times nearly brutally so, but in a healthful way. As competitors they gave no quarter. They would not undignify me in this way. They fought always to win with their own stock. While others tended to be protective, the stock farmers encouraged any type of daring.

Almost every day, at one of the country livestock shows, they would saddle a horse for me and point it to an open field and cheer me on to race at full speed just to get the feeling of "cutting loose," realizing that on horseback, as long as there were no obstacles, I had no handicap. Their open, easy-going acceptance and willingness to "neighbor"—to pitch in and help with any kind of work—was extended to me; and, more importantly, they expected it in return. I was often asked to feed another exhibitor's stock while he was away, or to judge his stock.

One day I overheard a visitor to the stock show in Fort Worth talking to one of the stockmen who had shown my stock. "Hell," he said to the visitor, "you don't need to feel sorry for him. He can do as good without his sight as the rest of us can with ours. He sure takes all the prizes."

Among no other group of men did I ever feel so equal, so whole, except with the monks at Solesmes. The stockmen were never overprotective and felt no guilt about enjoying a hearty laugh at my expense. As a group they were competitive but always fair. They did not take advantage of my blindness, but did not allow me to take any advantage of it either. For instance, I learned to play bridge, rummy, and poker with Braille cards. After a day at a stock show, we would all go out for dinner and then play cards. None of the stockmen would trust me to play poker with Braille cards. They feared that I could read their cards with my fingers as I dealt them. I had no such talent, but they were taking no chances!

During this period, several academics I knew expressed reservations about the farm experiment, and a few artistic friends thought it was a terrible comedown. Since I had studied music and monasticism, as well as medical science and the humanities, they thought I should teach or at least make use of this educational background. Many thought I should do something more distinguished, and they were not shy in letting me know of their views. It pained them that I should abandon all that "knowledge," and they saw this as the real defeat of my blindness. But my training in monasteries had taught the value of work, especially manual labor. It was the one blessed thing that carried me through, the reverence for work; to work with my hands was a new and restorative experience, no matter how humble it was.

I felt no loss of dignity when I sat in a farrowing pen in the middle of the night to help a sow farrow her pigs, drying them with a tow sack, clipping their umbilical cords and notching their ears before returning them. On the contrary, I felt satisfaction doing it, or raking stockpens or plucking the geese for down or rendering lard in a huge iron kettle over a wood fire. I found a parallel between the farm life and what I had loved at the Abbey of Solesmes. In both instances, in relative isolation and close to nature, I lived a simple, uncomplicated life. The liturgy, the chants, the silence were carried within when I worked. As it had been in France, so it was on the farm. Values held important by sighted society were supremely unimportant to me. I lived not behind cloister walls but in the solitude of pastures and trees. Time was no longer marked by bells but by the hunger of stock animals, by the woods in all their seasons and by the cycle of birth and death in nature.

It was not a matter of concern if it rained or was fair, since I relished all of it. To be in a freezing downpour before dawn to care for the stock and return to a warm kitchen for hot coffee, sausages, eggs, homemade bread, and fresh milk was enthralling. I could not prefer one moment or condition over another, and wondered why people grumbled about the times or the weather. I learned to cut wood for the fireplace and rode a sled, pulled by a horse over frozen ground, to deliver the firewood. In impossible weather, we sat by the open fire and listened to sleet skittle against windows while mother practiced Bach and Schubert. Profound contentment came not only in these feelings but in knowing the animals were safe and warmly bedded and fed in shelters, which by then included Toulouse geese, Golden Roller canaries, and the Poland China hogs.

I had rebelled against the attitude that placed a low ceiling and an empty future on the blind. I had refused to accept the provisions that society had made for us, including the pensions. I did approve of these things for others and did accept training and educational aids gratefully. It was necessary for me to know that what little I earned by my work had not come from the taxpayers' pockets. It had been the same with the military provisions, because I refused to accept the medals I had been awarded or the disability pension to which I was legally entitled.

No doubt some viewed these decisions as prideful but I did not. Even if there were an element of pride in this rebellion, I had been fortunate to have the support and understanding of my parents. Not every sightless person had that kind of gift. I condemned no one for taking the easier path, but it was not for me. The old monk at Solesmes had warned me to watch my pride and he had been right.

But I did not view the adjustments and the agricultural experiment as prideful, so much as necessary to self-determination and perseverance. And at that time, I had not realized that returning soldiers all around the country, blinded or otherwise disabled by the war, were refusing to accept that their conditions meant they were helpless. Others were doing the same in other fields—law, insurance, education, sports, and the arts, as well as in agriculture. Many labeled these efforts "aggressive" and considered us to be adjusting poorly. The well-adjusted, they said, did not attempt to do more than the handicap allowed. Such statements, and the general opinion among the workers for the blind, said that I should have stayed in town and been happy with group work. It burned, because these opinions and these statements were those of the sighted.

Edith Bell was not one of these, because she was blind herself. She had made an extraordinary life by helping others who were sightless, including Frances Smith and myself, whom she had encouraged to do anything we could.

My visits with Frances bore this out. We worked toward the day when the blind need no longer rebel, when the sighted world at last would be convinced that we could take our places as useful members of society. In fact, Frances was even more rebellious, and also she could laugh at many things that were still somber to me. Her laughter was never forced or strident. It was natural, and it was a far better reaction than mine.

I marveled and found hope in Frances's ability to run through their large home, to fix coffee or sandwiches. Always when she handed me a drink she would say: "Here it is," and make the ice clink against the glass so I would know to reach for the sound. It was strangely easy for us to forget all about being blind even when we talked of it. In every sense, Frances and Edith had been inspirations, and I had learned from their attitudes and accomplishments, from their humor and guidance.

As with Edith and Frances, nearly every blind person who adjusts does so by accepting without bitterness. This presupposes a potential of faith that is usually not brought into the clear light of religious activity. And there is one other crucial point about the sightless and religion. Often, the blind have natural mystical tendencies and these must never be allowed to become fanatical, but they should never be crushed out. The sightless person who can develop a deep mystical reality of faith, informed and balanced by good judgment and lived in humility and love, becomes immeasurably blessed.

With superb guidance, a mystical orientation can be cultivated with no distortion in perspective. It is the humility and wonder of mysticism that so naturally draw the sightless to its possibilities. I was drawn to it also, and particularly through the writings of St. John of the Cross, whom I had read while living in the villa in Solesmes before the total loss of sight. For me, the key was to balance the solitary contemplation of a mystical vision with active work. If this balance is struck, the open possibilities for not only a normal religious life but a sublime spiritual reality can be achieved in a special and powerful way of seeing.

The agricultural experiment, which had reconnected me to people in important ways, was supported by a very personal spiritual development that I kept secret. Eventually I accepted that the agricultural period did not represent my true vocation. If it had depended on my own tastes, I might have done it longer, for farm life had clarified things.

However, I knew that I would never be whole, never realize my full vocation, until I took the next step.

— Miss Sadie —

In the autumn of 1948, I delivered lectures on Gregorian Chant and classical music in Dallas and Fort Worth. Both series were well attended and well received. These programs involved speaking without notes and also playing fragments of the music under discussion at the piano and on a record player. I met many people and lost my fear of being in public. I knew that although I could advance in this area—lecturing, teaching, serving as a consultant—it was not to be my vocation. My nature demanded dedication, that I give myself wholly. This was entirely too pleasant, and it tended to spotlight me in a way that was uncomfortable. But since it was an enjoyable avocation, I did continue to lecture on music during the years that followed.

In January of 1949, I went on a concert tour through the south with Robert Casadesus. It was an opportunity to be with an old and dear friend and to hear music performed live by this master pianist. Between concerts we had a fine time together, staying in hotel rooms, talking about music, and also playing "dumb rummy" with Braille cards. At his performances, I would sit behind stage. During intermissions, he would pace back and forth talking of how the performance was going, or who might be in the crowd. We began the tour in Dallas. Backstage, he planted me in a chair and said: "Don't budge. Don't move a muscle. I'll return when I've finished the Beethoven. You want a mint?"

"No. Are you chewing mints?" I asked, thinking it incongruous to play the Beethoven *Emperor* with a Lifesaver in his mouth.

"I suck on it. Can you imagine the face I'd make if I swallowed it and got choked in the middle of the cadenza?"

I heard his footsteps walk heavily away. In the distance, one of the orchestra players spoke to him in French. I gathered they were talking about me, though they were too far away to be certain. In a moment he returned. I asked him who the fellow was and what they were saying.

"You knew we were discussing you, of course. Everyone wants to know about you. The poor fellow said that if he were you he'd commit suicide," Casadesus went on, as though he were slightly embarrassed. "So I told him that you had a good time, that we played cards, and that you didn't let it bother you." Among all my friends, Casadesus was unique. He was brutal about my blindness in a way that was strangely refreshing. I was blind and that was that, and yet he was extremely sensitive to anyone else's brutality. And he was curious about how I perceived the world.

In the hotel room the next evening, he spoke of painting, of literature, and of women. "It doesn't make any difference to you whether a woman's beautiful or not, does it?" he suggested.

"I really don't know," I said. "I suppose if I don't know, it doesn't make any difference, but when I'm told that a woman is beautiful or ugly, it changes the atmosphere somehow."

"I don't see how it could," he said, and let the matter drop.

That night we went to the home of a doctor for a reception. Events like these always presented a strange picture. All was confusion, voices, movements, perfumes. I never learned to separate voices in a crowd. If six people carried on different conversations in areas of the room, I heard all six with equal clarity and confusion. From the babble of voices, a clear and distinguished French broke out close by, someone conversing with Casadesus. Robert spoke with him for a moment and then introduced us.

"This is Professor Lon Tinkle," Robert said and then he disappeared.

The professor and I talked for quite a long time and he gave me the impression of being a man versed in literature and music, and he spoke French perfectly. We were enjoying ourselves when Casadesus drifted back, placed his hand on my shoulder and interrupted our conversation.

126

Blindness

In French, he said: "One of the most beautiful women I've ever seen just came in. She is dark, Mexican or Spanish, I suppose."

I was astonished at the change that came over the room. His words carried a tone of such admiration that a subtle radiance entered with the entrance of that beautiful woman. It was so tangible, I felt it.

"Find out who it is," I said. "I'd like to meet her."

I was curious to see if the resonance that I felt in the room with her at a distance would increase as I stood close to her, shook her hand, heard her voice. My impression was that it would spread out like a warmth and surround us up close.

It was then that Lon informed us that the beauty was his wife, Maria, and that he wanted very much for us to meet her.

I waited, speculating on the type of beauty I would meet. Would her voice be hard, in the way of many beautiful women I had met? The warmth did surround us and the voice was of another type of beauty— it was the soft voice of a woman who does not feel the need to hide behind glitter and glare. Maria's voice was natural, and it made her all the more beautiful in my imagination.

From that curious little experience, I carried away a recollection that never faded. I never realized that the Tinkles would return into my life a few years later, with Lon in the role of literary critic and friend.

The next day Casadesus and I boarded the train for New Orleans. It was carrying a great many doctors to a medical convention. After supper that evening, we went to the smoking car and began playing "dumb rummy" with my Braille cards. Our counting and conversation were entirely in French.

"Don't beat me in front of this crowd," Casadesus growled.

"What crowd?"

"Hell, there's a mob gathering around us. I'm supposed to be the famous one, but do they know me? No, they're looking at you as though you were some kind of damned phenomenon." He pretended to be outraged that I had stolen the show. Then, in a dry diagnostic tone, I heard one of the doctors say: "That's very interesting. You see how marvelously they train them in France."

When we arrived in New Orleans, Robert's friends Gladys and Harold Levy insisted that we cancel our hotel reservations and stay with them. They owned a home in the French Quarter and recently had converted the ancient slave quarters behind their house into a comfortable guest apartment. Years later I would stay in there while darkening my skin color to begin the *Black Like Me* experiment. The Levys urged me to contact a noted teacher for the blind in New Orleans, Miss Sadie Jacobs. They phoned her and arranged a meeting.

Miss Sadie, a short, energetic woman who had been blind since her third year, went over me with a fine-toothed comb in our first interview. She spoke in a half-shout. My cane was too big, too heavy, she insisted. "You'll ruin people's coffee tables with it." She provided a light one and taught me to listen for the echoes struck by its metal ferrule.

"But don't beat the floor with it," she said. "Here, just tap it lightly." We were only together a few moments, but it felt like a whirlwind had struck. She insisted on my staying in town and studying with her. That evening, I discussed our meeting with Casadesus and the Levys. Robert and I were due to leave the following morning for Atlanta. But my enthusiasm for what Miss Sadie could teach was obvious. Casadesus suggested that I stay on at the Levys and take advantage of Miss Sadie's generous offer to teach me. The Levys seconded him, and insisted that I stay in their guest apartment as long as I wished. So, I stayed on while Casadesus continued his tour alone.

Between lessons in advanced Braille and music Braille, Miss Sadie had me walk the streets of the French Quarter alone. She taught me to judge traffic by the sound, until I had learned to tell by my cane's echo how far I was from a wall or a curb or when I passed an open area. The Levys followed my progress with enthusiasm. Due to the huge amount of work Miss Sadie piled on me, however, we could only visit together a few minutes each evening over supper. Soon their guest apartment was filled with Braille books, a Braille writer, and other equipment.

One Sunday morning, Harold called me to ask if I'd like to walk over to the French market with him to shop for lunch. Since it was such a beautiful day, I was glad to go. We walked arm in arm the few blocks to the market and then, as we were about to return, I told him that I might as well use this as lesson time. "You're not allowed to help me. I'll find my way back. If you see me make a wrong turn or anything, just go on without saying anything." He agreed and we walked along talking, but he let me know each time a turn needed to be made.

We walked down Saint Anne's Street, where the houses rose directly up from the sidewalk, and the door stoops extended out onto the sidewalk. But I walked too close to the houses and after a few steps stumbled against one of the door stoops. I almost fell, but regained my balance. I heard Harold's voice: "Now, if you fall down, I'll help you up. But I'm not going to warn you about those obstacles."

This was the right and friendly thing for him to say, and both of us knew how he meant it. But two men standing at the corner had heard him and one of them said to the other: "How about that sonofabitch!" To them, it appeared that Harold was the meanest man in New Orleans.

Then Harold took my arm, saying: "Look, I have to live in this place. You can do your lessons alone, but when you're with me from now on, you're going to get helped."

Studying with Miss Sadie was like learning music from a master. I had thought I was fairly accomplished in the skills that nullify the handicap of blindness. Working with her, I quickly realized that I had made only the crudest beginnings. She opened up a new world to me.

Perhaps most importantly of all, she taught me to get rid of the "blind look." The sightless rarely look toward the person speaking to them. Like most, I tended to keep my head rigid and hold it too high, as if I was staring at the skies. The blind do this unconsciously. In some circles, it is brutally but accurately termed "the dumb look."

"Aim your face directly at the person's voice," she instructed. "Animate your face. Show expressions. Move your head frequently. Remember that to them you are not only Howard Griffin, you are a symbol of all blind people in the world. They will judge others by you."

Then she explained that "part of our problem now is that the sighted have seen too many beggars, too many ill-trained blind. So I want you to remember this: You will have succeeded only when you can make people forget that you are blind."

Though I had been without sight over two years, I still loathed the word "blind," even though I used it myself. I hated all it signified and could scarcely bear to discuss the condition with most sighted people. She taught me to say the word and to discuss its implications without blushing or wincing or feeling the oppressive sense of shame that had always pervaded my feelings. There was an element of brutality in adopting a more intelligent attitude about blindness. I had forced myself into this role, because it was the only sensible one, even though my feelings sometimes boiled beneath the surface. I rarely paid attention to my condition once I had developed some skills at home and on the farm. But my true attitude was revealed to me whenever I met another blind person or when I heard someone was losing their sight.

Every aspect of my experiences in New Orleans intrigued me. Daily, when I practiced cane-walking in the French Quarter, I was accosted by prostitutes, so openly and in such numbers that I remarked to Harold that never had I been in a city so heavily endowed with them.

"We don't have that many," he insisted.

The following afternoon as I walked down the sidewalk, a woman called down to me. "Hey, Sugah! Stop right there."

"What do you want?" I asked.

"Don't go away, honey. I want you to come upstairs. I got something nice for you."

I thanked her and walked on. She shouted: "Won't cost you *nothing*!"

This happened so frequently, and often with the added bonus of no charge, that I began to wonder what was going on. I spoke of it with our old family friend, Father Sherwood Clayton.

"I don't know," he confessed. "Maybe they think they could roll you without any trouble. But now, surely not all of them would have such baseness. Perhaps they just want to do you a favor," he chuckled.

Still I could not believe that New Orleans prostitutes were gifted with such universal charity. I had almost given up hope of solving the mystery when a woman accosted me in the street the next afternoon.

"Thank you. I'd like to," I said, "but I haven't got time."

When she insisted, I told her that I couldn't afford it.

"Won't cost you nothing, honey."

"Why not?"

"Never costs a blind man nothing. Didn't you know that?"

"Well that's very nice, but you're in business. Why give it away?"

"Honey, what country you come from, for heaven sakes?" she asked, as though astonished that I did not know about this.

"I'm from out of town. What's this all about?"

"Why, honey, don't you know it's positively the best luck in the world to get laid by a blind man?"

"No," I said laughing. "That's why they've all been after me?"

"Sugah, ain't a whore in Louisiana wouldn't jump at the chance," she went on. "But it's got to be free or there's no luck in it."

"About how many prostitutes do you think there are in Louisiana?"

"I don't know, a couple thousand, I guess."

"God, what an opportunity," I heard myself gasp. The magnitude of the charity demanded made me dizzy for a moment. I quickly calculated that two thousand adventures at one a day, taking off Sundays, sounded roughly like a seven year project! It was a titillating footnote to be a good luck charm to the ladies of the night in Louisiana, but it was not exactly the sort of footnote I would have chosen to explore, and it was not what I would remember most about New Orleans.

My most vivid memory had been those lessons with Miss Sadie Jacobs, who made a great change in my life. What I had learned from her was more important than all the previous encounters combined. After her lessons, I was no longer hesitant about going out in public. And after learning to walk in the French Quarter with the use of the new cane, it would be a relatively simple matter to navigate less complicated city streets. When I returned to the farm I felt liberated from many of the physical and psychological restraints of blindness.

⟶ The Writing Life ⟵

In the spring of 1949, a few weeks after returning from New Orleans, another significant change occurred that was also entirely unexpected. Some friends introduced me to John Mason Brown, the noted New York theater critic, who was in Fort Worth on a lecture tour.

We talked for a long time and Brown told me that I must write.

"How do I go about it?" I asked him.

"Get plenty of paper and a typewriter and start writing," he said.

"Surely it can't be that easy," I responded in amazement.

"You have told me some great stories, you talk like a writer, all you need to do is get started," he assured me.

Again, my training in obedience to those I considered masters, which dated back to my early student years at the French lycée, served me well. If a man of this caliber said I should write, then I would make every effort. I had never thought about the craft of writing and, except for technical writing in musicology and keeping a journal during my student days in France, I had written nothing.

The next day I called Edith Bell at the Lighthouse and asked if she could teach me to type. She told me to come in, that it should not be too difficult. Such things, in reality, are probably faster for the blind. I took a lesson on Thursday, another on Friday, and practiced on my mother's old Underwood over the weekend. By Monday I typed with fair facility.

Those who might be looking for dramatic inspirations in a writer will be disappointed, because neither did I become an instant expert at the keyboard nor did I know how to go about writing a novel. But as Brown had suggested, I started writing about what I had experienced in France.

I began the work by using the same method I had found efficient—speaking directly into the wire-recorder. I spoke in French rather than in English simply because I felt more comfortable in my adopted language at that time. The literature I knew best had been read and remembered in French, and it was the culture of France that had formed me. I had little knowledge of American literature and no training in literary forms or techniques. But I scarcely gave any thought to such matters.

My father helped to convert the feed room of the barn, a space roughly three long steps each way, into my writing studio. I carried the recorder and typewriter out there and began working. I decided to try to tell a story, hoping the writing would take care of itself. I worked at night, telling the story into the wire recorder. During the day, I transcribed the French into English directly on the typewriter. In the beginning typing was an impediment and the prose was stilted. Then the characters, who at first seemed dead, began coming to life and acting with a vitality of their own. I wondered if this might be my true vocation, so casually stumbled upon. All of my past studies seemed to have been a preparation for those long days and nights when I poured out pages of a first novel.

My past training in giving up to something beyond myself tempered life now. I immersed my being in the atmosphere, in the movements, and in the characters. The process became more hypnotically real than anything else. Soon the work took over so completely that I moved a cot into the feed room and lived there night and day. At the edge of the woods and amidst the farm animals, I led a solitary existence, living much like an animal myself. I forgot to feed the animals until the dog or one of the geese came into the studio to remind me. I forgot to shave, to eat. All the basic comforts became unimportant. I felt warm in the unheated room, sitting with an old quilt around my legs. The only thing that loomed important at all was the book. But new problems began to plague me.

How would I know if I had any talent? What was to be my attitude in the face of truths? Portions of the book I considered truths demanded by the story developed along lines that were an affront to my own tastes. I knew others would be offended, and I tried to determine where realism ended and pornography began.

I approached the solution to the problems simply. Each time I came to a passage where a truth appeared in conflict with current standards of good taste, I would ask myself if it would offend God. I soon discovered to my considerable amusement that God would appear to be much less narrow-minded than those who pretended to act in His name.

I believed that if I wrote for the good of the book and not for myself, my motives would be honest. I forgot what would glorify or shame me and concentrated only on what would make it truthful.

When I began writing fiction, I had a better knowledge of music than literature. I had, in fact, studied music so much that it had destroyed my creativity in that area. I had hoped to become a composer, and I ended up learning every damned rule in the book. I knew everything you *could not do*, and this silenced me as a composer. Even though I could write a technically correct work, I was too constricted by the rules and unable to breathe any life into it. When I began using words, I decided to avoid falling into the same trap. I did not really set about learning to write at all. Rather, I took musical forms and constructed my fiction on them.

In my first attempt at a novel, which became *The Devil Rides Outside*, I used the forms of Beethoven's String Quartet opus 131, a work that I knew intimately. The characters enter as Beethoven's themes enter and are developed in the same way. The novel's four principal female characters were created as the embodiments of four sensual types as the protagonist reacted to them. But I responded to them as representations of the four variations Beethoven had used in his quartet. When the thematics of the novel did not match the music, I changed the novel. Thus, I had chosen a musical form to write about a musical setting, confident Beethoven's spirituality during his final years would be consonant with the monastic spirituality of the eternal chants.

I did not name my protagonist—a young American music student who had lived in Paris and had come to the Benedictine monastery to study—so that his anonymity matched that of those unknown masters who had composed the chants centuries ago. I did not name the town or the river or the monastery either, hoping to evoke a sense of the eternal. I wrote in the present tense to feel the immediacy of experience in direct contrast to the eternal rhythms at Solesmes. The literary form of the novel was the journal, narrated through the voice of the American music student. I wrote the novel as a first-person narration because I could not tell a story from a viewpoint other than my own. The novel was not strictly autobiographical, but I was limited to telling a story in the only way I knew at that time. The novel and its narrator were fictional. I had not put my words into his mouth; rather, he had put his words into mine. The same was true of the other characters in the novel and the story itself, which developed with no preconceived plot or plan.

I completed the first draft of *The Devil Rides Outside* by the summer of 1949. The 600-page manuscript was typed in seven weeks. I did not know if the novel was publishable or even readable, and I had not the faintest idea who might publish such a work, or how one found a publisher. But unknown to me, word of my book was circulating locally, and people in Fort Worth were interested in reading it. None of this was of immediate concern, because my only desire was to continue writing.

After the novel, I turned to typing up the verbal "notes" I had been making about the condition of blindness and the experience of learning to adjust to it. The result was *Handbook for Darkness*, a brief monograph, which was a guide for the sighted who were in close contact with the blind. The American Foundation for the Blind produced printed and Braille versions of the work. In my introduction, I wrote:

Sightlessness places a man on a slightly different dimension from his sighted brother, yet he lives in a sighted world and remains in constant contact with the sighted. Too much superstition surrounds the blind and too few sighted people know what are his real needs and potentialities for overcoming his situation. The blind person's greatest unhappiness too often comes from those who tell him how tragic he is. It has become a commonly accepted social belief that blindness is unequivocally a tragedy. This is absolutely untrue, and it is the hope of most people who suffer with this so-called handicap, to prove it wrong. If a man is blind he does not consider himself less whole than the sighted man. Blindness is basically the inability to see with one's eyes and nothing else; but in practice, it is a great deal more due to the fact that those on whom the sightless depend for companionship are unaware of the truth.

Near the end of 1950, I began to keep a daily journal, which I typed directly on the typewriter without using the wire recorder. I was then proficient at the keyboard and serious enough to keep an honest journal, which had not been the case fifteen years earlier. During my student days in Tours, a teacher whom I greatly admired had suggested I keep a journal. He said it was one way of learning to know myself provided I let no one else see it, wrote it honestly, and wrote in it even when I felt I had nothing to say. The war changed all that.

When I had to leave France during the German occupation I entrusted my journals to Jacques Duthoo, who buried them at his family's country estate. After the war I retrieved the journals and began to read them. It was a sickening experience because the pages were filled with literary and musical analyses, the foods we ate, but with scarcely a word about the supreme reality of the war that had preoccupied us day and night. It was pure escape from that reality rather than any attempt to handle it. I was heartsick to find myself so false.

What I remembered was sitting beside a poor woman in a straitjacket, brushing flies from her face, and searching for better food for her and the other patients besides only the stale bread that was left at the asylum. I remembered dressing the wounds of the shocked Senegalese soldiers who had been used as cannon fodder by the French against the German army. And I remembered the faces of the Jewish parents who had handed over their children to us with the hope that we could save them from being shipped back to the concentration camps. But what I read through the faded ink of my juvenile handwriting were accounts of my reading of Gide and Sartre and I burned all those pages in disgust.

However, the reasons for keeping a journal were still valid, and total honesty was the only way toward detachment from prejudices and vanities, false values and inflated concepts. A private journal—with no thought of anyone else ever seeing it—allows the writer to rip the dull curtain off his thoughts, to record feelings, problems, emotions, reactions, temptations, and all of the private dramas and dreams. Most importantly, it is a way to recall those ideas and scenes that soon escape memory unless set down on paper. If honest, it will contain the tremendous advantage of giving him a truer self-knowledge, which can be horrifying, sometimes overwhelmingly so, for it is humbling to see oneself without illusions. But it is the best way to compassion and wisdom.

The journal allows the writer to create directly and without wending his way through all of the jungles of delusion and self-aggrandizement. The true writer, like the true painter, is an observer of all things, and quite especially of himself; but of himself in detachment, as though part of him stood away and appraised the rest, without love or partiality.

This is not to make factual use of experience—not at all—but rather that he understands the powerful insights that come through experience. If the writer experiences death close at hand, or the tragic break-up of his own marriage, or suffers any physical or mental discomfort, he has the strange consolation, even while hating the experience, of knowing that all of these things, the seemingly tragic along with the seemingly pleasant, will teach and develop him. He knows that this teaching and development will come out abstracted and refined as an enrichment to his own creative work.

For a real writer, then, life takes on a different significance. It will be only partially developed if too sheltered and too involved with creature comforts. He no longer acts or reacts in a stereotyped manner. If a writer gets caught in the rain, he does not curse his misfortune; instead he studies the feel of rain on his face, rolling down from his hair, stippling the backs of his hands. He studies its various sounds as it strikes the pavement or dirt or the leaves of a tree and he studies its odors and what it does to the colors of things. The writer does the same in all of the circumstances and conditions of his life, both good and bad. Unless he does this, he is more interested in himself than in this endless learning process that is his formation and greatest wealth.

In my case, I had been prepared to write about the effects of the

135

monastic experience on the narrator of *The Devil Rides Outside*. But I was *not* prepared to create a character who was losing eyesight or had been blind. And I could not imbue him with the wisdom to understand what I did not—the significance and the far-reaching effects that such an experience might have upon his spiritual evolution. In fact, since I was then agnostic, the novel was a lengthy argument *against* any spiritual evolution and a critique of organized religion. As to the spirituality of the narrator, he reflected only my most recalcitrant self, and he was not transformed any more than I had been at that time.

I had made a commitment at Solesmes, although it was anything but joyful in spirit. After the novel was drafted, I began making progress, yet my spirit was still as dry as dust. Without this powerful dimension of sightlessness, I know I would have remained as recalcitrant as ever, just like the narrator at the end of the novel. The important contradistinction was that I wrote the novel based only on what I knew to be true. But I was still learning about blindness and I knew nothing—or certainly not enough to evoke it convincingly in a first novel—about the hidden depths of spirituality. To have written about a spiritual conversion would have been not only false but out of character for the narrator, because I had yet to make that conversion real in my own life.

I knew about dedication to musical study, and I remembered my initial distaste for the monastic life at the monastery in Paris. I extrapolated from that and created a novel from those actual limitations. But I did not limit myself from imagining the rest of the story, which was entirely fictional, as long as I found certitude in the writing of the novel itself. While my actual experience at the villa was largely solitary and focused on dealing with oncoming blindness, the fictional lives of the characters in the village were much more involved and complex.

In any case, I never confused living with writing or fact with fiction. The truth of experience is what I am after as a writer. However, once a book is done it can only live for others. I believe that the true writer must avoid the error of attaching himself to a completed work. True, he must be immersed in it during the period of its creation, but when it is completed he must cast it off and then attach himself to a new one. A writer must not care what happens to the old one. The poetic idea of works being "the children of one's loins" is not only false, but needlessly distracting. It is impossible to dedicate yourself fully to a new work if you have one eye cocked to the reviews of the old one.

The act of creation is far more profound in its sources than we realize consciously. It comes up mysteriously from the very depths of our being, and that sound box of the spirit must be tempered and balanced as near as possible to the truth in order to produce the truest work. This is a point that needs constant exploration because it is vital to any act of creation. I constantly explore it, because I believe that the profoundest truth constitutes the greatest originality.

After typing the initial draft of *The Devil Rides Outside* and completing *Handbook for Darkness* in 1949, I poured my energies into the journal in 1950, recording daily observations and emerging ideas. Commenting in the journal about my efforts to write short stories, I felt the least bad ones that I made acceptable were those in which characters lived because I wrote with affection. How unbelievably trite were most of the stories I had been working on because the characterization was incomplete.

In the worst stories, all the amiable elements were carefully removed, and their cynicism was often hard and cruel, lacking the substance of affection to become believable and alive. But this was not true of the novel, according to our dear friend Sallie Gillespie, who had read the manuscript and remarked: "You write of all characters, even the worst ones, with such affection, without passing judgment."

I realized that I did that because living in the monastic atmosphere, being conscious of God in all of the characters, I loved them because God loved them, and they lived as characters because of that. Now, away from that, filled with worry, with disillusion in much of what I experienced from too close, the characters suffered from my lack of serenity.

However, I was shocked when one of these short stories, the one that I had written most rapidly and had considered the least significant, turned out to be the first accepted for publication. It had taken less than two hours to write the simplest story about a young farm boy and his favorite sow. But unlike the more sophisticated attempts, it was written without anxiety and with the assurance that I knew it was authentic. The story was based on my experiences raising livestock, except the narrator was half my age and, of course, he was not blind.

"The Big-Time Stockman" was accepted by a national magazine called *Farm and Ranch*, which was not the sort of literary debut most authors would have chosen to make. But I was delighted, because I had earned my first $35 as a writer in January of 1950. And the story was published in a magazine to which my family and also many of our farming and ranching neighbors subscribed.

Then on March 24, 1950, I signed a book contract with Smiths, Inc. of Fort Worth to publish *The Devil Rides Outside*. Gordon Smith and his brother, J. Hulbert Smith, owners of a successful public relations firm, decided to launch a new publishing venture with my novel.

During the rest of the year, Gordon and I worked over the manuscript. He was twenty-seven, and had earned a master's degree in contemporary British literature from Columbia University. He hired a reader to make a tape recording of my first draft. While I used the recording, Gordon used my typescript. We compared notes and then I revised parts of it four or five more times after that. Finally, I was sick of the work. Gordon had the final version typed professionally and that typescript was sent on to the printer to be typeset into galleys.

I had no idea how the final version read in English. Although it was the beginning for me—a novel that set up many problems of technique and content that I am still very much preoccupied with—I have never read the published version or attempted to evaluate it. I have a strong tendency, once the work is done, not only to detach myself thoroughly from it, but to feel very uncomfortable talking about it.

For me, the creation of works is an intense matter, a matter of almost hallucinatory concentration—and all that concentration must be focused on the creative process, on the work in progress.

⚊ Conversions ⚊

Good Friday of 1951 marked the fourth anniversary of my total loss of sight. The monastery had closed the book on my final visual images and opened a new book of spiritual awakenings. Nothing could be done about the old faded pictures, but as I listened to the silences of the country or caught the scent of pungent foliage or tasted dust in the breeze, I was returned unexpectedly to the essentials of that monastic experience. Yet I kept neglecting the spiritual part, even though it was the most satisfying.

The constant reproach of people was that I worked too hard, and that brought me to what I realized were the reasons. Going back through the *Primitive Rule* of St. Benedict, I had forgotten one of the rules that most affected me—murmuring against hardships. I had to accept them and thank God for sending them. It seemed that I had done nothing but "murmur" in my journal since I had begun keeping it, yet the acceptance had been something I once possessed.

I had never heard my friends murmur, the great ones who had risen to the summit in their fields. Far more significant than success to them was the fact that they had created something greater than was expected. The desire for fame was not really that, but merely an external symptom of a deep-rooted need in all of us not to have lived in vain. For them fame was a symbol of fruition. The most humble did not seek that but sought glory, something lasting—not to immortalize their names but to have the satisfaction of creating something that will give health and inspiration and goodness to succeeding generations.

I had seen greatness, true greatness from very close. I remembered those friends whose examples still meant the most—Pierre Reverdy and Abraham Rattner, Nadia Boulanger, the entire Casadesus family, both Friar Marie-Bruno and Friar Pierre Froger—the list could go on. Two things stood out with these artists of the spirit. The first was a personal dynamism, and I did not have it. The second was an enormous capacity for work and the need to work. I had the second. I prayed that someday, if I tried hard enough, I might have the first.

It seemed I had a core of rottenness inside which turned everything I touched slightly off-color. I felt that a sane and healthful marriage and the responsibility of children would be the great cauterizing element. But perhaps there was another way—to fight it constantly, to be always aware of it—to try to kill it? No, that would be dishonest. I wanted marriage and children with all my heart. Why deny it? But honesty had been my basic weakness in an odd sense—I was faithful because I made myself be. I was externally honest, scrupulously so, but it was a hard-bitten thing, of no spiritual value. In great crises I acted right, but I felt wrong, which was worse than acting wrong and feeling right.

There are two types of contributions a man could make. The one was immediate and necessary but lasted only for the now. The other was less immediate but lasted longer and touched a greater number of people. The thought of living, marking time in an office and gathering a few worldly goods and then dying, terrified me. That was why I worked so diligently at writing. That was why I was perhaps obsessed with work. I wanted something that will have made people think, act, be better, be more honest, if only during the moment when they were reading.

And there was the great gambling hope that if I worked hard enough, putting all of my love, all of my life into it, that the sweat would replace the genius denied me and allow something to emerge that would be beautiful and powerful. If God has *not* seen fit to give me a great talent, then He has given me the passion to work. If a genius can write beautifully in one hour with one rewrite, then perhaps a minor talent by working ten hours with ten rewrites could do the same.

Holy Saturday. Since there is not the strength or depth to write this morning, I type in my journal to ease my conscience. I write not because I understand and want to expose but because I understand nothing. I see newness every day and write of it as the first tasting of passionate interest. Mine is a quest for understanding.

Why the miracle of the heart, brain, and genitals, of renewed life and goodness and evil? Why the great love? How and for what reason is life? Will I ever know? Other people seem to know, others speak of it with authority, others seem to understand it without my struggle. It becomes a matter of converting these bouts of self-pity into the far ranges of compassion. There must be a new beginning now—I must become a Catholic. It is something that I dread and have put off for years. I must have the sacraments, however, and those are the only sacraments that mean anything to me. I dread it only because I have been so far away from that in these years since I left the monastery. I want to get back, but it is hard, a thousand times harder for me than for those who can accept on faith alone. I have to force myself to believe, to pray for faith, to pray for the love of God. Others seem to have it naturally. I do not.

I have slipped far, and it makes me miserable. I have left matters of judgment and decision up to me, when they should be up to God, to a constant awareness and adoration of the Divine. Why do I resist? Why do I confuse my shame of unworthiness with a sense of humility when I know it is pride? Why must I be so guarded and so secretive about everything? Why not tell the family that I need now to become a Catholic and let it go at that?

I must begin work with Monsignor Ernst Langenhorst, a theologian of incomparable insight. He is the first priest I have met since Marie-Bruno who understands my dread. I can communicate with him and confess my sins without fear or shame and yet some unhealthy desire for secrecy prevents me. Too many people have stared into the humiliating belly and seen and judged and, since their judgment is rarely valid, I can no longer bear their prying. Always I promise to begin instruction and something at the last moment prevents me. Why this heaviness, this feeling that I am not up to other men, this doubt as to the value of my work?

Perhaps it has been too much early success, too much over-confidence thrown back in my face? I must write not like the "author Griffin" but like an unknown and anonymous filter of life, offering works to God without sacrificing reality, without sacrificing truth as I see it. I embody more than one unsuccessful category: a Catholic who has denied himself Catholicism; a novelist without much talent; a musician and composer confined to the amateur ranks. I feel like a foreigner in my own country and an outsider to my own culture.

It would be easier, much easier, if I could only see. Seeing through the eyes of one's parents and friends might seem comforting but scarcely is it realistic or complete. How can I write when I don't know everything that goes on? In the meantime, there is this weight to be unburdened. If I do not make the effort to become a Catholic and to love God freely, what do I have to offer a wife, even an imaginary one? If I do not make a success of this creative work, how could I support a family? It is this lack of marriage and the gift of children that grounds my despair. Without spiritual union with God, the sacrament of marriage would be false for me and unfair to my bride. I need a communion of all these loves—of God, of wife and children, of creative work. But first I must make the effort and not allow blindness, the accidental catalyst for these spiritual beginnings, to become the pitiful excuse for giving up the effort.

By spring of 1951, I began my studies with Monsignor Langenhorst. He made it clear that my difficulty in becoming a Catholic would have nothing to do with learning the basic teachings of the Church. I knew the Bible from my adolescence as an Episcopalian altar boy, and I had read and studied the Catholic version in Braille. I had always been fascinated with theology and the lives of the saints, and I knew enough to carry on intelligent conversations. Rather than being intimidated by the Monsignor's knowledge of theology and the scriptures, I was utterly fascinated by his unpretentious fluency and humble guidance.

Since I had many times confessed to him in an "unofficial" way, I had no problem when it came time to confess my sins. That is to say that I had no fear of being honest with him, but there was another problem. At the moment of confession, I could never gather my wits to say all that I wanted to say, so I prepared a "General Confession" in writing.

Monsignor had the good sense to find humor in this, but also to make a point that was astonishingly simple and also very familiar. Essentially, he told me what Friar Marie-Bruno had said in Paris. My problem was giving too much power to my own sense of sinfulness, to my wickedness and unworthiness. Nothing I confessed that spring and summer alarmed the Monsignor in the least. He insisted that not only had he heard it all before but everyone had committed the same sins and had felt the same shame. Perhaps the only difference with me, he said, was that I seemed to be so proud of it!

That hit a sore spot because I had always hated pride as the most ugly sin, yet I had denied my own reeking hubris. How could I forget the old blind monk at Solesmes, who had warned me to watch my pride? He had seen right through my mask instantly even without being able to see my face. The Monsignor did not cackle like the old monk, but he did express tactful amusement when I handed him my "General

Confession" in typescript. What else to do but laugh with him and also at myself? It was a relief to do so.

When I went for instruction the next week, Monsignor said: "If there aren't any more questions, I think you are ready. When would you like to enter the Church?"

"Why not right now?" I said suddenly.

That afternoon I was baptized, making the Profession of Faith and a brief confession. I have dreamed of my conversion, planned it, prayed for it, hoped for it. I expected it to be an auspicious occasion. Instead, I was there wearing an old sport shirt and I needed a shave.

Thursday, July 12, 1951

Confession, absolution, penance. I became a Catholic convert at the age of thirty-one. I felt complete abandon for the first time in my life. And yet a strange calm. I was no longer counterfeit. On Saturday, I took my First Communion, feeling an inundation of warmth, of tenderness, feelings returning that had been dead since my time at Solesmes. There is no greater happiness. After the tensions of the decades, there was in this silence a profound peace, revealing a great leap away from all sus-picions and doubts about the Church.

Faith had replaced logic, erasing the need for further proof.

What change was there now? A sense of relief, a sense of gratitude deeper than I knew could exist. Although I feel no more "pious" today than I did yesterday, values fall into place, and the objections, my desire for spiritual independence, and all the old reservations have fallen into inconsequential ashes and dust.

I have learned more about the Church in these few days, by the fact of acceptance, than I learned in years of study. This because experience is a vastly better teacher than hypothesis and research. The mind can know, can even simulate, but only the soul can authenticate knowledge with feeling. Once again I felt the desire for innocence. Such innocence for me is the base of all joy, which is without color, without stain. It feels new to me now, appears possible, because I was no longer systematically trying to destroy it within myself. The marvel of this faith and adoration is my only health. It is a return to innocence, to simplicity.

I had known it once, but was too young to value it.

⚊ A True Friend ⚊

After these five years of loneliness and isolation, I had found a true friend. For a man who was deprived even of intimate correspondence with friends, it was a great gift. I had met Clyde Parker Holland through Monsignor Langenhorst and, while we did not then become close friends, we shared a few significant things in common.

We were both veterans who hated war and loved freedom. He was the first man from Mansfield to enlist in the military during World War I and he served in France. We both enjoyed France and had similar experiences in Paris. We shared a great admiration for Mark Twain, J. Frank Dobie, and the history of the real West. I loved farming, but my experiment was amateurish compared to Clyde's, because he grew up on a farm and had maintained a fifty-acre spread west of Mansfield. An insurance agent by trade, he worked his land during the evenings and on weekends, raising crops and livestock with the help of his wife of many years, Bess, who was a school teacher. They had an adopted daughter, Elizabeth Ann, who has been my mother's most gifted piano student for several years.

Clyde was intelligent, literate, savvy, and anything but a hick. Yet he was loved and respected by the locals, who considered him a bit of a "wise-acre" and a great storyteller. He was one of them in the best sense, having been raised as one of the commonsense rural folk, but without their prejudices. He was compassionate and humble enough to be one of them, but too worldly to ever be *only* one of them. He knew this and, perhaps, they suspected it; yet he was able to maintain a balance that allowed him to be both a trusted civic leader and an independent thinker who led a private life beyond the ken of most people.

The real difference was the genius of his wit—hilarious and even bawdy in some contexts but dry, acerbic, and ironic when called for. I recalled vividly my first experience with his sharp irony and quick wit.

As we were strolling back from lunch down the Main Street sidewalk toward his insurance agency, we passed the usual group of old men who sat on the wooden bench in good weather. Clyde referred to them as the "mourners"—because either they sat in silence as if at a funeral or they gossiped about the death of the good old days. Once we had walked past them, they began talking about me and one of them said: "Look at that poor blind fellow—jeez, ain't that a pity." When I heard that I moaned to let Clyde know I wanted to get the hell out of there.

But instead of walking faster, Clyde stopped and turned toward the hangers-on and called out in a loud voice: "Yeah, ain't it terrible . . . and the poor sonuvabitch can't hear either!" I stopped a few steps further away, transfixed by the heavy silence that had followed his thunderbolt. Then we bellowed with laughter and, before they could recover, moved swiftly down the block. I never forgot that, and it endeared me to him forever. The "mourners" have not muttered a word in my presence since.

Clyde became my business manager, guiding me through the basics of contracts and negotiating with the Book of the Month Club to have my novel be one of their selections. In July of 1952, however, we received a registered letter from the Book of the Month Club, informing us that the jury had decided against *The Devil Rides Outside*, although it would be designated as a recommended title of the Club.

All the judges thought the novel was remarkably written, but their other reactions were all violently for or violently against. Thus, because of the lack of unanimity, the novel would not be chosen as the one title. The primary objection was that the novel was too pro-Catholic, and it was to its "sectarian conclusions" that the unnamed dissenting judges objected. Finally, they decided that it would be "too controversial" for the Club's mass audience. In a way, it was an extremely encouraging letter. It felt good, actually, that the novel produced "violent reactions," although I could not imagine two of the judges, Clifton Fadiman or John P. Marquand, being violent about anything.

I felt two basic responses. First, of course, I would have liked to have the Club selection for the income it would bring. More than anything in the world I should have liked to help a lot of people financially, and this would have solved a lot of problems. Second, however, I was relieved that it would not be chosen, particularly because it would be by-passed for reasons of religious interpretation. It was, therefore, a question of policy rather than merit. In my heart I felt relief, because it allowed for much better and more independent work to come without the brass ring of success to sour the taste and to infatuate me with self-importance.

My publishers were disappointed. But as businessmen, they also knew that even a recommendation from the Club would promote the novel in ways they could not. It was not disastrous, for how could the brass ring be expected by a first-time novelist and a regional publisher? I thought it strange that others could despair in such a case, perhaps thinking that I would take the decision as a rejection. On the contrary, something I had lost had returned—the passion to work in that way that does not exhaust but nourishes. My creative energies had been dormant for a time, and I felt renewed.

There was a serenity, an enthusiasm, a sureness in the new work and, to a nature like mine, that was happiness. I did not think of "success" in the way that word is usually interpreted, as a refuge or a false escape, for I felt no hint of delusion. In addition, I had gained a little time in which all of the paraphernalia of success had been spared me. I did not have to be bothered with all the ballyhoo, the hysterics for a while yet.

My only grief was being unable to help those who had helped me—my parents obviously and Clyde and Bess Holland. I sensed disappointment in all of them, but they remained supportive and never uttered a negative word about the situation.

In August of 1952, with the Book of the Month Club recommendation and the novel's publication set for September, I decided to take a brief vacation before the upcoming promotional tour. I needed to be alone, not only to sort out some formal problems with my second novel, but simply to create some distance from the perception that I was unhappy.

I took the bus to Galveston, about 300 miles southeast, because I loved the sounds of sea birds and surf, and would be invigorated by the salt breeze off the Gulf. I knew this would be an opportunity to immerse myself in something different and at the same time be absolutely anonymous. I never minded bus rides, even though this one took many hours and the bus made countless stops, because I was able make notes on a novel that would be based on a Pacific island. The Gulf of Mexico was not the Pacific, but it could evoke similar impressions to the senses.

I arrived in Galveston, took a cab from the bus station to the sea wall, and began a lovely, restorative few days. The vacation was uneventful in the conventional sense, which was just what I had hoped for, but very productive. In fact, only one simple "event" occurred during that week. I was seated on the sea wall with my legs dangling over the edge. A large farewell dinner at one of the nearby pier restaurants and the long hours of fishing were combining to make me drowsy. As I was about to return to the hotel across the street, I became aware of a shuffling beside me.

"You had any luck, Kid?" an aged and shaking voice asked above the roar of the surf.

Since I was dressed in fishing khakis, I said, "Nope, not a bite all day."

"Not a bite, eh?" he said in disgust. All grunts and groans, he eased down beside me on the concrete wall. "I'll swear, it does look like people'd shell out for somebody like you."

"What're you talking about?" I asked, turning toward the tobacco odor from which the voice emanated.

"You're on the bum, ain't you?" he asked, but before I could answer, he assured me. "Don't worry, I am too. Anyway, I wouldn't squawk on you for the world," he said in tones of connivance. "But they ain't too bad on vagrants here—long as you keep in line, you know."

I was about to protest when some impulse to adventure, or perhaps the hope of getting information about a way of life unknown made me keep silent and let him think what he was thinking.

"They ain't no jobs around here for people like us," he pointed out. "I know 'cause I've tried. But I'm so old and crippled-up, they don't even ask what I can do. They just look at me and say no."

"How old are you, Pop?"

"Lord, I'm awful old. Must be around 79 now. Well, it sure is a nice evening, ain't it?" he sighed.

"It sure is. Is it dark yet, Pop?"

"It's still a little daylighty over west, but there's a few stars out."

We talked about bumming in the immediacy of finding brotherhood in poverty. His old voice rattled on, half lost beneath the wash of breakers below us. He knew the best places in town for eating— "mooching" he called it—and where to rent a bed for pocket change. We discussed the intricacies of keeping clean and well-shaven when you had to carry your entire wardrobe and toilet articles with you. He suggested that I'd have a better chance of avoiding arrest if I'd shave, and rinse out my clothes.

I wondered why he didn't go about his business of mooching, until I realized why he was sitting there talking instead. He was trying to help me. He remarked that the worst thing about being down and out was that there was no one to turn to or even talk to and, of course, everyone looked down on you. Then he said that if I wanted him to help me shave, we could walk down to the bus station. "The washroom is nice and clean and they've got plenty of towels."

"I'm too worn out, Pop," I apologized. He patted my shoulder slowly, as if to reassure himself that I was okay.

"I do believe I'm better off'n you, after all," he observed. "At least I can see." And then he fell into immediate stammerings. "I didn't mean it that way, Son, I just . . . "

"That's okay, Pop."

"I mean I'd never mention something you might be touchy about, you know. It just slipped out."

"Sure. Don't worry about it. I got over being touchy a long time ago."

"Well, that's awful nice of you to say that, but still I wouldn't never—say, Son," he interrupted himself, "it's getting pretty late. Must be close to eight or so. If I don't get me some supper soon, I'll just about cave in. What about you?"

146

Blindness

The idea of more food sickened me after the supper I'd eaten, so I told him I guessed I'd do without tonight.

"Hell no," he protested. "You ain't going without supper. I'll guarantee you that. I know you're broke, and I'll bet you ain't ate all day, right?"

When I could find no words to answer, he said, "Well, you've got to eat, Son. You can't go against something like that because you don't have the price to buy a meal now can you? The Galvez is nice if you sit over by the kitchen door about this time of night. I'll go over and find us something to eat, don't you worry. You want to come along?"

Since I was staying at the Galvez, I was afraid I might be recognized, so I told him I was too tired. He commiserated and said he would mooch enough food for both of us. He balanced himself with his hand on my shoulder and got to his feet, stifling a groan.

I listened to his footsteps sloughing away and felt guilty that I was leading the old man on about being a bum. Yet he felt apparent delight in my company and in his intention to help out a blind man.

Cars passed behind me on the seawall and vacationers strolled along at my back, parents and children exclaiming the wonders of the Gulf. As their heels tapped and scraped rapid syncopation, I heard some whisper how it saddened them to see someone like me. I stopped listening to that and breathed in the sounds of the Gulf and in the distance, I could hear the carnival music of the calliope wheezing faintly. I thought of people at the amusement park, imagining them on merry-go-rounds, in the penny arcades and shooting galleries.

Then the voice of the old man cackled behind me.

"Boy, they're giving that stuff away tonight, just throwed it at me!"

"Are you back already?"

I was astonished at my joy in hearing his voice, feeling the same gratification he felt earlier when he thought he had found another bum. He sat down, rattling his sack and jubilantly describing its contents of steak scraps, poppy seed rolls, some lettuce and a tomato. "And a whole big old cup of tarty sauce," he added.

I laughed at the way he said tarty sauce for tartar sauce, uncertain if he was aware of his wordplay.

"I was wondering," he said cautiously, "about maybe saying Grace. If you're religious, you know. I don't want to butt into your business, but if you're in the habit of saying it, you know?"

"Sure, if you want to?"

"I kind of think it's a nice thing to do sometimes. Do you want to say one? Do you know one by heart?"

"Yes, but don't you want to say yours?"

"No, you go ahead before this mess gets cold."

"Bless us O Lord for these Thy gifts which we are about to receive from Thy bounty through Christ our Lord, Amen," I recited.

He remained quiet for some time before asking, "Is that all?"

"Yes. Wasn't that all right, Pop?"

"It was fine except it was so dinging short."

He made sandwiches from rolls and the rinds and fatty trimmings of broiled steaks left on plates by customers, seasoned them with tartar sauce and placed one carefully in my hand. I nibbled it, repelled by the idea of eating someone else's scraps.

"Did I put on too much tarty sauce?" he asked uneasily. And I realized that he was sitting there, his face close to mine, waiting for my reaction. I bit into the sandwich as though I was starving.

"It's good, Pop," I said enthusiastically.

"It's really all right?"

"It's delicious. Just perfect."

We had our strange picnic, perched above the sea and isolated from the greater world of vacationers around us. We feasted heartily.

"There's a bench over there," he said, once we had finished the last of our scraps and wiped our greasy hands on the paper sacking. "Let's go sit down there where we can digest and rest our backs a little."

He hobbled along beside me, so stooped that his voice was coming from far beneath my chin. "Here we are," he said, facing me to the water and backing me up until I could feel the bench touching my calves. "Just plop yourself right down and you'll be comfortable."

"Thanks very much, Pop."

"Oh, don't thank me, Son. It's a pleasure," he grunted, sitting down beside me. "You smoke don't you, Son?"

"Yes sir."

"Want me to see if I can find us some snipes?"

I told him I still had a few cigarettes left, and we lighted them.

"Ain't this nice?" he asked as we leaned back.

"It sure is."

"You really enjoyed the meal, didn't you?"

"I sure did."

"And you got enough?"

"You know I did."

"Well, people are good about giving you things, you know. They can tell when you deserved it and when you're just poor white-trashy. I'll tell you what. If you'd like to, why don't we meet here again tomorrow night and have supper together. I'll get something real nice for both of us."

We sat in comfortable silence, listening to the waves slosh in among the rocks with the rising tide and to the distant calliope waltzes.

"You know what, Son?" the old man asked after a time, his voice soft and thoughtful.

"What's that, Pop?"

"You know, after a good meal like that, there just ain't nothing that tastes so good as a good cigarette, is there?"

"There sure ain't, Pop."

An hour later we went our separate ways, without even knowing each other's name, but it had been memorable sharing such scraps for a feast.

⏤ She Played Chopin ⏤

When I had returned from Galveston, Clyde and I continued meeting every week when he brought his daughter across town for piano lessons with my mother. While Elizabeth Ann practiced under mother's tutelage in the house, Clyde and I visited in the barn studio.

Later that summer, sometime before she was to step up to advanced music at Our Lady of Victory Academy in Fort Worth, I began to listen closely to Elizabeth's final lessons. She would soon be learning from the finest piano teacher in the area, Sister Mary Albertine, who requested that I coach the gifted student for her senior recital. So, instead of meeting with my business manager once a week, I began music lessons with his daughter.

Even though she had been my mother's best student for a few years, I had paid little attention to her, other than noting that she was a perfectly mannered girl with genuine talent. I was a demanding teacher—as my teachers had always been—and we never drank tea or chatted but got right to work. I coached her on pieces by Bach, Mozart, Schumann and Chopin. She worked diligently, never complained, and her playing was beyond the technical level needed for a high school recital.

But nothing I had ever heard from her could have prepared me for what I heard a few weeks later. On a warm afternoon in early September, I sat there and listened to my pupil, a charming teenager, playing Chopin. The next moment, I heard something altogether different, and it seemed that a new dimension had happened to the music. It sang out. I heard the soul of Chopin's nocturne liberated into the phrases, no longer performed by a teenager but by a woman.

The music projected not by mere fingers but by a heart that drew from it the secrets most of us miss. The realization was a radiance that brought all elements of the day into sharper focus and, for a moment, all my defenses were destroyed. I opened myself to her, as she had opened herself to the music. Feelings of nothingness were replaced by those of longing and a deep tenderness for the soul that allowed Chopin's nocturne to sing in such a way.

I caught myself abruptly. It was too ridiculous. My reactions warned me. I must not let myself feel tenderness toward her. I gathered my wits and showed none of my feelings. I talked as I had always talked. And yet I knew that I would never look on her as a youngster again. She had become a woman, a lovely woman in that moment.

I went out to the barn and tried to busy myself with work, sternly telling myself many sensible things. But then I would catch myself drifting into daydreams of scenes shared with her. When I fed my stock I imagined her there, watching me, and the scene was different. It was the same in all things—sitting in the chair, I would see images of walking with her in the woods or having breakfast with her in our kitchen.

"It is your loneliness," I rationalized. "There is nothing but infatuation in this reaction. You know this. Stop thinking about it. It is impossible. This is too sudden to be real. You heard something in her playing. You don't hang your hopes on such intangibles. Next week her playing will probably resume the tone of childish perceptions."

I hoped it would. I saw myself in a classic farce—a blind man falls in love with a student because of the way she plays, because he sees her in the music. I, who detested such clichés, was living one. I became painfully aware of it and embarrassed. The classicist whose instincts drove him toward romanticism, even temporarily, cannot fail to blush. My emotion was classic, the emotion of love, but it was framed in a romantic situation.

Elizabeth Ann was at that very minute visiting with my mother in the kitchen, perhaps having a cup of tea as they often did after lessons, a girl waiting for her father to pick her up from a music lesson. Meanwhile, out in the barn studio, her recital coach was immersed in a fantasy of a life with her that sailed on the music of Chopin while she chatted over tea. I tore myself away from thoughts of her. Could a man love a young woman he's never touched, never even seen? Of course, I told myself, but not in this case. Was I not substituting for the reality a profound wish?

In the vast confusions of blindness, of a life in so many ways stymied, the thirst for all that is most normal to man becomes overwhelming. It fogs logic, obliterates taste and twists the mind to its needs. I had to think clearly, and yet I could not. The image of a kitchen, of a breakfast table, a shared bedroom settled over me and possessed all my thoughts and feelings. It was a good image, one that made everything right, one that gave to nature the sense of health and expansion.

I stopped, forced myself to breathe deeply.

Would it be fair to her? I presumed instinctively that it would work out merely because I wanted it. But that was not good enough. The real responsibility to her had to fall on my shoulders, and my responsibility just then was to stop this madness before I said anything to anyone.

I heard a car drive up toward the house. I figured it was Clyde and I ambled out to greet him. Before reaching the car, he had stepped out and said, "Hey Buddy," and touched my arm. Without hesitation, I asked him if we might talk down at the studio. He agreed, and as we walked I wondered what I would say, surprised at my involuntary request.

As soon as we were inside the barn, I closed the door and sat down. I heard him scrape the other chair on the floor, pull it directly in front of me, asking "Is anything wrong?"

I heard my voice ask: "Clyde, do you pity me?"

"Why, hell, you know I don't."

"If I ask you something, will you tell me the truth," I stammered.

"Of course."

"No matter if you think it would hurt me?"

"What is it?"

"I promise you I've given Elizabeth Ann no indication of my feelings. I wanted to talk to you first. I could fall in love with her. I think I already have. As far as you're concerned, is there any hope in that direction? I can understand why parents would not want their daughter to marry a blind man. Please, you can just tell me yes or no . . . "

After a brief silence, his voice sounded old, cracked. "No," he said.

"That's what I expected. Then I'll have to ask you to keep her away from me."

"Now for the first time since I've known you," he said, "I do pity you."

I remained silent and leaned back from his voice.

"I'll tell you this," he said, "if she were a few years older, I would never say no. As it stands, it wouldn't be fair to either of you. She's never been in love. She doesn't know anything about it. It would be too risky for both of you."

"I know," I sighed. "I've been telling myself all those things."

Heat poured in the window, bringing with it the parched odor of late summer in the country. His refusal went with the day somehow, fitted into it, deadened the air.

I accepted what he had said in complete numbness, aware only of the sudden emptiness. I thanked him for his honesty and felt no bitterness. He said nothing, put the chair back in the corner, and walked out. Within a minute I heard the car doors open and close. They drove away.

Stupefied by the void of a future without companionship, even though I had expected it, I walked up to the house. Without saying a word to my mother, I sat at the piano and began practicing scales.

During supper I realized my clumsiness in trying to eat, realized that once again I was blind, after having lost it in the naturalness of her. The darkness behind my eyes was once again a supreme preoccupation. I said nothing, except to respond automatically to what my parents said at the table. I felt like crying, but I also felt calm. After supper I took a cold shower, very cold. Then I took a long time drying off.

As I returned to the living room, my parents were on their way out to the store. The door closed and I felt uncomfortable with the silence. I switched on the radio to a channel featuring a hillbilly announcer and laughed at every frightful thing he said. Then I clipped my fingernails.

When my parents returned, I talked with my father about the price of chickens, about how to make garlic bread. I drank glass after glass of tap water. The wind began to stir the trees outside. No lonelier sound than that. In all of it, the obsession of time was erased. I said good night and went off to bed early, rare for me, but they didn't make a point of it.

In the bedroom I opened a window before lying down atop the covers. I listened to the wind as it began to howl. A soft wind blew in moisture through the screen and onto my face. Soon a late summer storm blew in to lash the trees and throw a limb against the window screen. I tossed about the bed, fully clothed, in the clutches of insomnia. I raged against my stupidity, my selfishness, my doubt. Why had I said a word to my friend, why had I indulged a fantasy with his daughter I could not make real, why had I cast my darkness into their light?

He had been right to say no—and for all the right reasons.

I expected everyone to understand what it was like to be blind yet failed to see his view. I had claimed to hate being an object of pity yet turned myself into that very thing in my friend's eyes. So, he pitied me— and why not?—for I had been pitiful and false in the face of his mercy and truth. He had responded as the man he is but I had acted like an idiotic schoolboy. Damn, he deserved better than that. And I got exactly what I deserved—his pity—for giving him nothing better than my putrid pride. I must apologize for being so damned false to our friendship, apologize for debasing his pure trust.

I ripped off my shoes and almost threw them across the room. Instead I threw my sweaty socks. There, happy now I thought, but thankful I had not thrown the shoes, which would have startled my parents. I slumped back in the bed, too old for tantrums, too tired to pull off my clothes, but still kept awake by guilt.

I listened to the slackening rain, the dying wind, and then the slow drips lingering over the edge of the eaves. I, too, lingered on the edge of a question: Could my friend forgive me, would he?

The last drop of rain clung then dropped to the soggy earth. But its brief silence brought no answer. I lay silent on the ledge of sleep, waiting, praying without words. Then a vague thought formed into one clear unspoken syllable: Yes. And I believed it and I slept.

The following day I began again and I believed that I would make it. Everything seems clear after a storm. I prayed with all my force that this blackness would not return, and in the emotional depths I felt that the crisis had passed and I had been spared.

I called Clyde and, in his usual natural way, he brushed off yesterday's conversation, insisting he understood and that I needed no forgiveness from him. "Thanks, Old Man," I told him with great relief, "but there must be something I can do to make this right."

Without hesitation he said: "Just make sure you prepare your pupil as well as possible for her recital."

I told him that she was well-prepared now, but that I would give the performance pieces a final tune-up, implying that I would be altogether mature and professional about it. And that was that.

Nonetheless, there were some things I had to realize coldly. I had to become detached from what was purely instinctive. I had to command a certain action, control that part attached by nerves to the heart of my being. There was only one solution and that was to grab hold and fight the inclination to give up, to wake myself to a state of health that would cause them to be happy. Those things that blocked me were defeats that had to be accepted. The self-torture of struggling against the fact that I could not see had to cease. I had to accept that I would never see the faces of those loved ones and I had to give up the furious desire to see.

The struggle to overcome sightlessness had to be a healthful thing, without pathos. But also I had tended to deny its existence, which is like listening for the footsteps of the dead. I had to struggle constantly to reduce the face of blindness to its minimum disadvantage but never to deny its existence. I had to realize that sighted people obviously operated from a different point of view, a different criterion for judging the gravity of things. For them, each word or act or gesture was not, in itself, the ultimate expression but only a passing one.

Since I had been sighted, I should have understood this from the beginning. What seems crucial to the blind is generally insignificant to the sighted. With patience, the blind will be reassured, because the tone of voice will change, the silence will be broken, and the tiredness will disappear in the natural process of conversation.

Sightlessness is an unnatural condition, a minority condition, thus it is largely up to the sightless to adjust themselves to the rest of the world and not the contrary. It was in those things that I had allowed myself to react spontaneously but without understanding. Another phenomenon is that blindness inevitably renders its vessels away from externals and back to what seems like a somewhat childlike state, which becomes a form of compensation. Blindness isolates a man; he never sees ugliness at very close range. Contacts are usually limited to those who modulate information for his benefit. His isolation from externals—the hardening surface of society—is much more complete than the sighted imagine. Strip a man of that and he will return to fundamentals, as a child does. He seeks normalcy in simplicity, abandoning all the adult refinements.

Around those whom we love, the tendency is to abandon the façade that the sighted can never abandon, because it is part of their lives. And when we do abandon the façade, they fear that we are not adult enough. Thus, I had to accept coldly that the façade can rarely be abandoned. I had to stand aside and force myself to be that which would make me like the sighted; and in that very fact was the motive necessary to carry it through, because their unhappiness became mine.

It takes sensitive awareness to all the nuances of the sighted and to all the dissonance of the sightless. For both it is a continuous struggle, but the ultimate goal must be the communication of insights, those which are beyond the physical limits of darkness or light, yet never losing awareness of those limits.

For the sightless person this is the first insight, and it must always be remembered and understood before it can be communicated. And it is in the realm of the spirit, that crucial realm most difficult to understand and nearly impossible to communicate, that I still struggled unceasingly.

My loneliness for a wife would not be allowed to destroy the pleasures of the spirit. However, only she would one day enhance those pleasures of the spirit while sharing those pleasures of the flesh. I longed for that knowledge of love and the pleasures that would lead to happiness.

➤ Fame and the Devil ➤

Local reviews of *The Devil Rides Outside* appeared in September, after a deluge of news features long before the novel's publication. I became concerned that the many letters we had been receiving could balloon into thousands once the feature appeared in *Look* magazine, along with news about the Book of the Month Club recommendation and several national reviews that had been scheduled.

My mother had been recording the printed materials so that I might listen to them on tape later. She also recorded some letters, apparently only the positive ones, for I suspected she had kept the negative ones to herself. Unable to handle the flow, it would have been impossible for her to read everything into the tape recorder. I asked her not to over-extend herself, because I had no intention of replying to fan mail. The Mansfield post office feared it could not handle the flood if hundreds of letters became thousands.

The newspaper features were embarrassing. If I had to listen to one more line about the "blind war hero" who has written a torrid tome of "the epic war of good and evil" or about the "Catholic convert" whose "spiritual search has overcome the guilt of the flesh," I would die of apoplexy. My deepest embarrassment was that the press had written sparingly about the novel and seemed interested only in the author's story. The local headlines reeked of boosterism:

BLIND WAR HERO CONQUERS
NEW YORK LITERARY SOCIETY!

When I insisted in phone interviews that what mattered was the book and not its author, the more they poured on the clichés. I knew that one of my many stylistic faults had been the use of hyperbole, but compared to what they had written about my so-called gargantuan tome, even my naive excesses withered in horror from the bombast!

A second printing was scheduled for October 27, because the first five thousand copies had sold out. The perceived tidal wave of "success and fame" rolled over us, matched only by the actual undertow of near-poverty. I had not seen a dime from the book. My parents worried because there was no money to buy a new suit to go to New York. Why should there be embarrassment if I wore an old suit? The blessed security of feeling like writing once again was all that mattered. To live like a human being—not to be on display, not having to submit to the whims of publicists.

The first round of local book reviews were only slightly more intelligent than the features. I wanted to see if reviewers would actually seek to interpret the author's intention, to evaluate his realization of it, rather than merely to express their personal tastes or, worse, the tastes he wanted the readers to think he possessed. It seemed that most of these critiques ended up being mere opinions. I meant this not from the point of view of the mistreated author, but from that of the critic, for I was preparing to write reviews of new books and these things preoccupied me. I did not want to bring to the fore such clichés or those pathetic little involuntary confessions of the critic. At first I believed that I should study other criticisms, but I quickly found that it was best not to read them at all. They were too full of the critics and too empty of discourse about the works under review.

For instance, the Catholic press had reviewed *The Devil Rides Outside* strictly as a contribution, or lack thereof, to what they saw as a so-called American Catholic Literature. This was idiocy and just as idiotic as the local press calling me a "Texas author." The fatal error, of course, was when the writer misguidedly *attempted* to write like a Texan, an American, or a Catholic—then he was a poisoner of the first rank. I believed it was crucial not to write like any of these things, not to try to be medieval or, above all, not to try to be modern.

I did not find this sort of closed-mindedness in the reviews published in the national publications during the fall of 1952. I had traveled to New York to meet with people in the publishing industry, and we negotiated paperback and translation rights. I did several interviews for newspaper critics and radio shows, which were interesting but exhausting. The national reviews were more insightful, because those critics had written about the novel pure and simple. I have always appreciated genuine criticism, believing that nothing can mean more to a serious writer than to be edified by an insightful reading of one's work.

For instance, John K. Hutchens in the *New York Herald Tribune* said something that might discourage a first novelist, but it was accurate.

The book is overwritten in the flooding sense that Thomas Wolfe overwrote. It is repetitious, and it is often and lengthily bemused with theological meditation. Yet there remains about it the massiveness of the big, symphonic novel that sets up a theme worth writing about and then attacks it with passion, knowledge and the authority of experience. But you will not fail to note that almost anything at all that he touches upon takes on vividness and depth as only a true writer can make it do, whether mystical vision or carnality or a peasant's child dying. He will be a better writer

when he is a more disciplined one, and yet there is something gratifying, isn't there, about a writer whose fault is overabundance
instead of meagerness?

Orville Prescott's review in the New York Times was just as critical
in general, but singled out Madame Renée as "one magnificent full-
length character" for praise. "This is a gruesomely expert study of a
hysterical woman consumed by vanity, hypocrisy and old-fashioned
meanness," Prescott wrote. "His Madame Renée is a frightful and horrible creature, but never a monster. She is pitifully human, too. She is a
character such as Balzac would have enjoyed writing about. Any first
novelist capable of creating her is blessed with uncommon talents."
   The most gratifying response of all came from Father Gerald Vann,
the renowned Dominican scholar and philosopher, who reviewed the
novel in the Catholic Herald of London. He wrote:

This is an outstanding book, both vivid and subtle . . . and as a
statement of the Catholic view of life, of holiness, of human love
and the love of God, it is magnificent. In this respect it is precisely
this novel's communicating of an outsider's inside knowledge of
monasticism that is so compelling. The insider's main criticism
here (and, apart from a number of small points, his only one)
would be that the author's admiration and affection have led him
to paint a picture in which the real approaches the ideal more
closely than is generally to be expected in our fallen world.

What struck home was not the praise but the clarity of his criticism into
the narrator's "outsider's inside knowledge," as opposed to Vann's own
insider's view of the monastic reality.
   It was important to me that such a lucid theological mind had taken
the novel seriously, and without being offended by its raw language and
depiction of sexuality. On the other hand, the Catholic press reviewers
were scandalized by the "foul" language and what they believed to be
"pornographic" scenes. How strange, considering that the most
detailed account of the sexual act in the book I repeated word for word
is the account of the raptures of prayer. That, I suppose is the main
point, that sexual and spiritual love are the same.
   Other Catholic press reviewers, who tended to forgive the novel's
indiscretions, believed that the narrator had survived his agony and had
been "converted" by the end of the book. But if the novel gave the
impression—certainly not my intention—that man conquers the evil
within him and then abandons himself once and for all to God, then the
novel was wrong and I had failed to clarify this distinction. My sense of

the narrator's state of mind at the end of the novel was that he remains attached to his intellectual agnosticism. True, the monastic experience changes him, as it had changed me, but he was no more capable of a dramatic leap of faith than I had been. The novel ends with a certain peacefulness on his part, but not with the promise of a conversion.

Yet some reviewers still seemed to demand that dramatic leap. Either they had imposed it upon the narrator's actions or had expressed their disgust when the novel failed to deliver their wish. The most perplexing review was written by a critic I respected, but he had overidentified the author with the narrator. Because he knew I had begun contemplating conversion at the Abbey of Solesmes, perhaps he assumed that the narrator had done the same. The opposite was true.

Yet he interpreted the ending as the narrator's failure to be changed by his experience and as the novelist's failure to create a convincing leap of faith. "Above all," concluded Lon Tinkle in the *Dallas Morning News*, "the final salvation of a hero so capricious, brutal, ungenerous and socially unsympathetic, is beyond even Mr. Griffin's verbal power. "The hero may have seen the light, but this reader is not at all persuaded that he has really adhered to the true, the beautiful and the good."

However, the narrator's sense of acceptance, as he returns to the monastery at the end of the novel, is but a phase in his life. The moment such a phase appears to be final we face the immense delusion of seeing it fall to pieces. There must be victories, but these are only transitory. There is never permanent victory, and the transitory ones are dangerous in that they put us off guard. If we think we have won, and we relax, we will find ourselves more hopelessly defeated than we thought possible. Conversion has to be won over and over again, every day, every hour if necessary. At least that was my experience of conversion.

When I had returned to France after the war, in 1946, I was doggedly determined *not* to become a Catholic. I held onto that early Protestant training as a defense against Catholicism, but in truth I was slipping toward an agnosticism that questioned all forms of Christianity. The novel presents every possible argument against Catholicism.

I wrote it to please and instruct myself, never expecting it to be published. The novel is *not* autobiographical, but one might say it records my intellectual history. I found the solution I was seeking in self-criticism and I had to abdicate all compromises in order to have a clear conscience.

I became a convert to Catholicism because in it you do not depend on the stiff-necked morality of your own willpower, which was what I had felt both as a Protestant and as an agnostic. The origin of my novel lay in the wish to apply these ideals of medieval Christianity that I had encountered to the diluted, sanctimonious Christianity of modern life. I wanted an answer to the aimlessness of the twentieth century, especially during the years following the great wars.

I needed above all else a solution to the problems of discovering a tranquil conscience; of striking a balance between the sensual and the spiritual, but without truncating the naturalness of either urge. I chose not to be silenced on these issues because my generation, then called the Silent Generation, was faced with a peculiarly silencing situation.

As writers, we were faced with a culture so derivative and many-sided as to be without sharply defined characteristics; faced with a nation that was going through the purifying processes of crisis; faced with a public the statisticians had wrongly labeled mentally pubescent; and faced with a cult of self-styled critics, unbelievably transparent in their techniques, and so shallow and self-infatuated in their critical gowns.

The writer was faced also with a commercial proposition wherein the two best-selling commodities were religion and sex—not as integrated qualities but as extreme opposites, vulgarized to the point that sex was robbed of its natural beauty by being couched in fake terms that achieved precisely the opposite effects of their benevolent contentions.

The result has been withdrawal. The good talents, unable to focus on the whole scene, preferred to deal with only minute portions of it. The mistake was dealing with portions lifted out of the context of humanity rather than those portions common to all humanity. Too refined to dirty their hands on the livingness of their material, they were afraid of the heartbeat, afraid of the warmth, afraid of the sneers of the little coteries.

But this withdrawal had justification. It was a result of a culture wherein certain concepts of "goodness" had been so horribly exploited as to make them repugnant to some source of truth within us. Nobility had become a questionable virtue because the showiest practicants were so un-noble as to disgust us with that false light.

But I believed, and will always believe, that the artist must utilize all of these raw materials, not reject them. The artist must be dedicated enough and humble enough to choose subject matter from the universal aspects of the human apparatus, not from its aberrations.

The artist must—as a combination priest, physician, jester, and lover—give readers what the heart of all people claims: insight, nourishment, entertainment, and the substance of affection.

And most of all, the writer must find a legitimate way of returning such words as *nobility, loftiness, virtue, merriment, ribaldry, humility,* and *compassion* to the spiritual vocabulary of our age. If this can be done without prudery or fear, then the artist will be writing for all time and quite especially for one's own time.

— Love and Marriage —

Initially Bess and Clyde Holland were against my marrying Elizabeth, but as it turned out their daughter felt equal love for me. All the while I thought it was nothing but wishful projection; however, it was genuinely shared. I had accepted that it would not happen, but now it will. I could not be more fortunate than to marry a lovely girl who seemed to be wise beyond her seventeen years. Of course, people will talk. They will say why should this beautiful girl marry a thirty-three-year-old blind man? They look upon me as a sort of cripple even as Elizabeth does not and my parents-in-law do not. Once we are engaged it becomes at least semi-official, and the gossip will fly.

Apparently Elizabeth was not in love with "the blind novelist," but in love with the man she knew during those months of studying piano, of being with me in the context of her own family. She would be a true wife and a wonderful mother. My only concern was that I would be the true husband she needed and the father I wanted to be. I gave her my heart, as I had given God my soul. These essentials were in no way handicapped by sightlessness. This was something I could see without eyes.

I had always been considered controversial, yet I felt not controversial at all. I was sightless but refused to live down to the sighted view that I was handicapped. I was a writer who refused to spin out popular books. If I allowed myself to become average—a totally dependent blind man or an unscrupulous writer—I could never be normal or live naturally. This was not bravery on my part but simply survival.

Christmas 1952

I spent the evening with Elizabeth and her parents and we had a fine meal before going to church. Midnight Mass was lovely and Elizabeth was delighted with the engagement ring. At Mass I prayed to St. Jude, helper of desperate causes and the appropriate patron saint for my own case, asking for a moral miracle that would help make this marriage a true sacrament. My heart was filled with peace that this portion of my life was settled in the happiest possible manner.

January 1953

The weight of the past months—the heavy promotion schedule, the preoccupations with career decisions, the immense amount of mail, and the inner necessity for getting the next novel in shape—had required the brain to be twisted into some sort of logic when that cried out only for rest. This day, instead of writing all morning in the journal about the ephemeral, about the tortures of the spirit and the useless defenses against the unknown that caused the heart to become stagnant, I took a long walk in the woods. I found a nest of duck eggs while bending down on one knee to smell the dampness of the ground, and it was so natural and reassuring that I immediately felt the country around me and thought of my future children gathering duck eggs or pestering their daddy to take them into the fields. This thought was a moment of total health, and I realized how far I had strayed from such earthy things. As I had so many times in the past, I lost my balance.

It was all cake, and I realized that I needed bread, needed to step in cowshit and laugh and pray and forget my damned immortal dedications. Let them be in life, in earth, in children, and in making people's hearts glad—not this deadly serious pursuit that had lost spontaneity. The danger of this type of fame was that everyone urged you to hurry, to take advantage of an imagined hot market, to produce inferior work.

I went out to the far end of the woods to a little amphitheater with a grassy bank leading to a brook. I discovered this on one of my walks last year and have gone there to bathe often. I took a towel, soap and a large sponge and had one of the dogs go along to warn me of snakes.

There, in the profoundest stillness, I undressed and bathed in water so icy I could scarcely bear it. I lingered a long time, dunking in the cold water, walking barefoot in the sun to dry, and then plunging in the water again. My bathroom walls were a barrier of trees and underbrush, my ceiling the sky, and my tub the shale-bottomed rocks. After such a vigorous cleansing I felt suitably anonymous and naked; I felt entirely restored to health and spontaneity. I trailed the dog back to the studio.

During those next few months, Elizabeth Ann and I experienced only the profoundest contentment in being together. The expectation of our marriage filled me with soul-bursting vitality and such sentimentality! In fact, I had become nauseatingly tender-hearted after all those years of trying to crush that quality. The return of such feelings after so long was all the more magnificent in being totally unexpected.

I imagined myself in the role of a papa and how splendidly infatuating that felt. I envisioned walking down hospital corridors, waiting anxiously for the delivery. I dreamed of awakening in the middle of the night to check on our sleeping baby. No man was ever so completely in quest of that life, and no man would ever be more grateful for its fulfillment.

However, I was not prepared to be grateful for what the hygienic state of Texas had in store for us when the month of May arrived. We were obliged by law to be massacred—blood tests and vaccinations, plus additional tests for syphilis, gonorrhea, tuberculosis, and God knows what else—which left our arms more or less paralyzed for days.

In addition, the doctor, whom I had never met before, felt it his duty to give me a little lecture on the more intimate aspects of married life, which ended up implying that: "We all have to go sometime, but this is a hell of a way to go." He hastily added that he was one of those rare individuals who was a perfectly married man and would never exchange "the little woman" for anyone in the world. But his voice sounded tired.

The clichés poured in from all quarters—in cards and letters and hints in conversations—about how "marriage is a partnership" and "remember, it is by these that marriage attains its full measure of perfection," and how "it takes patience and generosity, a lot of give and take, to make a marriage work out," and so on. But we decided that if you had to do all of that to obtain perfection, we would be content to be miserable and wretched and mismatched, and to hell with it.

And of course there was always the scene about the church music for the wedding. Nearly all organists and nearly all mothers insist on having either the most mournful music possible. The bridegroom, unable to bear it, suggested that he would not go through with the wedding but take his darling to a nearby town for a tawdry little civil ceremony if they did not choose something else.

The mothers and the organist said: "Of course, what would you like?"

The bridegroom said: "None of that Wagner tripe. All Bach."

They agreed, then the organist said that there was a Bach chorale called "Oh, Sacred Heart Now Wounded," and how would that be?

He countered: "How about 'My Jesus in Gethsemane' in my honor?"

They thought it unfitting.

Then the bridegroom threw the bombshell: "I want something lively."

"Something lively," they asked in horror, "at a wedding?"

Through clenched teeth he said, "Yes, dear ladies, you may not believe it, but we are happy. This isn't Good Friday, you know." Meanwhile, the couple stood aside while the arrangers-of-things went on arranging their marriage after The Gospel According to Emily Post.

Despite it all, I felt I could marry without doing any injustice to the young woman I loved, and on June 2, 1953 we were. We honeymooned in Mexico City, going to sophisticated restaurants and nightclubs, and stayed in a posh hotel. It had been Elizabeth's first visit to a foreign country, and she was enchanted with the flavor of Mexico City. We vowed to return someday, and we would.

Returning to Mansfield, we moved into our first home, which was a charming cottage on the Holland farm. As a wedding present, Bess and Clyde had deeded twenty-four acres to us, which was about half of their property, along with the former chicken house, which had been re-designed into a stucco cottage. The remodeling was expensive, since we added a fireplace, complete plumbing, a wood beam ceiling and a tile floor. But we loved living there, forty yards from the Holland's old farm house, surrounded by a grove of oaks.

I still maintained the solitary writing studio at my parent's place, about five miles from the Holland farm, catching a ride with Clyde each morning and riding home most evenings with my father. On some nights I stayed at the studio and worked all night on my second novel.

A few months after our marriage, I fell and shattered my shoulder. In the hospital the doctors discovered that I had diabetes of a type diffi-cult to control. This explained several blackouts I had experienced in the past, as well as rages that had struck fear in all those around me—rages of which I had no recollection. How many others were going through this same experience, wherein the blood sugar reaches a low enough point to cause this blocking of conscious awareness but not low enough to throw you into shock? The diabetes would be my compan-ion for life. I had to brace against the diabetic assaults, watching the blood sugar levels, the diet, and injecting the correct amount of insulin at the proper time. This condition was dramatic in its mood swings, and I had not come close to mastering an awareness of its radical shifts and warning signs.

On top of all this, I began having painful foot tumors, like those my father had suffered. His had been benign, and it was assumed that mine would be the same. The first operation removed three tumors and, thank God, the material was benign.

But the hospital was the worst I had been in and when I left, after all their bungling, I felt as though I were escaping an actual danger. They did everything wrong, because they refused to say what medications they were giving me. I asked if I were getting NPH insulin and they said yes. But it turned out they were giving me a type of insulin to which I was violently allergic. I insisted on being discharged early and returned home in a wheelchair, to which I was glued for weeks.

Because it was impossible to put either foot on the floor, I learned to crawl out of the wheelchair onto the high bed, making all the fidgeting movements required to get into position when there was no further use of the foot leverage. All of this interested me, but very little physical effort was exhausting.

Finally relaxed during that first day back from the hospital, something rumbled in the back of my mind concerning the truth of happiness and suffering. The true ingredients of happiness were really nothing, for one can be happy with much less than considered necessary. I had grown to need less material things to be perfectly contented. I was happier than I had ever been.

— Lost Souls —

In need of further spiritual guidance, I began making trips by taxi to Fort Worth to meet with Monsignor Langenhorst. I told him I wanted to love God, but that I had drifted far from the adoration, the joy, the peace that once filled every hour. I had drifted so far that it seemed almost too difficult to make the trek back. I meant not a return to the superficial elements of form and action, but to that training of the emotions that cuts the crusts of callousness. I needed to pray, but it was impossible to concentrate on the core of the prayers. I went through the mechanics but ended up with no more than my prayers to St. Jude.

And I told him that I wanted my marriage to Elizabeth to reflect that same warm adoration, for she had made generous adjustments to my needs while I had not been as generous, perhaps using my blindness as an excuse not to change. She was my greatest joy on earth, and she had made our marriage both sweetly romantic and deeply sacramental. I felt that I had not done my share, and wanted to do more.

Monsignor began guiding me back to the path by reading from Aquinas and discussing the philosophy and theology courses on tape that I had received from Father J. Stanley Murphy of the Basilian Fathers in Canada. Father Stan also sent taped lectures of the series' outstanding lecturers in the Christian Culture Series, which he had founded in 1946. Thus, I had as tutors, thinkers like Etienne Gilson, Jacques Maritain, Gerald Vann, and others to discuss at our weekly meetings.

From the beginning, a taxi driver named Wooly made himself available every week for the ride to Fort Worth and often, on the return home, he would take me on side trips without running the meter. On the first day, he asked me how I "pictured" people, a question I had not heard since I had stayed away from the city.

Blindness

For a time, because it appeared to amuse people and it was awkward to do otherwise, I made a few tentative guesses. I could judge height by the level of the voice, but such things had not interested me in a long time. In the beginning, sighted habits clung, and I would ask what someone looked like. But after almost six years of blindness, I did not have the slightest interest in making pictures of them. The imagination was content to leave the physical portions blank. And I realized, too, that many things which had been sharp in my recollection—memories of stars or dew on grass—had now faded.

When Wooly first arrived at the Holland farm, he half-frightened me. He seemed delighted that I was blind. "Can't you see nothing at all?" he asked as soon as I got in the cab.

"Not a thing," I told him.

"Well, I'll be damned," he said in a pleased voice.

As we drove toward Fort Worth, he drew me into conversation with all the verve of a child with a new toy. My initial resentment at his attitude changed to vague curiosity. At least he was a different type of inquisitor.

That afternoon Wooly was waiting at the steps of the church in his taxi. He drove through the park, made me get out and smell the plum blossoms. "Take a whiff of that man," he said in a croaking voice that was strangely gentle. Then he held the back of my head with one hand and shoved a blossom-covered branch in my face. "Ain't that sweet?"

"It sure is," I agreed.

"I thought maybe you'd get a kick out of that," he said. "Nothing smells so sweet as plum blossoms."

When we started up again, I discovered that I was sitting beside him, for he had put me in the front seat instead of the back. I sensed an immense, whiskey-scented warmth beside me. I suggested that he take me by my sister's house since we were still in Forth Worth. I had not seen Kate in months and gave him the address.

"Sure thing," he said with great enthusiasm.

When we arrived, he would not let me go to the door alone, as I am accustomed to doing, having memorized the way up to my sister's porch. He insisted on parking the cab and helping me out. Then, with a death grip on my arm, he half-dragged, half-led me across the lawn. This kept me off balance and made me even clumsier than I would ordinarily be. I was ready to tell him I could walk much better without his help, when he said: "I really know how to take care of you, don't I?" He said it with such eagerness that I did not have the heart to contradict him.

When he finally left me at my sister's house, he said, "Look, you call for me anytime. Just ask for Wooly. Tell the dispatcher I'm the only one that knows how to take care of you."

"I'll do that," I said.

He left me on the porch after having rung the bell. Before my sister reached the front door, he had sped away in the taxi.

The following week I had forgotten all about asking for Wooly. I was focusing on my lesson with Monsignor, and how I was going to get to the church in Fort Worth was not on my mind. I simply called the cab company and directed them to my parents' farm that day, since I had stayed up late in the studio working and had not returned home.

The cab pulled up in the gravel lane and honked. When I went out from the studio to intercept my mother from responding to the cab, I heard a loud friendly voice. "Hi-yuh, Buddy. Gimme five."

"Five what?" I asked.

"Five fingers. Shake hands, man," he shouted as though I were his greatest friend standing a mile away. I shifted the cane to my left hand and offered him the right hand to shake. He pumped it for a moment and then once again put me in the front seat. He explained he had heard my name called over the short-wave radio system, and he had broken in on the circuit to tell the dispatcher that I was blind and he wanted to take the call. His exaggerated delight in my company bewildered me again.

This bewilderment ceased in the presence of Monsignor Langenhorst. The sessions were proving to be extremely edifying and every time I visited him he handed over a new tape he had made from various books. In this way, I was able to carry over our work at the studio, taking not only the new tapes but the memory of his marvelous discourse. Slowly, by way of focusing on ideas and voices more fascinating than my own, I moved away from self-absorption toward health. This renewal pervaded our marriage and my relationships with our two families. It also pervaded solitary hours of work with fresh energy. No longer was I feeling like a lost soul. I could see past the horizon.

Over the summer months and into the autumn, every time I called a cab, Wooly would show up. My reactions were invariably mixed. His effusiveness embarrassed me, but I was touched by his kindness and by his apparent joy in seeing me. He talked of taking me fishing, of taking me on a drunk if I wished. I always declined and dreaded being with him, but when we were together his contagious good spirits made me glad.

On one trip to Fort Worth, we went to have lunch before going to the church. He became serious for the first time. He was trying to say something that was obviously painful to him. "Do you, you know, imagine in your mind how people look?" he asked.

"As I've told you before, Wooly, not any more. I used to when I first lost my sight, but I never think of it now. I can remember how certain places used to look, but because I was blind when I first came here and I had never seen Mansfield before, of course I have no recollection of it. As for faces, they are too vague to recall. Frankly, I don't even remember how I looked."

"Well, I'll be," he said. "But if you don't remember how people look, how do you imagine somebody now?"

"Oh, just by the way he acts." Instinctively I had come to know a lie or a truth in the people I encountered. I could discover the essential truth in the timbre of the voice, in the sound of gestures disturbing the air, in the silences—but I did not tell Wooly this.

"Well, how do you think I look?"

"I've never thought about it, Wooly."

"Well, just guess how you think I look?" His voice was urgent.

"I can tell you're a big man. You're strong. Probably overweight."

"That's right. But what about my face?"

I paused. "Well, I expect you've got a heavy-set face, which is probably red-nosed from drinking."

"That's right. But I wonder, do you think it's a good face?"

"Oh, I know it's a good face," I told him in all honesty.

"Boy," he chuckled, "I don't know how you do it."

For several weeks after that, although I never asked for him, Wooly would continue to break in when he heard my name over the dispatcher's radio. Each time, whether tight or sober, he acted the same, with such delight that I became more and more mystified.

Then one day in October I called for a cab and another driver came to the studio. I wondered about it, but did not say anything because it did not seem important. However, when this happened several times, I was surprised to note that I was missing our strange trips together, and I began to fear that something might have happened to Wooly. I did not follow up my concern immediately, but made a mental note to check with the taxi company about Wooly if he was not the driver next time I called.

When next I went to Fort Worth to visit Monsignor at the church to receive Holy Communion and to continue our discussions, it was with yet another different taxi driver. I mentioned Wooly to Monsignor and he found the tale peculiar and suggested that I might ask after Wooly. I told him I had intended to and that I felt guilty because I had not fulfilled that promise. I called the taxi company on Monsignor's phone.

I felt somewhat foolish when I reached the manager and asked: "Do you know a driver named Wooly?"

"Yeah," the manager answered curtly.

"Well, he used to drive me a good bit, and . . . "

"Don't worry. He won't anymore," he snapped.

"Why is that?" I wondered aloud.

"Because I fired him a few months back," he said.

"What for?" I asked, a bit stunned.

"You kidding? Didn't you call to complain?"

"No, he was always nice to me."

"I never heard of him being nice to anyone," he explained. "You must have the wrong guy."

"I don't think so. He was hoarse-voiced, elderly . . . "

"That's him, all right. He was a hot-head. We lost too much business on account of him. I had to let him go."

"I can't understand that. He was wonderful to me. Do you know where he works now?"

"Sure don't. I think he left town. Never stayed in one place very long."

"Why not?"

"Couldn't hold a job, Mister. He couldn't get along with anybody."

I thanked him and was about to hang up when it occurred to me to ask: "You don't happen to know where he lived in Fort Worth, do you?"

"I think he had a room over at the old Majestic, but I'm sure he's gone by now." I thanked him and vowed to myself to investigate the story.

The next week I asked the driver who had taxied me a few times if he knew Wooly. He affirmed what the manager had said. He said that Wooly was the hardest man to get along with they had ever seen. Was this the same man who had treated me with such generosity?

Instead of going to the church that day, I decided to inquire at the Majestic, and had the driver drop me off at the skid-row hotel. The desk clerk half-whispered through loose-fitting false teeth, in a confidential, conniving way. "He was kinda hermit-like and never talked to no one that I saw. Never sat here in the lobby like the others."

"What did he do in the evenings, do you know?"

"Oh, every day he'd come in after work, about six-thirty. Then he'd buy a sandwich and a bottle of milk over at the cigar stand. And he'd get his newspaper. And I believe that was all. He'd carry all that right up to his room and just stay there by his-self." He said that Wooly had no personal possessions except a small radio. "You could hear it playing sad-like music programs late at night. He always listened to 'Moon River'—it's one that comes on real late."

"Did he have any family?"

"Not's I know of. He sure never had no company visit him."

"Is that all you know about him?"

"That's about all. He just didn't have anything to do with folks. Oh yeah, about once a week he'd go across the street and see a late movie."

I left the hotel feeling guilty that I had once been so irritated by this lonely man's overtures of friendship. Wooly's life was becoming known in fragments, and it was forming a desolate picture. Yet there had never been any hint of that with me; nothing but good humor and a childish affection that I had not bothered to return.

He appeared to be three different persons. On the job he was an active bully, thoroughly detested by all who knew him. At the hotel he was very solitary, keeping to himself, listening to his bedside radio, going out to break the monotony with an occasional late movie. With me he had been all sunlight and happiness. I was puzzled but asked no more questions of the hotel clerk, who called a cab for me.

When it arrived, I asked that driver if he knew Wooly.

"Everybody knew that s.o.b.," he grunted.

"Well, what did he look like?"

"Oh, he was uglier'n sin," he said disgustedly.

"He was?"

"Hell, yes. He had a big scar running clean down his face, you know."

"No, I didn't know . . ."

"Oh, of course not. Well, it was awful. I mean it was sickening just to look at him. It screwed his face all out of kilter."

The answer slapped me in the face. Here was the missing fragment to the puzzle of this lost soul. Wooly had been on the defensive against people who drew back from him in horror. It had soured him until he apparently hated the whole world, because the world could not see beyond his deformity, beyond his very face. This explained his jubilation that I could not see, that I could not see him as others had, but that I saw beyond his scar just as he had seen beyond my blindness.

All those with whom I had spoken implied that I really did not know Wooly. But I was sure then that I was the only one who did. With me, he had been like any other man; with me, he knew that his face could not blind me to the quality of his heart.

I imagined him in some other town, grubbing, living in cheap hotels, flaring with anger and hatred at the way people revealed their disgust at his scar. He had left no forwarding address, which seemed strange at first, but now I realized that he had no reason in the world to leave one.

His story haunted me. Its ramifications grew in imagination, disturbing me with a feeling of pity and futility. How could a thing that had been so casual to me have been so important to him? I had thrown the poor man scraps, never realizing they were his only sustenance in the sense of relating as himself to other people.

That night I brought the radio down to my cell in the barn. I listened to that program called "Moon River." It consisted of muted organ music as a background to a ghostly voiced reading of sappy poetry, saddening in its obvious sentimentality, and all about lovers, alternately walking on a beach or in the moonlit woods or sitting together before a fire. The man smoked a pipe and the woman had damp fragrant hair and they just strolled or sat together, musing introspectively about their contentment and the beauty of it all.

Somewhere in the night Wooly probably lay alone on a bed, listening, living still another life of substitute romance and fulfillment. For a few moments I saw it as he might have seen it, imagined him escaping into those nocturnal sounds of a world he would never inhabit. During those times he was not the deformed brute. He was the man in the poetry, casually smoking his pipe—mature, knowledgeable, comfortably but elegantly dressed. He surrounded the damp-haired girl with his love and protectiveness. In this intolerable cheapness he was not a lost soul; in this nocturnal world of romance he became whole.

⸺ A Different Species ⸺

During 1954, I entered into a period of deeper isolation, attempting to adapt to another physical limitation. The following journal entries are an account of those events in their immediacy.

May 4, 1954

I write here because I hope it will help me to arrive at some solution that might combine my almost uncontrollable reactions with an ingredient of wisdom. I am rapidly losing the use of my legs, and a superficial opinion seems to indicate that it is due to the gross damage of the nerves at the base of my spinal cord. I am to have a thorough examination of that the day after tomorrow. I am faced with a decision in the event that it proves correct—the decision of how I shall learn to live indefinitely in this wheelchair. This means not merely spending days or weeks, as was the case when the foot tumors had been removed and I acquired this chair, but possibly hereafter with no cure on the horizon.

These facts are obvious. The prospect of the loss in no way saddens me but it is almost maddening to have to be dependent on others for the simplest necessities. Second, I can scarcely bear to be observed by those I love during the clumsy initial learning period, because it is too sad for them in such things. Third, I am deeply pained to think that I am giving Elizabeth this for a husband, and the pain is more intense because she is so sweet about it. My inclination is to leave her, to seek an annulment so that she may find her proper happiness with someone else, when she has got over the initial loss and has adjusted herself back to life again.

If I go somewhere, I should want to be alone, to cook my meals and care for myself, and not be embarrassed to drag myself across a room if necessary. My only suffering now comes from that embarrassment. I cannot bear to be pathetic. I never feel pitiful or pathetic when alone. It is only when I see myself in the context of loved ones that I feel cut to the quick with my own pitifulness in their eyes, and then in my own. This is, of course, the basis of maladjustment and defeat. Perhaps it is merely pride, I don't know, but the point is clear. There is no such thing as tragedy in these losses of sight and legs, for they do not have any effect on my hands and the ability to work. My heart and vital organs are in good shape. I am relieved to be spared those necessary parts of the machine that I cannot for a moment regret the loss of the unnecessary ones.

The experience of losing my sight has prepared me for this, so that what will appear tragic to others will in no way cause the slightest ruffle of personal resentment. I do not mourn the loss of walks in the woods because it is nothing compared to my anxiety over the actual mechanics of reconciling my adjustment to the necessary changes of my loved ones.

My problem will be to find some means of controlling the nightmare of being pitiable, because I tend to react to that with a violence that goes beyond the realm of self-control. The only way of erasing the pitiable is to erase the one controllable ingredient—other human beings during that period of fumbling beginnings. I cannot, for something within me—pride no doubt—will simply not permit it, bring myself to ask others for things. I will sit and wait for them to offer those things which obviously they have no way of knowing I need, and the resentment within me grows into vertigo when I must finally, through clenched teeth, mutter my request.

Scattered Shadows

But I am obviously going ahead of myself, and I hope that all of this will prove curable, but the chances are not favorable for doing anything to arrest this nerve atrophy that destroys the use of my legs from the hips down. This brings up the question of my attempt to solve the riddle of these two poverties—the sightlessness and the loss of mobility. In itself, and in my intimate self, this recent poverty is more interesting than distressing as my loss of sight had been. But when the dissonant element of its effect on the lives of others enters, it becomes a source of turgidity, nervousness, and guilt that destroy its positive characteristics.

Again the truth of the experiments on readjustment is brought home: that all persons, gravely handicapped through lost of eyesight or limbs, when left completely alone at the very outset begin to compensate for the loss. Only when the adjustment involves the sighted does the element of pity and the idea of tragedy enter. The opposite, of course, is even worse, when those who attempt not to treat the sightless person as an object of pity make him an object of contempt and brutality. The middle route of encouragement and tranquillity and love minimizes the difficulties of the adjustment. We must realize that a legless man crawling across a room is acting no less naturally to his condition than is the legged man who walks across that same room and takes that ability for granted.

The man, socially labeled as handicapped, will know and suffer from his actions as though they were obscenities only through the presence of one who has no obvious physical handicap. This gets perhaps into the secret of why the handicapped can accept help from some but never from others, because these invisible reactions are felt with great acuteness and cannot be hidden. When the handicapped man is forced to accept the nauseating narcotic of pity, he will soon become addicted to it, and then he is truly unwhole. Most can scarcely bear to accept help from hearts that bleed with pity, but we can accept help from those whose hearts understand that we are something else besides mangled bodies.

Again I ask myself if I would prefer to have Elizabeth remain with me under such ennobling conditions, consoling myself in the fact that she grows adult and beautiful under these difficulties? Or does this viewpoint merely romanticize the truth? On the other hand, would I prefer to spare her this nobility in favor of giving her a happier life without me? Or does this opposite view well up from my own self-pity? I do not know. I think it would be perhaps more bearable to know that she was happy and that I had at least the tranquillity of relief from the constant remorse of giving her an incomplete life.

Perhaps nothing is more gratifying than to have a noble role to play and to know that you can play it perfectly. However it seems equally true that nothing would be worse than having a noble role but without being sure if you can measure up to it. When I encounter a nice person, like the taxi driver Wooly for instance, who has become nasty because of some misfortune, I look to this as a cover-up for shame and despair. The ones he loves are not the cause but merely the existing agents, before whom he feels profoundly unworthy and resentful. The whole person can feel that he deserves to be loved and is loved and therefore needs little reassurance. The unwhole person believes deeply that he feels a burden attached to the affections of another, feels that he does not deserve even the love offered, and this belief is so acutely ingrained that he needs constant reassurance.

Man's potential for experiencing misery is in direct proportion to his capacity for loving. The man who lives very little, or who is capable of living only in a small way, experiences misery in a small way. He is never either very happy or very pained. This is a relatively good state, since it is essentially an egocentric one, and it would be desirable if he were not capable of feeling the emptiness of his limbo. Great love transforms misery into privilege. The man who takes small pleasure in things must never be confused with the one who takes pleasure in small things. The criterion should be based on the proportion of his pleasure and not on the size of its source. It is better to be enchanted by a gopher hole than to be bored by the Grand Canyon.

Now I am immensely tired and emptied of strength. Each step is like walking a long distance. And I must prepare and wait for the moment of strength in order to undertake the project of walking across the room. A bird chirps outside the open window and then I hear a fluttering of wings as it flies from tree to tree. His world is full of greenery to explore and I wonder at anything that is not tied to a given spot.

This has been a very long day, as I conclude this late in the afternoon. It has been a day of emotional intensity, but things have begun to make some sense. I should like to describe something very beautiful, but all my attentions are filled with the animal curiosity of trying to coax muscles in legs and feet to do what my head commands. I tell my legs to uncross yet they remain crossed, and it is a strange feeling when they take minutes of coaxing before responding, quite often now five or six minutes. I sit and concentrate on getting them to lift the body from this chair so I can walk across the room, and there is simply nothing to do but wait for that concentration to find some response in action. While waiting, I try to find ways of making the immensely complicated process of moving my legs become less complex. I try to lift one up and place it across the knee of the other, and it simply will not respond. So I must reach down with a hand and place it where it should go. However, when I get up in the mornings, I can still walk fairly well, although very slowly.

July 13, 1954

Received word from Valley Gorge Hospital. Very pessimistic prognosis for the paralysis. They say it will undoubtedly return and there is nothing that can be done for it now, and that I must be prepared to accept years of legless existence. There was a moment of tearfulness on hearing that, even though I expected it in a way; but that flash of realization passed quickly, almost immediately, and I feel nothing but a vague naturalness about it now, no dread, no sadness at all. It is as though this were what should be and it is indeed a small thing as long as it happens to me. If it were to happen to another, I suppose I would find it monstrous.

People talk of my calm and patience in the face of this misfortune. I see no virtue in my acceptance and it simply does not bother me now. It is a status like the color of my hair or the size of my feet, that is as it is and I give it no more thought than that today. Strangely, I did want to cry. I felt the urge to cry for a time when the news came. But it was that other part, as though outside like a friend, looking on and regretting what was happening while the inside part did not really regret it or feel tearful about it at all. That outside or "social" part reacts as society does rather than as I should. The degree of success in overcoming a handicap depends on how truly we can become the new creature we are rather than remaining merely a social being who has been deprived of eyes and legs.

It would sound fatuous to say it in public, but I am no longer capable of living the lie of the maimed individual. I am no longer able to conceive of myself as others conceive of me: as a man who has lost his eyesight and the use of his legs, as a man in whom pain has replaced comfort.

I am not that: I am a different species, as legitimate and normal as that other animal whom I resemble in some ways: I am an eyeless and legless man in whom pain is the norm. I am a completely different entity, completely normal to the potentialities and drawbacks of my state (I do not say *condition* now). It would be ridiculous for me to mourn the fact that I have no eyes and legs as it would be for another to mourn that he has not four eyes and six legs.

He is a two-legged, two-eyed type and I am a no-legged, no-eyed type, and I know, although he would find it difficult to believe, that what I am and what he thinks I am are two different things entirely, because he is incapable of judging me except by his own standards.

Blindness

So he grieves my loss, whereas I can feel no loss, but only confidence that God made me this way because He wants me this way. His reasons do not need probing. It is enough that God wanted me this way; enough to make me *completely whole*, content, and thankful that I can rest in the security of His wisdom, knowing that whatever God wants of me is exactly what I want also (even though it might not seem like what I should or would normally want). The only difficult thing is not in the state of my body, but in trying to live with it among the two-eyed and two-legged men who have geared the world to their size. But perhaps that is part of it too and need not concern me.

I recall a photo I saw of Frederick Delius when I was an adolescent in Tours. It was the photo of an old man, blind and paralyzed, and of my immense and searing pity for him. Now, years later, I come to be the face in that picture, and the only thing that worries me is that others will see it and be torn as I was, never realizing the truth, or to what extent they are bound in judgment by their bodies. They will never realize that they will feel pity for a whole man who is different, neither more nor less. This area of dissonance expands, but its intensity will be less.

It has been seven years since I lost my eyesight, and I do not feel that dissonance as acutely as I did in the beginning. That was the danger, for the dissonant element of blindness was at one time almost more than I could cope with. Some do, by becoming tough; others do by drawing more closely into the enfolding bosom of God and not worrying about anything except the unassailable safety to be found there and in the incomparable rightness of that resting place. We are the lucky ones, for what God takes away He replaces. We gain great intimacy with God without doing anything voluntarily ourselves. For others who must create such occasions through voluntary sacrifice, it is much more difficult.

July 14, 1954

This is the third anniversary of my First Communion and it is Bastille Day, a day significantly commemorating independence. Have I been a Catholic such a short time? No day in my life was more important, and I was determined never to miss celebrating the anniversary by going to Mass. But today I must miss it, for it is impossible to go anywhere.

I will spend the day working on what most fascinates: the analysis of human sanctification through the creation of fictional characters. How critics can say there is nothing interesting left for contemporary authors is beyond my wildest understanding. I think of this in conjunction with *Nuni* and its narrator, Professor Harper. Inspiration works in the most logically possible manner. When we are well and with pain or trouble, we usually write of pain and trouble. But when pain and struggle are our daily lot, our inspiration seeks to express itself only in the clear and joyous. That is perhaps the adult-child which suffering turns one into; rather than the child-adult who's merely a shell without the experience. The child-adult is the adolescent in an imagined world of lusts and successes, usually with no comprehension of charity; whereas the adult-child must be burned through with charity, and no source of charity is richer than suffering when suffering can no longer embitter one.

July 16, 1954

One hundred and ten degrees in the shade! My poor fan makes little relief as it purrs to battle against torpid air. I sit working, sweating. The metal brace binds close to sweating flesh on my back and sides and down over the hips, reminding me constantly of its dominion, not through its stiffness so much as because it is hot to the touch, hotter than my body. My eyes sweat and fill as though I were weeping, and feel raw from it.

But there is an undercurrent, a background of jubilant happiness, as civilized understandings give uneasily away to a series of emotions that seem to stem from other ages. The sensation of grace: the idea that God sends ample graces to help you in any sacrifice demanded. Not the grace of courage, but the grace of complete joy, of overflowing happiness and richness in the work. It is the grace of enormous vigor that bursts forth in all that I think, in my speech, in writing, in prayers. It is a grace that, for the first time perhaps in many years, loves God.

I have always struggled, sought to find God, sought and cried out for God's grace in moral temptation and too often lost. Both the temptation to despair, and the assaults of impurity are seeking entrance, seeping through the fringes of my being, and for the first time I laugh at them, mock them, deride them. Nowhere is sex more invigorating and more nourishing than in marriage, which in no way nullifies impure desires and fantasies. This sounds heavy and medieval, I know, but it is not. It is light and invigorating, an inner indication that seems to grow gigantic manna on which to feed the Christ within us. You ride life like some sunlit ocean wave; all is large, spacious, and clean—not in the lifeless antiseptic soul, but in the cleanness of country kitchens, of fields, of digging in the earth and planting.

I think of my paralysis and spit on the somberness it should entail within me, and there is no hint of dread, but only the most joyous and complete acceptance. When I accepted blindness, I did so with immense sadness, wholeheartedly but sadly. But with this paralysis, I have grown into total joy now that it appears to be definite.

Now the sensations have fled and there is nothing at which to laugh. I am filled with emptiness, as though in dizzying hunger, and I ache all over and am very tired. Jubilation, when sustained on such a plane of concentration, can be as exhausting as grief, and as emptying. But they are not comparable except as physical effects, for exhaustion of sustained grace leads to peaceful sleep and undiminished love, whereas that of grief often leads to sleeping pills, neck aches and nocturnal sweatings. Only the degrees of tiredness are the same.

Infused contemplation: ever distant, ever in the haze of distances that seem impossible to traverse. But all the complexities of science can be resolved in the instant of God's choosing, and He will lead me where He wants. I do not want anything at all but that, so there is no problem: only cooperation, only allowing Him to grow, only laughing at the devil, only making sure that he does not crowd God out of this hovel. I started to call it a temple, but what is a temple with windows blown out and the foundations crumbling? It is a hovel, and that is the best place. Perhaps that is why the devil does not make too great a struggle to inhabit it—the soul of this body.

July 21, 1954

Unutterable peace to the accompaniment of increasing pain that almost breaks my back. I am filled with such extraordinary graces that I remain dumb before the joy that flows into my heart with ceaseless richness. In this instance, man is reduced to nothingness before the greatest of gifts he can no longer understand, which are gratuitous and overwhelming in generosity. I can do nothing other than to be silent and no longer seek to understand and allow my heart to pour out its gratitude and worship.

I know that the greatest of all handicaps, that of the spirit, has been removed and that beside it, these physical handicaps are nothing. Gladly would I have exchanged far more suffering; and the stunning thing is that I expected to. I expected to give all of this with nothing in return. But the nothing has been replaced with superabundant joy, which is not of me and no way merited, but is given out of the vastness of grace.

I cannot help but wonder what would have happened to me without the faith? How could I have taken all of this without becoming bitter and full of revolt? I think back on thoughts I had while going through baptism, those horrible doubts and the determination to offer them to

God as a gift, but with a queasy sensation of sadness. Then the long, slow work of the sacraments, erasing all former education and giving me a new one—not only of the mind but above all of the heart and the affections for the logic of natural law. What medicine, what science, what social system can accomplish this incomparable sublimation of pain in man's heart and body? What logic can touch the logic of heaven?

The example of one saint can teach us more than all the theologians in the world. The saints taught me the longing for spiritual poverty, the longing for nothing except what God chooses to work in and through me.

St. John of the Cross taught that total absorption into God, desiring nothing, forgetting the things of the past, allowing imagination and soul to become absorbed in Him above all. St. Teresa of Avila taught not to be sour-faced in physical pain. St. Benedict taught not to murmur against anything that might be sent, but to give thanks for it because it would destroy self-love, and leave the way clear for the love of God.

And that is the beauty of the faith. You can conform to the highest levels no matter who you are or what you are. The greatest intellect or the most ignorant peasant can be equal in sanctity, each complete and whole in one's own way, through the routes open to one's nature.

⌐ Artists and Smut Hunters ⌐

July 28, 1954
I try to keep this journal, for it is important that the events of these days be catalogued if only briefly. The summer turned hotter, and so did the censorship case surrounding *The Devil Rides Outside*. The Supreme Court of Michigan agreed with the Detroit municipal ruling, which had removed the novel from libraries and bookstores in that city. Hereafter, the book will be banned throughout the state as well. The *Michigan Catholic* has come out with an idiot editorial, after previously publishing an excellent and impartial report about the test case of my novel in Detroit.

Father Stan Murphy sent the article along with this note: "Renewed hope! There is reason for plenty of it. Anyone who eschews pseudo-prudence and bravely blazes a trail will always offend the status quo, ecclesiastics included." Also received a magnificent letter from Monsignor Langenhorst, who has just returned from Rome with a rosary blessed by the Pope as a gift for me. After seeing and feeling the viciousness, the serpentine goodness of many priests these past weeks in reference to the novel, priests who condemn without ever having read a word of my work, but knowing only that it contains obscenities like "bastard" and "bitch"—such a letter from priests like these make me tearfully grateful.

July 29, 1954
Have written and sent the rebuttal to the *Michigan Catholic*. I am truly amazed, though, that a Catholic newspaper should come out with such an irresponsible view, indicating they have no understanding of the issue at all, and which further makes gross implications against the motives and integrity of those involved in this case. It has been a tremendous job to bring all of this into some focus of clarity, and I have worked literally every free moment this week.

August 1, 1954
Today under the headline TEXAN FIGHTS BAN ON HIS NOVEL, the *Dallas Morning News* published my counterattack—I do not say *defense*—against the censorship circus surrounding the test case, which reads as follows:

> The censorship system in Detroit is based on a "containing" statute that says any book containing objectionable words, phrases, etc. can be banned from public sale, on the grounds that it will be harmful to children. The books are read by someone appointed by the police department, who simply copies down all such objectionable words and sends a typed list of them to the chief of police, who puts the book on his banned list without considering the book as a whole. Those who banned my book never bothered to read it. They went on a smut hunt for any passage "containing obscene, immoral, lewd or lascivious language, tending to incite minors to violence or depraved or immoral acts."

The ramifications of such a statute are staggering, because logically everything from the Bible to Shakespeare could be banned on this basis. So the choice of my book for a test case was really only a peg on which to hang some clarification as to the constitutional legality of a containing statute. Any number of novels could have been chosen to serve the same purpose. Three points had to be considered in this very important case:

1. Can any work of art be judged piecemeal? This is like calling a great statue ugly because you throw a veil over it and leave only

the umbilicus exposed. In order to have any influence on humanity's understanding, art must exist whole. This statute denies the existence of that essential quality of wholeness, and allows a book to be judged obscene because of one or two words taken out of context. It is like judging a man's soul by a hand that has been severed from his body in an anatomy lab.

2. Must serious novelists, who wish to treat with essentially adult emotions and problems, aim their dramatic incidents through the filter of juvenile concepts and capacities. Can there be no such thing as adult fiction? This statute obviously demands that if you wish to have your book sold, you must exclude from it anything capable of "impressing" children. Could they not as legitimately ban cigarettes, medicines, and insecticides on the same basis of possible harm to children?

3. If such works as those banned in Detroit, which are admittedly adult fare—although many of them, including the novel in question, have been highly recommended by theologians for adult reading—are legally banned from sale in stores, must the banning city not face the responsibility that, in depriving children of books that everyone agrees were not intended for them, they are automatically depriving adults of books that were intended for them and to which they have every right of access.

This statute is one of expediency, and such legislation can prove disastrous in establishing an illegal precedent. That was what we were trying to nullify by our test suit. It is such innocent-appearing cracks as this in the foundation of constitutional law that cause it eventually to crumble. Admittedly, there is a grave problem, for unethical publishers abuse the right of freedom of the press. As an author, I have received requests from some of these publishers, and they are of a cynicism to make an honest man sick.

We are in complete sympathy with any attempt to curb this abuse of freedom when such a freedom is not accepted with the necessary responsibility; but this law, which is illegal and very dangerous, has not succeeded. It was inevitable that it fail. Publishers of scabrous material have simply deleted the "objectionable" words from their texts and go right on selling. If Huxley, Dos Passos, Hemingway, and hundreds of others cannot be sold in Detroit, you can still buy such trash as *Midnight Passion* or *Violent Honeymoon* or others of that ilk everywhere.

If banning must be, we ought at least to get the containing statute changed so that a book would be restricted as a whole and not because of a list of questionable words and phrases taken out of the body of the text. The difference between these trashy books and those that profess to be serious is that an editor can alter the former without doing it either much good or harm.

When I was asked by the prosecuting attorney why I used a substitute word for "illegitimate son," I said that the character who spoke it in the novel would be completely nullified and unreal if I had him switch over into such Victorian elegances—and I would sooner strike him from the book than alter him in such a ridiculous way.

Burke, in one of his great judgments wrote: "Any decision which is both new and persecuting is a monster." And as such this statute applies. It is not persecuting so much to the authors as it is to the adult public who are deprived of their rights of access to these books.

The case, as a test of the law, is going to the Supreme Court for ultimate decision. There is much more that should be said about this problem. If this type of legal precedent becomes generally accepted, we are well on our way to becoming a country where all books are banned and where there is no more literature at all. The censors are about to reach the point of putting fig leaves on anatomy books next. They seem not to be able to distinguish between pornography and realism.

August 3, 1954

Called the doctor this morning to see if he could extend this brace up to my shoulders. It is painful to make the slightest movement now. He said that I should be in traction, but that we will try something else first to stop the spasms. I cannot go through a long treatment that will require inactivity at this moment. There is simply not the time to spare. It seems as though there should be some method of bracing the shoulder that will be better than this. I am in the frankest of miseries. The pain comes from the spinal cord; there is not simply a muscular spasm as we had hoped. Nothing can be done except to put me in traction, and I do not think I can bear that. Pain paralyzes and makes it impossible for me to sleep. This morning, at 4:30, Elizabeth finally had to get up and give me some codeine, which leaves me groggy now, hours later, but which relieved the pain enough to return to sleep.

When I awakened, I thought of the farm things I enjoyed that I must dismiss now, and I must dismiss them. But I am immensely frustrated that my legs and back will no longer allow me to get out and occupy myself with those tasks that are so pleasant and so health-giving. I cannot turn my head without turning my body, not because my neck is stiff, but because the spinal cord aches all the way down whenever I turn my head. I begin to feel like an old Steinway on which students have practiced *fortissimo* passages for years. I dread the *fortissimo* noises of painful emotion now and long only for the Bachian counterpoint, the Mozartian line of melody, the Beethovian variations of the last quartets.

August 8, 1954

Intense pain, making it impossible to sleep more than thirty or forty minutes at a time. I have decided not to let them put me in traction. And meanwhile, book banning is sweeping the country. Now they want to ban all sorts of comic books, magazines, and pocket books from sale where children might fall on them.

Later at the barn studio, I jot down briefly my reactions, for it is past midnight and I am falling from exhaustion. My left leg gradually lost all feeling during the day. There is no pain, but I felt as though I would break down if I did not have something to take my attention from the numbness in my leg, so I asked Clyde to bring me here.

All of the windows are open and the night air pours in to the accompaniment of crickets close at hand and those distantly heard from the woods. To my back, the bed, with a thin pillow, the bed of timbers, covered only with a thin cool cotton comforter. To my right, through the screen door, the birds silent except for occasional stirrings and chirpings.

All the country sleeps and I am awake, sitting here in underwear and brace with the feel of warm cement beneath my feet and the clacking of this typewriter. From the north window I can hear the monotonous hum of the air conditioner from the house, and I think of it pouring coolness in on my parents. Out here the air is different. It remains warm, without a hint of any dampness or coolness, without a hint of dew. It is perfumed with dryness from the fields that were scorched by one-hundred-degree temperatures today. But it is fragrant, like the smell of hay at noon; delicate and flavorful at midnight. I could turn on my fan, but I do not. I want the ruffling silence of natural sounds, the scraping of my feet against the floor, the occasional rustle of a breeze in the woods outside the east window. Distantly there is an odor of cattle and dried grasses, a faint odor of manure. Sweat spots form on my back where it touches the chair. It is like day, except for the silence of the birds. I am aware of pain as a vague normalcy centered in my spinal cord, but not distracting from the pleasure of the moment.

August 10, 1954

The day is finished, and there has been much work and a frustrating amount of work not yet accomplished. I have not found a moment to bathe and shave. I feel like some beggar in a street of Mexico, and would not mind being one for a few hours. I realize that I am very tired,

tired of struggling against my legs, but it is the tiredness of the ending day, not the defeat of the struggle. Something within me yearns for adventure while I remain tied to this chair, but I can have it in this chair if only I will! The real adventure is at home, where Elizabeth, probably curled up asleep on the couch, has our first child growing within her.

August 12, 1954

Received a request this morning from Macmillan, who want to publish "Sauce for the Gander" in an anthology for college students. Strange, this little story about a simple monk (Friar Clud patterned after Clyde), which I dashed off quickly and with so little thought, makes its mark instead of works over which I have truly labored.

Meanwhile, this censorship idiocy of moralistic organizations goes on demanding anything "positive" at the expense of the solidly truthful. Apparently one cannot be a smut hunter unless one is deeply suspicious of all mankind. They constantly suggest that the kind of reading they do from high and pure motives is done by the rest of mankind from base and prurient motives. They dedicate all the energies of their septic minds and consciences to the task of keeping ours antiseptic. Those prudes who can see in themselves nothing but evil will see only the evil of the art; but they will see it as evil because it provides them with the discomforting revelation of those portions of themselves which they have learned to see as ugly, or as sources of tension which they resolve simply by ignoring or denying their existence.

Responsible people seriously concerned with questions of pornography and obscenity distinguish themselves from the smut hunters by a certain discretion of the intellect that prevents them from seeing as intrinsically evil many things God obviously created as good. The responsible person does not confuse nudity with provocative stripped-down nakedness, never confuses classic Greek sculpture with cheesecake. Sex, for him, is not synonymous with sin. He understands that innocence is not based on non-knowledge of evil, but on non-love of evil, and that innocence encompasses a profound knowledge of evil. Unlike the smut hunter, he feels no need to glut himself on every four-letter word or nude photo in order to deal with the problems of obscenity or pornography in society, since he knows, of course, that the mere existence of such terms or pictures does not necessarily constitute pornography.

August 14, 1954

Robert Ellis, our painter friend, spent Thursday night at the cottage. We talked until two in the morning about his book on the Tarahumaras of Mexico. Such an experience as he has had living among them! He claims that not since the Greeks has there been a nation so totally in harmony with nature, with the philosophical compound of the male and female elements of nature. He says that all Tarahumara are philosophers and contemplatives of the highest order, though living in the most isolated and primitive conditions, that for them there is no concept of sin, that they place their soul's reality far above any concepts of morality. It is obvious that, as an artist, he is not just a quiet, patient, meditative person but a true contemplative. I wonder coldly and for purposes of work if I have ever been graced by such contemplation? What a distance from Bob Ellis contemplating the cave paintings of the Tarahumara and my being forced to defend the printed word against the censors and smut hunters!

The distance covers millennia, and the resultant regression for our "advanced" civilization strikes me not as merely ironic but tragic. How sad that the lovableness and decency of the individual is pitted against the cruelty of society, how depressing that noisy civilizations drown out the silence of contemplation.

August 24, 1954

Elizabeth attended a lecture on censorship last night in Fort Worth, helping me to research the local scene. She returned home dazed, saying she felt as though she had been "pietistically raped." The deadly debate continues, as I make these notes for pieces recently commissioned.

Smut hunters invariably present an obscene and absurd spectacle: the spectacle of good men and women whose noses are poked into every conceivable source of obscenity in order to ferret it out for the purpose of protecting society from the very thing that has proved such a fascination to the smut hunters themselves. If they were aware of the obscenity of their actions as they are of the obscene elements of human language, they would quickly censor themselves into oblivion. Instead they are trying to censor writers into oblivion.

I have not met a smut hunter who admitted that constant exposure to the "lewd, lascivious, obscene, salacious and pornographic" had for one moment menaced his body or soul. No, he pursues his apostolate to protect the rest of mankind from the kind of "appalling dangers" which have never apparently endangered him. He absorbs more filth than the victims he seeks to protect, all in the cause of purity, he insists. If you want to feel completely depraved, ask a censor to show you the collection of pornography he has gathered. A Chicago cleric reportedly claims to have the country's largest collection of dirty books and films, and he invites concerned or skeptical adults to attend his private showings. No audience at a stag party gets half the show regularly given when our guardians of civil purity meet to show their latest "discoveries" of filth. Semanticists, jurists, philosophers, and theologians have searched for valid criteria by which to judge pornography. But the smut hunter sees it clearly and simply.

One of the most dedicated professional lecturers on this subject, in a private conference for Catholic religious, explained his infallible criteria for detecting pornography. He contended that you could be sure a work was pornographic if it contained any passages that gave you "a kind of feverish feeling in the cheeks and a grinding feeling in the stomach." When the lecturer died shortly thereafter in the midst of his arduous tour, one of the theologians promptly diagnosed the death as stemming from an occupational hazard: "undoubtedly too much grinding of the stomach," he declared, without any hint of irony or humor.

⏤ Waiting for the Child ⏤

September 1, 1954

I force myself to write about this so those who do not know now will be able to go back and someday understand.

Am I to be completely paralyzed? This secret conflict, which I can tell no one now, this bewildering conflict against something that bandies me about, brings on the need to answer questions and to make difficult decisions. Each day the numbness makes further headway in my hands and I am able to keep my legs fairly stable only through daily exercise. They knew that, and half expect for me to lose the use of my legs completely, but they have no hint that I am losing the use of my hands and arms also. How can a blind man do anything without this being known? How can I consult with doctors without the family learning of it and being horrified into grief?

Last night Elizabeth had a shower for the baby and returned radiant and excited with the evening and wanted to show off the gifts. I took one of them, a night light made like an inoffensive cricket, and as I was feeling it, it slipped out of my hand. I was shocked. Later when I wheeled into the kitchen to get a glass of water, it was impossible to hold the slight weight upright. The glass flopped to the side, but after intense concentration, I got it to my mouth and drank.

I do not know what to do. Everyone feels great joy over the baby's imminent arrival and I cannot bear to let them know about this latest downturn. I need to work it out alone and I think I have hit on a way to help without anyone's knowing. This typing does not seem to help, since all of it is in my fingers.

But while everyone was gone this morning, I wheeled from the studio to my parents' house and began, after such a long time, to practice again the piano. All was sloppy and uncontrolled, but I put the metronome on slowly enough to be able to concentrate on striking and releasing each note and doing those exercises that require the most muscles. I practiced the diminished chord, broken arpeggios in both hands simultaneously to stretch the hand muscles and forearms. Then I did the Czerny five-note exercises with double mordants, the scales and regular arpeggios, and the held chord with released notes. Finally, and very slowly so that I could control them, short works by Bach and Mozart.

The numbness remains, but if I can keep doing these piano exercises each day, under the guise of wanting to get back into practice, perhaps I can retain the use of those muscles. I must concentrate again and again on one thing. I must not let this show, for the only unbearable thing is their pain in seeing me degenerate like this. I feel now that being blind and diabetic and, perhaps, to be paralyzed not just from the waist but from the neck down, brings on a stage when it becomes senseless to fight against it. I must seek to salvage my sanity if that is the case.

I know the dissonance of such situations and have a large capacity for supporting it. But if I arrive at complete dependence, when I will have the torture of hearing our infant crying but being unable to do anything to comfort the child, that would be maddening. When the body goes and only the brain remains, then you must have the use of someone else's body for nearly all things. No man has a right to demand that from his wife. In a practical sense, since I am a large man, Elizabeth could not do those things in any case; and it would sear me continually with anguish to have her obliged to attempt it.

I must accept this. But I pray now that God will spare me that. I have never prayed for God to stop taking of me physically, and now I do it for the sake of loved ones. But if it is not His will, then I must accept all of it and seek solution elsewhere. I am not strong. My heart weeps within, but deep beneath that immediate pathos of dread to face what I shall, God forbid, perhaps have to face, there is true thanksgiving. It is horrible and yet it is magnificent in that God should demand heroism of those who care for me, and perhaps of myself. And there is no false humility when I say that it is all the more splendid in view of my weakness, in view of the laziness that has lain over my soul for so long. What is my life to be? God gives me the chance to become a living martyr, I suppose, for I have the choice of obeying His will in all of this or of following other inclinations and fighting against it. I am given the rare opportunity to be generous—to give up everything, even my body, even my love in life.

September 5, 1954

Late in the night of a full day's work, I jot these notes down hurriedly. Went to the doctor's yesterday. Atrophy of the left leg, very rapid. The therapist came bursting in and put her head down close to mine on the therapy table and screamed: "Did you notice how hot it is today?"

"Lord yes, it's terrible. The worst yet."

"I came driving out of the underpass and felt that hot air and I just thought that the gates of hell had opened up!"

She tested my muscles and gave her own unequivocal diagnosis: "Piss poor, Howard, you know that?"

I winced and smiled. Then throughout the afternoon as I lay under the heat lamps, I could hear her voice booming back from other rooms: "My God, I thought the gates of hell had opened up!"

September 7, 1954

Phyllis and Bruce Marshall sent us a book on *Mothercraft*, which gives the Truby King method for feeding and caring for the perfect baby. All of it is simple, natural, very appealing, and widely used with great success. There is a chapter on "Grandmother," stressing that she can be a great source of joy and help, providing she remembers that this is *not* her baby.

Elizabeth had scarcely finished reading that to me when her mother came down and visited for a time. All of it was pleasant until Elizabeth mentioned the new book we had just received. "According to that," she said enthusiastically, "the more you leave the baby outside on an enclosed porch the better it is, and we have to have a green-lined cap and a screen to protect the baby's eyes from the sun."

"Oh, no," Bess groaned in heavy disgust. "You're not going to go into that old sunbathing thing with the baby I hope!"

"Well, the baby's got to have sunshine," Elizabeth insisted, as I began to smile, thinking of the chapter on grandmothers. "It's an important source of vitamin D," she pointed out.

"You can get vitamin D in a bottle," Bess snorted in disapproval.

"And the baby must have plenty of fresh air, too," I added.

"What's wrong with just plain good ordinary living conditions?"

Bess asked. "I can tell you about raising babies and chickens. It's all very simple. All you need to do is keep them dry and warm and well-fed."

"There's a wonderful little chapter on grandmothers," I offered.

"Oh Lord, what's it say, something silly I suppose."

"It says that grandmothers can do so much and can make things very pleasant, providing they do just one thing," I said gently.

"What's that—die?" Bess retorted.

"Briefly, it says that as long as the grandmother is careful not to give unsought for advice and that she never dismisses the methods of the child's parents, she can be a great help," Elizabeth explained.

"Hum," Bess said, as though she had swallowed a fish bone. Then she burst out laughing and said: "Don't worry. I'll be too busy to help at all."

"But there's some things you're supposed to do," Elizabeth said.

"Well, unless I can get rid of some of the problem children in my classes, I won't have time to do anything."

I blessed Sir Truby King quietly to myself for including that chapter.

October 11, 1954

Early in the morning, a cool morning, I listen to the lucid music of Bach's French Suites for Clavichord, and the incomparable music makes the morning full of jubilation of the spirits and the heart and the affections. Affections particularly for Bach. No wonder, after writing such pages as these, and then playing them for his wife, they would produce another child! The joy of the animal spirits made into a vehicle of the tenderest affection and vigor, combined with the sanity of the man, and the love of God, all of these together and centered in the family, in the loftiest concepts of soul and body, but without ever sacrificing the gaiety and exuberance of genius. Only a man of the most profound sentiments could produce such light-hearted music.

November 3, 1954

Strange reaction to diabetes. Any day can dawdle off into its own inner hummings, having nothing more to do with me and leaving me alone in a diabetic vertigo. Today I was stunned as if I had been struck on the head, bewildered and only vaguely aware of time. I put the writing aside, drank a cup of coffee, and then stumbled back to make these notes. Stumbled, indeed, but at least I have been able to move short distances these past several days without having to utilize the wheelchair. As for the diabetic vertigos, I am aware of all that goes on, even within, but almost as an objective bystander. All thoughts and actions seem to reverberate through a long tunnel, with reality pinpointed at the distant end. I know that although I am aware in this eerie manner, tomorrow I will not be able to recall any of it. Thus, I write it down now.

After supper, I came back out to work, walking slowly and painfully, a few steps at a time, from my parents' house to the studio. The air is full of winter outside, spacious and nose-biting. But when I stepped into the barn, warmth that seemed alive with birds and crispness and health greeted me, and I felt sudden relaxation and an overwhelming tiredness from my bout with the diabetic coma this afternoon. I plopped in the chair and listened to the birds chatter their *Compline* before settling into quietness for the night, and I did not think but only felt the invasion of an infinite peace and contentment.

Then it occurred to me that all of this was so familiar, reminding of an earlier time when I lived in this little bare room day and night, working and dying of a desolate loneliness that was nevertheless full of passion and richness. But with the hinted terrors of dusk folding in, the reality of my present is good and I am no longer lonely, for I have a home and a wife and an expected child. When I finish working, instead of sitting here dumbly and feeling the crush of night close in, I can go home to a fire, a good supper, and the companionship of wife and family. I thought about something that rarely enters my mind, wondering how it would be to see, to see all of this, to see my wife and child, to see the walls of this place, the trees, the pastures and the animals.

I wondered how I should feel if I could suddenly see my face in a mirror after these seven years of blindness. What did I look like? What do I look like now? I remember no face in a mirror, but recall photographs of myself. Would I be shocked at the change? I have been told that my hair is graying, and perhaps my face has deeper wrinkles, but what of the expression? Would I look anything like I think I look, but then it occurs to me that I have not thought whatsoever of how I look. This must have been the concept man had before the invention of mirrors. And it seemed truly amazing and unbelievable that I have really never seen any of this, although all of it is as familiar as the slow throb of my own pulse. I suspect that all would seem strange if I were allowed to see, and probably all of it would seem completely different from the concepts I have now. And I remember years ago when I drove a car, but now such an idea seems almost miraculous. But I feel no mournfulness, just an occasional flooding of realization with an ingredient of harmless curiosity.

Now the birds have retired, and it is utterly silent in this barn, so I gather that it has become dark outside. In here there is never any feeling of daylight or darkness, for they come only in sounds, and these walls are so thick they seem to shelter me both day and night, held suspended in a neutral time. It is all pleasant and complete, like the atmosphere within your proper brain; for indeed this entirely familiar room seems merely an expansion of the mind, intruding nothing on concentrations, giving space in which to breathe, akin to some larger outer skull.

November 5, 1954

Constant knowledge in the back of all thoughts that Elizabeth may call at any time to say the baby is ready to be delivered. Jubilant knowledge, yet nonetheless nervous on the brink of this great event.

During my visit to the doctor's office yesterday, I could feel the grins, the happiness of everyone for our baby. Also, the doctor began a new treatment for the progressive paralysis. He is attempting to attack the infection with tiny doses of strychnine. The idea is simple. To introduce enough poison into the system to kill the infection but not the patient. We now know that this disease, a form of spinal malaria that has a very long incubation period, was contracted in the South Seas. All around the country there are cases of soldiers returning with the same infection, and it seems the strychnine might be the answer.

Now that I am taking the strychnine I realize that I have been very ill and that my mind has been profoundly affected by this illness. When I thought I was doing well and the degeneration of mental spontaneity was so gradual as to pass unnoticed—from this vantage of gusto, I can now see that I have gone through a steady decline. The full weight of my deterioration strikes home as I look back on this depression, as I feel inspiration and inventiveness return to stimulate the excitement that had always been normal. If the strychnine can reverse the paralysis and the insulin can better control the diabetes, I will have only sightlessness to deal with. That would be a great relief, because it is a static situation, whereas the paralysis and the diabetes are unpredictable.

November 19, 1954

We came to the hospital at six yesterday morning, but the pains were so mild we were not certain we would stay. I brought the typewriter and set it up in the chaplain's quarters here at St. Joseph's Hospital.

About a half-hour after we had checked in, I was in the waiting room and they called to say I could go into the labor room. Sister Mary Andrew wheeled me in and left the wheelchair beside Elizabeth's bed. I felt for her hand, and she responded faintly, although she was already under heavy sedation. The room smelled of alcohol and ether, and I listened to her even breathing, interrupted every few minutes by a stirring as the pains hit her; but she did not call out. After an hour, the nurse said they were real pains and a little later the doctor showed up and reassured me that we would have a baby probably before breakfast tomorrow morning. They suggested I stay until time for her to go into the delivery room.

I stayed with her and about every hour I would slip my hand out from hers and wheel back to the waiting room to smoke a cigarette and get some cooler air, for they kept it stifling in the labor room.

The tension was constantly being broken, because Elizabeth would suddenly start talking. Once, she squeezed my hand and laughed.

"What's the matter?" I asked.

"That grease, it's running round and round in the pan."

"It is?"

"Uh-hum. I just cooked some bacon, and now the grease is running round and round in the pan so I can't turn over my eggs."

"Well, maybe it'll slow down after a while."

"I guess so. Did you have breakfast yet?" she asked.

"Yes, I had a good breakfast."

She asked me this constantly during the night. Later she squeezed my hand again and I leaned forward in the wheelchair.

"I found a little child's scapular," she said.

"You did? Where?"

"I don't know."

"What did you do with it?"

"I think I cooked it and ate it."

Elizabeth was a marvelous patient; she said she was having a wonderful time, but she kept talking strangely, worried that I might get "all haggard" sitting there so long.

November 20, 1954

The doctor returned at six this morning to say that it was going to be slower than they had anticipated, and suggested I return home to sleep. I did not want to leave but went out for breakfast.

I spent most of the day with Elizabeth and she was completely dotty from the dope, but happily talked and laughed. The doctors decided to wait a few more hours before falling back on the cesarean. Bess and Clyde held up very well, but finally went home during the afternoon for a nap. I felt drained of all emotion, keeping preoccupied in that strange way one does in the center of desperate worry.

That night things began to happen, finally. While I was away from her bedside, she began having serious labor pains. Another of the prospective fathers wheeled me toward the room. As we were about to go in, I heard a groan and the nurse stepped out.

"Your wife asks if you would mind waiting a moment. She doesn't want you to see her in pain." The prospective father wheeled me back to the waiting room while I swallowed back the unbearable poignancy of that simple sentence.

A little later the nurse retrieved me. I went to Elizabeth's bed as she mumbled something to the wall. I asked: "What is it, Honey?"

I heard her turn over in bed and apologize: "Oh, excuse me a minute, Darling. I'm just talking to the seamstress," and went on about buttons and flounces to the bare wall.

It was more than I could stand. I rolled to the door as the nurse came toward me. "She thinks she's talking to a seamstress. Do you think she's all right? Is she supposed to be that gone?"

"Just be glad she's got a seamstress to talk to, Mr. Griffin."

The doctors returned and examined her. They decided that it would be safe to proceed with the natural birth and that was a great relief.

At nine that night, after fifty-one hours of labor, I sat in the waiting room in great anxiety. The doctor came in and my heart stopped beating. He asked: "Will you go into room 422 and lie down on the bed?"

I was paralyzed with fear, thinking the news must be very bad, but I was beyond doing anything but obeying. Clyde wheeled me down the hall and the doctor accompanied us.

As soon as we got into the room, he said: "Everything is all right. You must get some rest. It's still going very slowly, but there is absolutely nothing to worry about."

Clyde helped me up on the hospital bed. And then the tension had to break and we laughed ourselves silly, thinking how strange it was that I was being put to bed in a maternity ward. Then I did manage to nap.

Later that night, a few minutes after ten, I heard footsteps out in the hall and Dr. Grogan's voice asking someone: "Do you think I should wake him up?"

"I'm awake. Come in!" I shouted.

He opened the door and said: "We had a devil of a time but you've got a baby girl."

"Is Elizabeth all right?"

"Both are fine."

People crowded into the room, and I felt suddenly not tired at all, and not happy either, just numb and relieved. They all went to see the baby and came back raving about how beautiful she was. Daddy and Clyde, the two grandfathers, were weeping with relief, but all I felt was a dumb sort of gratitude that I had both my wife and our baby, Susan Michelle.

November 26, 1954
After a long stay in the hospital, we brought Elizabeth and Susan home. Tonight I helped feed the baby, preparing a bottle after she had finished breast-feeding. Then, a little later, she set up a howl, and I sat back in the lounge chair and cradled her against my chest. That was the only way she would be silent and Elizabeth could get any sleep. It was only then that I felt she was my daughter, that she was a part of me.

I held her against my shoulder, and could feel her stomach contract against my chest and then the discomfort left as she gradually drifted off to sleep. With my wife asleep and our baby sleeping against me, I felt the first full strength of my paternity and the almost intolerable quietness of joy to hear her breathing against my face.

⌁ *Nuni* and Solitude ⌁

By January of 1955, I had begun using two recording machines, transferring spoken text from the first, along with the edited changes, to the second. This sped up the process and I was spared tedious retypings by working out the problems orally. I used the first machine to edit all the bridge passages and, when that was complete and correct, I transferred it to the second in unbroken sequence.

This was when the actual fascination of *Nuni* entered the picture; this was the element of construction that must give strength and solidity to a novel without ever being made obvious to the reader, like putting on the undercoat of a painting. It was a brain-crushing job, however, cataloging the specific sensual details of sounds, sights, smells, along with the progression of actions, which had to be made consistent with the general mood of the scene, or in contrast to it.

Those first months of the year, too cold to go out anyway, had been days of intense and unrelenting work, when it seemed as though I had four hands and two typewriters, so rapidly and consistently did I work.

Nuni drew to its close and became tremendously absorbing. I had no thoughts disconnected from it, but felt unreasonably irritated with the constant interruptions. Then it occurred to me that such breaks from concentrated work were precisely the same as suddenly waking one from a dream into a raw world that was momentarily unfamiliar.

I realized also that my own tears had interrupted the work. I had felt this many times in *Nuni*, when I would become so moved over a scene that I would begin weeping; and the weeping would destroy the fire of the work and the writing would come out dull and forced. In one instance I had worked out a scene in the bedroom between the narrator Harper and his wife, but I was overwhelmed by a tremendous desolation in the fact that Harper would never again have that. A pressure of tears came, but I held them back and began to type. Although it took longer for that to bring the relief that comes from tears, it eventually did precisely that.

Perhaps art, then, can be produced as the product of this intense transferal—perhaps art was the unshed tear, the brush stroke that evolved from the same speck of tension and energy as the tear and was put into form rather than into the evaporative liquid.

In *Nuni*, I had come to see the details of life through the magnified lens of a telescope; but I had to fit them so that the overall picture was actually seen through the wrong end of a telescope. It does no good to describe the smell, sound, and color of a leaf, without connecting it with the tree and even with the forest of emotion it must elicit. This sense of proportionate perception pertained even to the blind, as vivid in memory.

Beneath my ape-skull of density was an unexplored perception. The effort of penetrating it, of going deeper and deeper into this domain of interconnection between all things, all thoughts, all emotions, was killing. When there was that sudden flooding of perception, the work was good; when there was not, it was mediocre and therefore useless. I sought some way of attracting it, of hanging on to it, but there seemed to be no formula other than writing, uninterrupted and without tears, in that direction.

February 1955

Meditations on solitude. The degree of our loss of the memory of God was in direct proportion to our fear and discomfort with solitude. Solitude need not indicate inactivity but did need to indicate freedom from distractions. The artist should not be deprived of pleasure and live in asceticism. Rather, the artist must have the security and serenity of uninterrupted time devoted only to it, without fear of distractions.

During these winter months of solitude, the bitter cold and frequent rains had prevented nearly everyone from distracting my concentration on the novel. I had been very close to *Nuni*—aware perhaps that I had been putting the problems of my own life into the lap of Professor Harper, desperate for the narrator to solve them. I had stripped him of everything that men generally consider necessary to function at the human level—family, friends, even clothing—and plunged him into a world in which he was ill-prepared to live. My prospect was similar, though I never mentioned it aloud.

Love cannot exist without this quality of innocence, a quality never lost in love, except when it turned evil. I have experienced this when I talked from the "godhead" of my own mind, from the stupidity of my own self-filled heart, and had fallen silent in the midst of an idea or a phrase, silent and embarrassed by the sudden perception of their clarity. In all cases, my own humiliation had been burning, and my gratitude to them had been both great and full of resentment, because my pride sought to tell me they were merely being superior. What strange irony in the fact that the intellectual will spend half of life exhausting intelligence to discover the basic standards for all life, always arriving at exactly those despised truths that the simplest person knew by intuition.

So, I trusted these instincts, leaving them naked and innocent in this divine darkness in which God enveloped me. This was enough, the richness of innocence, feeling the instinctual value of solitude, of life itself, without giving in to the clatter of a devalued world.

March 16, 1955

Today, for five minutes, I have known what it is to be a saint, and all else is unimportant. Not the writing this morning, not the crackling fire, not the treatment at the doctor's office. For these minutes I have known the greatest happiness I can know on this earth. Deep in my heart, despite its momentary vigor and robustness, despite the new blood coursing through my entire being, I know that some devil of smallness, some lust-splashed image will turn me out of this sunlight into that drab middle-plain of myself, and that I shall diminish back to who I am.

The man who half lives and who seeks his happiness where it can never really be found—*of himself.* Although *in oneself* it can be found, for there it exists, but never in ego. That is the difference, an inexpressibly subtle difference, between the absolutes that lead to sanctity and those in-betweens which lead only to the self-justifying lie that is a type of piety. And even that is touching, touching as a false hope, as the whistle in the dark of my blindness, the blindness that tells me to listen to logic and intellect, senses and flesh, but not to my soul.

April 18, 1955

I have just finished wrapping and mailing *Nuni.* I have stayed awake almost every night—napping an hour occasionally—for a long time doing the final draft. Parts had to be redone twenty or more times. Elizabeth has fed me and bedded me and been marvelous in letting me go through this final draft period as the energies came.

Now, a hot and sticky night. I sit here in a near daze, in my shorts, listening to the quietness of the woods. The birds are silent and there is no sound except the distant passing of a train. Is *Nuni* any good? God only knows. I have worked at it three years, too long, and sent it away with fear and trembling. I think Harper found himself along the lines of humanity rather than those of civilization. Stripped of everything that we think makes a man a man, he in fact became a man.

Now it is gone. They are all gone, all of these characters who have been more real than many people I know during these past years. They walked out the door with stamps on them. Their existence disappears when words stiffen into print. The printed word is the tomb of human spoken utterance. The body of the speaker is elsewhere.

I do not regret it. Now to come out of it. There is neither jubilance nor sadness, and there never is when I finish a work. I feel only a dullness, an overwhelming fatigue, a need to go and just be quiet with my wife and child, perhaps to bake some bread or help her cook a meal.

⌐ Parenthood ⌐

May 2, 1955

There is no one here today. My parents are in town and I worked all morning in the cool of this cell and at noon went to fix my lunch. Then, when I left my parents' house to come back to the barn studio, the sun blasted me full in the face and drowsiness seemed to bear down in my legs. I would probably sleep all afternoon if I did not do something to wake up, so I decided to hobble about the barn, breathe the fresh air, and see if that would do it. After a few moments, it occurred to me to take off my clothes and get a little sun.

I began to make my way toward the woods, and the ground was level enough to carry me quite a distance, the furthest I have gone in over a year, since I first became crippled. And, being alone, I decided to try to go as far as I could. The wind was strong, and from the roar above, I knew I was well into the edge of the woods and on a good and safe path.

The odors were magnificent. The leaves from last fall were crisp and very dry, giving up a slightly fragrant dusty odor that I usually think of as coming from grain fields in mid-summer. Mingling with that were odors from greenery, from wild clover and sun-baked vetch blossoms.

When the path passed into sunlight, the heat burned into my shoulders, but in the shade it was cool, almost chilly. After I had gone a few yards, I came to the barbed-wire fence that is deep in the woods at the edge of the creek. I could hear the water bubbling fast over the rocks below. I was wearing nothing except shoes and the scapular on its chain around my neck, and carrying my cane. Health and sweetness seemed to flow out of the wilds surrounding me, to envelop my nakedness with the softest balm of freedom. I knew there was no one around to see, and quickly dismissed the turgidity of modesty. I was as free as God created man to be, unencumbered in the midst of His nature, and there was a marvelous upsurge of jubilation in all of it.

Before me I could hear the leaves rustling as lizards must have run and a crow flew screaming away, sounding outraged. Walking, listening, smelling, feeling the atmosphere of deep woods, prayer came naturally, and I found my little amphitheater and hobbled around its circular path, saying the scapular prayers and the rosary, in the greatest calm, in the peace that was all mortality akin to all immortality.

When I had gone as far as I felt I could go, I returned to the barn across the field, grazed short by the cattle and holding their lingering odors under the brilliant sunlight. It had something of the sweet smell of udders, of drying dung, of grasses full of nourishment, but I am sure no cattle were around, because I heard none and because they were probably under the shade trees, waiting for the sun to lose some of its blaze.

I sat in this cool barn, typing these few lines before returning to work, dressed only in my shorts and shoes, burning around the shoulders and covered with sweats that linger from the sun's thirst. The wind howls in the trees and the birds in the aviary beyond the wall are somewhat quiet, chattering only occasionally. Rarely has life ever seemed so good. Rarely has God seemed so close to the barest essentials of this life, to man reduced to his primitive state.

May 3, 1955

My heart is frequently torn with tenderness for those involuntary little gestures of humanity that occasionally slip out from guileless hearts without ever realizing it; and I know that no other emotion is quite so perfect as this one which is love that is completely outgoing, love that is soft and good, like the love between parents and children.

This morning, while I was having coffee in my parents' house, mother was sitting with me and we heard a mockingbird in the front. It sounded so near that I went to the front door and located its sound.

"I believe it's over in the corner of the yard, in the hedge roses," I said.

"Why it is, I can see it," she said in the private thrill of such things. "I do hope they'll nest there this year. Wouldn't that be grand to have them so close?" I exclaimed that it certainly would, and then she said, in such an innocent way: "I'm going to wait a little bit to see how the doctor bills have run, and if they aren't too high, I'm going to see if I can't work it some way to get a birdbath to put out there."

Such care in spending their tiny income. The birdbath would not cost more than three or four dollars. And yet that is an amount to contend with when you are as poor as we are. But something about it is good. There is achievement in "working it out." It means more to us who are made simple in our hearts by the lack of excess. But it hurt a little, melting me, and I thought how I must work to ease this situation.

Returning to the barn, I counted the money in my pocket, all I had in the world at the moment. It came to $7.09. So I put two dollars in an envelope and ordered a Mother's Day gift, a copy of My Way of Life by Aquinas. She will love that and has long wanted it. I know that the reason I offer it at this special moment is my gratitude for being allowed to hear her charming plan. Then the mockingbirds will be close by.

Another such incident was last night, when Elizabeth, overwhelmed by anguish when the baby fell off the bed, sat rocking her and talking to ease my mind, talking of insignificant things while her voice trembled. Where does nobleness ever shine so authentically as in those moments when it is the least intended, the least obvious? These things stir me and make my love helpless, like a bird batting its wings in the desire to rise ever higher beyond the barriers that are bearable to its heart.

May 4, 1955

Spring in the country. They told me last night that a small cottontail rabbit had taken up quarters with a setting guinea, that he had been there with her in her nesting house for three days, entering and leaving by the tiny door that allows the guinea to enter and leave, but sitting most of the time directly in front of her, giving her companionship as she passes the hours until her eggs hatch out. Strange pair, a white guinea and a young rabbit, sharing a naturalness we find odd but they do not.

It occurs that my finest work has been the product of what I thought was my greatest boredom, but in an atmosphere of peace, of isolation. How much work did I do in Tours as a student, and in Solesmes during those months of great happiness and solitude, when there was literally nothing else in the world to do except work. I feel that if I could ever get caught up with myself, could ever forget deadlines and promises to have work out, I would do far better work and probably far more, although it would be more leisurely done.

The world is vastly different from what it was then. What we knew is almost totally unknown today, with such a frightful amount of activity. Then we measured time in hours; now it is measured in seconds. Then it was considered perfectly normal to spend many hours drinking coffee, reading, or doing nothing. Nowadays there is some guilt attached to it, some guilt in the air which I can feel and cannot escape—a terrible thing in a way. Never is it possible to rest in long intervals, without a sense of guilt as it was in the days when I was in France. Here you are caught up in the prevailing atmosphere, and here you become part of it, and you lose by it. I am determined to retain as much of the other as I can—to produce slowly and leisurely, better works than I could possibly produce rapidly and commercially. I remove myself as far from this consumer culture as possible, but never far enough.

Our dear friend Robert Ellis has removed himself entirely from this noise and clutter. His letter today tells us that he is living and working in a little village below Mexico City, cultivating orchids in his spare time, painting and writing in solitude—he has the right idea.

To create independently of all opinions and criteria, seeking never to create a portrait of your wisdom but only of those things in life that you understand and experience, created anew in the forms of your private art. What does this amount to? Nothing more than an art based on truth, not on what someone else thinks, not even on truths that a majority embraces. The leaven of experience, of your individual humanity, is a vast backdrop for truth. The artist who has lived fully need never report what he has lived, but reconstructs from the basis of that living. The married artist, for instance, who has experienced the full gamut of emotions in a marriage, immediately applies a different coloration to his portrait than would one who never married. And parenthood creates a similar distance between parents and those who only fantasize about how it would be.

It is rather strange how parenthood has changed me. Before our child, I was writing of a father's feeling for his infant daughter in *Nuni*, and noted that he rather dreaded her growing up and leaving him, dreaded the thought of her marriage; but now all of that is altered. I do not fear Susan's marriage, do not fear the hardships she will undoubtedly have to endure (as do all married people), but instead am enthusiastic about it for her. Last night, lying beside her on the bed and playing with her while she giggled and cooed, I placed my hand on her stomach and thought: "God, let this stomach know all of life, let it know love, good love and ecstasy, and let it know its own children." And those thoughts caused an immense and painless tenderness to well up in me for her.

June 1, 1955

I volunteered to stay home and take care of Susan while Elizabeth went to Mass. Always before, Susan has taken her bottle and then a good long nap during most of the morning, but not today. As soon as her mother was out of earshot, she let out a roar that demanded my taking her up from the bed. As soon as I did, she got happy. So I gathered up all her toys and put her on her stomach on the mat on the floor, and she began playing and having a good time. When her attention was distracted, I sneaked into the kitchen and started washing the breakfast dishes. But the water had hardly started running when she discovered my absence and let out a wail.

I returned quickly, thinking she had been hurt, and picked her up to examine her. She cooed and giggled and pulled my hair and said "da-da" and kissed me on the cheek, and then I felt the warmth dribbling down my stomach and turning cold as it soaked my pajama pants.

She had wet me thoroughly, so I hauled her into the kitchen to turn off the water, and then to the bed to change the diapers, powdered her and returned her to the toys on the mat. As I left to change, she screamed in agony, and I slipped into shorts in a hurry.

"Are your little gums hurting you," I said.

"Wow," she bawled.

I hauled her into the kitchen to get cool-a-gum from the refrigerator. She grabbed the gum and shoved it in her mouth. I told myself that you can never guess, that when they cry there is always a reason. She drooled all over my chest and sucked the gum happily, so happily that I put her down in a high chair in order to return to washing the dishes.

As soon as she was seated in the high chair, she threw the gum with all her force into my face and began whimpering. I got the medicine and massaged her gums. Then she clamped down and bit almost through the flesh of my finger. I held her nose to make her let go of the bulldog bite. And then I petted her on the head, kissed her cheek, and she crooned "da-da-da-dy," grabbing a handful of hair and kissing my cheek. I left her, seemingly contented, in the high chair.

But before I had the first dish washed, she screamed, so I ran back and picked her up and rocked her, thinking she might be coaxed to sleep. But she wanted to play. The morning was passing, we were expecting company in the afternoon, and I had to get some of the housework done before Elizabeth returned from Mass. So I decided to feed her. I carried her into the kitchen, found an open can of baby apricots in the refrigerator, warmed them, and carried all of the paraphernalia back into the living room where I arranged it on the little table next to the rocking chair. This was my first attempt to spoon-feed the baby.

I cradled her in my left arm, found her mouth, shoved a spoonful of apricots in. She blew like a hurricane, splattering it all over my face and into my hair. I told her to behave and she laughed, continuing to make sounds like the Bronx cheer. I filled the spoon again and poked it gently to her lips, but she did not cooperate and would not even part her lips. So I sat there with the baby in one hand and a spoonful of apricots in the other, not knowing what to do, not daring to set it down on the table with all that mush in it, so I could only decide to eat it.

"Why don't you behave," I growled at her.

"Da-da-da-dy!" she cajoled.

"You're sweet and adorable, but dammit, behave!"

I hauled her into the bathroom, tried to wash my face with one hand, slopped the washrag across her face which vastly amused her. Then I carried her back to the bed to take off her soaking diapers and change them again. She kicked and giggled through that, and I left her in a jubilant mood, although I was beginning to feel destroyed.

I had not gone three steps toward the bathroom to brush my teeth when she screamed. I returned, picked her up and carried her into the kitchen. I held her on one hip while I washed the dishes with my free hand. She grabbed at everything.

Finally, with nothing done but the dishes, I brought her back to the rocking chair, told her to go to sleep, and rocked until she finally did. Susan slept less than ten minutes when her mother came in from Mass, very silently so as not to awaken the baby.

"That's the most ungodly-spoiled child in the county," I informed her. My words woke up the little angel and she lay there, glaring at me.

Enchanted, my wife said: "She's hurt. She's sulking at you."

"Okay, I'm sulking at her, too," I answered.

Elizabeth laughed sweetly and it made me laugh. This was something she did every day, not just this day.

What a powerful force a child can be: Susan was changing our lives and Elizabeth was pregnant with our second child, promising a greater dynamism that our family quartet would become in the near future.

November 30, 1955

After a long silence I begin writing in these journal pages again—on a drizzling afternoon of rain and sleet when the cold penetrates the bone and feet remain frozen in shoes in spite of the gas heater which sputters out its tiny warmth.

Two days ago Susan began walking, and her pride in that achievement melts us to pure adoration for her. How much we do learn from them, how naturally does their joy come and how simply they communicate it to us, lightening our lives and making them almost magical during these days and nights when we huddle against fatigue and cold, isolated in the country. The miseries are so superficial and the joys so profound that even the discomforts and privations never manage to put us out of sorts.

We spent our last penny on the November 9th birth of our son Johnny, and for buying a stove which has not yet been delivered. No, it should not be different and I think that secretly neither of us wants it different, for then we would have missed an experience that was energizing and infinitely touching. Strange that there should be this union of reactions to what most people would see as a grave misfortune.

Johnny awakens in the middle of the night. I bring him into our bed for feeding, and then he ends up not digesting the milk and spitting up all over everyone, which means we must change him. But before we can do that, I must build up the fire in the fireplace. When this is repeated again and again and the temperature howls at twenty degrees outside and fatigue becomes almost a mania, one would think there might be an outburst of irritation, of complaint from either of us.

Then Elizabeth makes me go back to bed, and I lie there listening to the squeak of the rocking chair moving back and forth on the brick floor as she sits before the open fire while the baby sleeps, listening to wind and sleet ravaging the eaves and windows.

⭢ A Death in the Family ⭢

Tuesday, January 10, 1956

I force myself to write this entry, for the heart does not need or want the pain of arousing itself from numbness to speak, yet I feel that I must tell what has happened.

Blindness

Saturday night Clyde and Bess Holland went out to dinner at friends and I was up at their house cooking a turkey over hickory coals in their fireplace while Elizabeth was making cornbread for the dressing and a cranberry relish.

They came in about ten, happy and warmer than I have seen them in a long time. He was in pain, but made so light of it we all thought it a slight indisposition. We said our good nights and went to our cottage.

At 2:45 in the morning the phone rang and I answered it.

"I think Clyde's dead," Bess said and hung up.

I returned to the bed to put on my shoes, unable to hurry because I was shaking so violently and was scarcely conscious of what I was doing.

"What is it?" Elizabeth asked.

"It was Bess, Honey. She thinks Clyde has gone."

Elizabeth was out of bed, whimpering, and ran out the door in bare feet toward her parents' house. I put on my shoes and hurried out.

The night was frozen and utterly still. My legs would not work well enough to run. So I walked, struggling up the hill, and I began to pray, to offer my grief to God for Clyde's dear soul, and the most unbelievable calm came over me.

I would have thought I would go almost out of my mind with grief, but it was as though I heard him saying, "You can do better than that, can't you son? You've got to help them." And I said out loud on that path: "All right, Pappy, I will. I'll do what you want me to do."

I was at the door when Elizabeth said, strangely calm and intense: "Honey, do you know how to give artificial respiration?"

"Yes."

She led me to the couch where her father was lying on his back, not apparently breathing. I lifted and rolled him over on his stomach and began the pumping, counting one, two, three and four—over and over again with utmost calm.

Elizabeth called the ambulance, the doctor and the priest.

I pumped and Clyde began to respond, began breathing. Then the ambulance arrived and with a pull motor lifted his pajama-clad body to turn him over on his back to receive the oxygen when I heard his mouth, almost touching my ear, issue a sigh and stop breathing. The oxygen was pumped to him, but he had expired.

I touched his head, hands, and feet and recited the *De Profundis* and then the priest arrived to administer the last rights.

Bess was almost in a state of collapse. The doctor gave her a heavy sedative, which could not control her. Elizabeth, thank God, was calm and superb under pressure.

The priest took me aside and said that Clyde was in a state of grace, that he knew almost exactly when he would die and that he had prepared for it well. Then the gallantry, the foolish and magnificent gallantry of it struck more deeply than anything else—his knowing that he was dying, knowing when the spasms became regular but never telling any of us how serious was his condition over the past few months. Knowing that he could do that while making the slow walk to infinity struck like a blast.

Again I was on the verge of breaking down and losing all control and again I felt his presence, instructing me that I could do better than that, saying in essence that while we had him only during those moments when we were together, now we had him with us always, every moment in our hearts and that the body lying there was no longer Clyde, that he would not be in the grave, and that his spirit was happy.

After that, all was simple enough, for we were given the grace, the incomprehensible grace to be at peace and to be happy for him. At the recitation of the rosary we were impelled, without knowing it until later, to say the joyful mysteries rather than the traditional sorrowful ones. I was tremendously proud of Elizabeth, as I know Clyde was, for rarely has a father been so adored as he was by her. In all of this, then, the sharp edge of grief was transformed into this essence of tenderness for him.

Wednesday, January 11, 1956

We are at peace, completely, and we work now to shorten Clyde's stay in purgatory by offering up all of our actions and thoughts and prayers for his intention. And, as he would have wanted us to, we are back in our work and in our lives—addled, yes, but all right.

Today, here in my studio, there is the peculiar, detached business of writing many letters to inform people of Clyde's death. I write and then forget almost immediately what I have written. I write in automation while the sunlit countryside, still and cold, lies utterly silent and the little gas stove sputters its bit of heat in the background of this clacking.

There is a light thread of loneliness around my heart, but it is serene and peaceful, and whenever I falter or feel the expansion of tears, again I become aware of Clyde's desires and his heroic example of kindness, and I catch myself and go on trying to do what he wants me to do, trying to act as he wants, trying to be what I must be. How near is sublimity to the depths of despair, into which I could easily have fallen but which I have escaped through nothing less than the grace of God, granted in answer to my prayers and shown to me in Clyde's own last gallantry.

I fall into prayer, and in the prayers comes the knowledge and the will to overflow my tenderness for his soul into the realm of the living here on earth. None of this is in me. All of it is the infusion of strength from beyond, for which I am profoundly grateful. All in all, I learn that man is nothing of himself, learn it again and deeply.

I know that if it were only *of* myself I would be encircled and enclosed in grief, but *beyond* myself I am opened to grace and love, and those are the salvaging things that lift and sustain us in the majestic consolation of our God. For if I am selfishly aware of this new and vast loneliness, I am simultaneously and equally aware of great happiness for Clyde. That is the better and stronger emotion, the predominant one.

The soul, the spirit, the affections: These are the only nonmaterial elements of man, created by God, that cannot be destroyed. They have flown from the animal shell of Clyde, have ceased to vitalize his body, but remain around us today and forever. When I think that dear Clyde is destined for Heaven, destined for the dazzlement of glorious union with God, then I am indeed selfish not to experience the core of profoundest joy in the midst of this superficial sorrow.

I will scarcely admit it, but is it not little more than mourning over a suit of his clothes to mourn his physical absence, when we are assured of the presence of all that is most important to him, all that made him who he was in his spirit, his soul, his affections? These still live in us.

And to think of this man who sneezed and laughed and was known more in his flesh than in his spirit, who sat next to me in his car the morning of his death and cheerfully made the morning offering of all his prayers, works, and sufferings in union with the Sacred Heart of Jesus. Then he said the Hail Mary for the intention to be granted the graces of the things of God and the grace to love God ever more deeply.

Then Clyde made his usual hilarious wisecracks and drove away. To think of him now as a saint, or at least assured that he is on his way to being one, it is too touching. Yet that is the one certainty in my mind, for he died in a state of grace and received the last sacrament validly and is at this moment intensely happy in the knowledge that he will soon share the ultimate felicity. And what we call the harsh design of God is only harsh to us who must remain without him. But harsh to Clyde? No. God loved him enough to take him to paradise, to cherish him and give him infinite happiness for his struggles while here on earth, because he struggled valiantly for a faith which it was always difficult for him to accept. Clyde wanted to accept, to immerse himself in it, but did it only with the most tremendous effort in humility.

Now he need no longer believe, for he knows and is there where all souls must long to be. He is where we may hope to join him after living good lives and dying well. And on this day when we are so close to the reality of his departure, we can see once again that of all the things in this life, the most important is to struggle to be with God, and secondly to be with those whom we love and who preceded us there.

It was with pure intention that Clyde was the model for the little hero of my Friar Clud stories, both because of his humor and his humility. He enjoyed those stories, without our specifically discussing that he was the model for the friar in "Sauce for the Gander" and other unfinished tales about the humble Clud. If Clyde did not know then, he knows now.

Sunday, January 15, 1956

We celebrated Mass for Clyde this morning at our little church here in Mansfield. Clyde's brother, Bob Holland, who was very close to him but who did not become a convert as Clyde and Bess had, told me this morning that he had given up smoking in honor of his brother.

"I don't know much about your faith," Bob said, "but I understand he maybe has some time in purgatory, is that right?"

"No one knows, but we imagine so," I said.

"Well, your priest said that if you make some sacrifice and offer it up for Clyde's intention, that'll shorten his stay, is that right?"

"Yes, that's right."

"Do you reckon it'll count if I do it, even though I'm not a Catholic?"

"I'm sure it will, Bob."

"Well, I'm going to do that then, to help him shorten his stay."

At the cemetery, Bess could not stop sobbing. Before they could lower the casket into the gravesite she threw her body over it, shrieking wildly and begging Clyde not to leave her. It caused a commotion I could not see, but which was so heart-wrenching to the ears I shuddered. Members of the family pulled Bess away from the casket and tried to console her. But there was no consoling her then or in the weeks to come. Her grief was dramatic and entirely unlike Elizabeth's dignified sadness.

Wednesday, January 25, 1956

These are days at the studio when it is very difficult to work, because Clyde absorbs all thoughts, and even when I am the busiest, I find myself forgetting what I am doing and becoming immersed in these recollections of him, and particularly of his death. It is the most difficult discipline I have ever subjected myself to, but it is absolutely necessary.

I say each day the full rosary for him and another rosary for our regular intentions.

I find compensation for not seeing him in the more intense feelings I have for my children. These are days of fatigue and overwork, but of a quiet happiness which binds all of the hours together and makes sleep good when it comes at night.

After working all day in the studio, how much I enjoy the evenings at home when I can relax with the family, listen to the radio, sit around in pajamas shortly after supper and lie down until sleep takes me. There is a steady pulse to it, a pulse of contentment that does not flag, does not produce monotony. We both need it and savor it after the emotional loss of Clyde. How much more tender and nourishing is quietness in love. It tears your heart but does not break it or injure it. It is good to love in this way, to a point of acuteness, simply and undramatically.

I am aware, in a thousand ways, that I am no longer young, that I am becoming familiar with middle age, but all of that without in any way being old or feeling any degeneration in any aspect of life, an aging but not in a morose sense.

May 15, 1956
It has been four months since I have written about our lives in these pages, but instead have been setting down a first draft of the new novel.

Today I awakened feeling strange. It took some time to realize what this new and wonderful feeling was. For the first time in three years I was out of pain. And today *Nuni* has been published, and whether it does anything or not, it was nevertheless a very important point in my life—the result of three years of labor and loving care and the end, I pray, of an epoch of sickness and pain.

I worked through the day, in calm, in quietness. The air is fresh and chilly after good rains last night. Above the incessant chirping of birds in the aviary, I hear from across the woods the tinkle of a cowbell and the occasional whinnying of a horse. I feel immense peace, a prayerfulness without words, immersed in the desire only to work on the new novel.

— Crisis in a Small Town —

October 14, 1956
The most touching gesture this morning from Susan. I was in a hurry to leave, was forgetting things. Without making a sound, she fetched

them, met me at the door with a package of cigarettes and my cane. It was a moment when I was overwhelmed by the infant's quiet thoughtfulness.

Other touching things: Susan imitates me now. She walks about the house with her eyes closed in imitation of my blindness, according to Elizabeth, delighted with herself, thinking she is being like me and thinking this pleases me. Last night, gaining confidence, she walked into the door-facing and bruised her forehead, striking it with enough force to send her falling backwards. I held her for a long time, but she was more humiliated at her failure than she was at her hurt. She clung to me in absolute silence, not even weeping, but holding on with her arms about my neck in an intensity of feeling that could not be denied. I think this made her realize something of what it means to be blind— rather even more, since she has experienced it now in a far worse way than it really is, except in the beginning.

Last night, she was very attentive to me, but quieter than usual, and when I went to bed she insisted on going with me, and she lay there in the dark beside me for the longest time, patting my cheek and head as though to console me. Unspoken things from an infant, communicated in ways that cannot be doubted, poignant things.

October 15, 1956

A dark and somber and rainy day, early in the morning. The day that the Supreme Court decides whether or not I am a pornographer, a writer of obscene literature. Strange, it is the Feast of St. Teresa of Avila, the last day when I should allow burdens to get me down, when I should be sour-faced, and yet I have a feeling that they will find me a pornographer. I try to forget it, to work, but work is dazed, from some spreading numbness within me, glassy and feelingless, and only is there an awareness of exhaustion, deep and pervasive. How difficult it is to love—not to hate. Much work to do and no heart for doing any of it.

October 20, 1956

A norther blew in a moment ago, and now the air is still, utterly still in that fecund way of hanging in suspense before the unleashing of a storm. It is eerie. All is silence at mid-morning and there is a feeling of dampness hanging breathless in the air. The birds are silenced, the geese mute. Everything waits, hypnotized by nature, and now, distantly I hear the rumble of thunder, the growlings and belchings of hatred, and a breeze springs up to an accompanying rustle in the trees outside the window.

Still again. Still. We wait. And I must work in this strange half-fright of elements become communicative, telling things on paper while all of the rest of me listens and knows things that have no words, knows that the norther is on the prowl, sending its massed clouds sneaking like some great cat across the heavens, ready to pounce on this quivering lamb-world.

When I returned home from the studio, I learned that the Associated Press story broke about the Court's ruling on *The Devil Rides Outside*. The novel has been exonerated, and I am innocent of smut-peddling. It was a relief, of course, but I felt exactly as Elizabeth did when she sighed and said, "I don't know whether to laugh or cry."

October 23, 1956

A ravishing morning, chilly and sunlit. I put on the new tape recording of Alec Wyton's J. S. Bach performed on the cathedral organ at St. John the Divine. I place the large speakers in the windows of this studio, facing out toward the woods, and turn it up full blast. The air is utterly still and the sun warms. I sit under the trees and listen to this magnificent music, so robustly and superbly played; and it is amplified that you can hear it clearly far away. The entire countryside is permeated with its health, and all animals react to it. From the back porch fifteen canaries begin to sing and trill; the geese foregather under the windows from which the sound is pouring and they squat there in a great batch.

Never have I spent a more entrancing hour hearing this music become a part of the very atmosphere, penetrating into the woods, spreading over the pastures. I have the impression that every animal, every rabbit and squirrel and raccoon and fox, every frog and crayfish—all of them are listening wherever they are out there, and wondering what happened to the day to make it so much better than those before. During the music, a great flock of wild geese flew over and added their honkings to Bach's counterpoint. Surely I've never heard Bach to better advantage, nor under such perfect conditions.

October 24, 1956

I napped and dreamed of an elderly man dying like a child—not as an animal, as Hemingway says. No, I have seen too much death, seen too many die; there is a helplessness, a sudden frankness that never ceases to tear my heart and haunt my dreams. No, not with the terror of death, but with the unreserved tenderness that is renewed for them, as for children with their eyes closed in fever, for the feeling is the same. Nothing of farewell, nothing of grandeur or eternity enters it—no, only the moment, only the man dying like a child, unable to do anything or help himself or hold back, and that strange awed look on his face, no matter how peaceful his death, the look that says: "I didn't have enough time. I should have combed my hair at least," and the viewer's reaction that we can do at least that much for you.

That is what tears me, the poignancy rather than the sadness, the pity that is tenderness rather than sentimentality or fright. A man walks away from it with eternity understood in his heart once again, as though a beautiful day in autumn were being experienced. It is not dissonant. Rather, it is conformable to this exquisite Mass, something of the order of God's universe, with death as the transition passage, striking the soul with an awareness of reality and reducing man either to serenity and internal harmony or to terror and disharmony—and this music, it melts the crusts within the soul, the crusts of foolishness and fear and gives a glimpse of eternal truths and eternal loveliness.

December 6, 1956

It is a disconsolate night, because I received word that the two television dramas on which I had so counted to tide us over are not going to sell—"too original, too intellectual," according to my agent. Now that my agent has pointed this out to me, I see clearly their unsuitability to a mass commercial audience. My mother read the letter, and knowing how desperately broke we are, I think it hit her harder than it did me. But I am feeling that desolation of being cornered tonight, too, for seeming to be unable to make a living with the only thing I really know to do and want most to do. Mother encouraged me, certain that the plays are good, that they will sell, but she knows that we have nothing further to eat and no money to buy Christmas presents, not even to buy groceries.

I came out to the studio to work, but all I can do is sit here and try to face these problems, try to decide what I do wrong, and it comes to me that I know only the most savage of men and conditions thoroughly, along with the most intellectual, but I am completely nil to that vast middle area of living wherein my family and friends live. No problem is solved with this realization. It only creates doubt that I can do anything in this field except on a slow and long-term basis, and that then leaves the problem of supporting my family. I must do something fast for a medium I cannot even see! But art is very slow, and when there is no food, then it must give way to the belly, to the family's survival.

It tears my heart out to think of closing up this typewriter and going to take a job, but I see no alternative. I have not been successful enough and there is not more time. I cannot turn out hack work, my work takes time and peace, and there is neither when we face the blank wall of such total poverty. A man must quit, then, in this day and in this land, and go make some money. I cannot do it commercially, only artistically, and therefore I must leave the typewriter—but how, to go where and do what?

The little economies do not depress me, but touch me, and I would have great joy and enthusiasm in them were it not that others worry about them, were it not that they are depriving my family of what is rightfully theirs—peace and financial security. Otherwise, we gain by this experience, and it would be beautiful indeed were it not becoming of such crucial sharpness.

It is very strange. Both of my novels have been nominated the best of their respective years, both have received extravagant critical success. I am acclaimed as one of the important writers of our day by serious and respected critics. But I cannot make a living, not even a humble one. I have great prestige in the literary world, and no money in the Mansfield bank. If I had a few more months, another year perhaps, the tide might have turned. Up until now it has been the gentle poverty, the healthful frugality, but now it becomes the brutal, sharp, agonizing poverty. I pray to God for a solution, for the whole family's sake, where would we be now without the gallant help of my parents and Elizabeth's parents?

Instead of dwelling on this any longer, I put on a heavy wool jacket, rummaged around the tool room until I found the ax, and slipped away to the wood pile on the edge of the woods. The ax was very sharp and I chopped with no effort a good stack of kindling. It was delicious. I felt transplanted into another role, another century. I was one of those wilderness settlers with a wife and children huddled in their cabin, for our cottage is as small and primitive as a cabin, and I was providing fuel and warmth for them.

By the time I had finished, my blood was well stirred and I dreaded to quit, dreaded to break the spell. I was, for a time, the outdoor man, the pioneer who works hard outside all day long. No wonder they had so many children! Because after working, all crampings are gone from the chest and one feels lovable and robust and full of fun. Even though tired, it makes you feel like making love.

III

Vision

― What It Means to See ―

Mount Carmel Monastery, January 13, 1957
Last Wednesday, the ninth of January, as I was walking from the barn studio to my parents' house to prepare lunch—redness swirled in front of my eyes. Then I thought I saw the back door, cut in portions, dancing at crazy angles. I stood dumbfounded. Elements continued to dance and there was pain in my eyes and head.

I stumbled inside and found the telephone. I got the number dialed. I heard my wife's voice answer.

"I think . . ." I began, and then collapsed into weeping.

"What is it? What's happening?" she asked urgently.

"I think I can see."

I could not talk anymore. Only mumblings came out, until I managed to say: "Call the doctor. Please hurry."

Her voice was quiet, awe-struck. "All right. Oh, Lord, go lie down. I'll have the doctor there in a minute."

"You come too," I said.

"Yes, I'll be right there. Don't move. Don't do anything."

I sat in a chair at the table. The room was broken up. Triangles of color faded and swirled. Weird designs of floor and wall and ceiling fused. It was like being hit a terrible blow on the head. My system could not bear the shock. Numbness filled me.

Dimly I thought of all those sightless people who had for so long been my brothers and sisters. Was I actually leaving their world, to which I had become so accustomed? I prayed for the presence of mind never to forget them, to do or say nothing that would build false hopes in them or hurt them. Was something happening to me that would never happen to them? Dear God, would this hurt them, would this make them feel more lonely? And I was concerned with my family. Was I really seeing? Would their hopes be built up only to crash when this incredible storm passed?

Another thought struck me and almost twisted my brain. Was ever a man in a stranger position? My own wife and children, people who were my life, and yet if I saw them in the street I would not even know them! From the swirl of my own confusion, I thought of how my wife must feel. Should she run immediately to me? Should she take time to dress, fix herself up, so I could see her first in the best possible light?

I felt my brain tossing it out, refusing to believe. Desperately I clung to consciousness, struggling not to collapse, struggling to hang on to the light and movement.

Then the doctor was there, but I couldn't see him. Only a splotch of blue there in the corner.

The monumental effort of keeping my eyelids open was exhausting. My eyes ached from the effort to focus. But there was no focus, only lights and colors in constant movement.

The doctor's voice was deadly calm. "Are you really seeing?"

"I think so," I heard myself saying, as though another's voice spoke.

"What color is my suit?" the doctor asked gently.

"Blue, I think." I was trembling violently.

He was saying things about how wonderful it was.

"You've got to give me something. I can't stand it."

He gave me a shot and talked. I no longer remember the words, for my mind was blotting out, trying then to become unconscious. I sat, holding myself up, drained of all strength, all intelligence. The sedative made me withdraw into a deep calm, far into myself. It closed out the world. I heard myself asking what the sedative was.

"Demerol, a light sedative. I want you to be aware of everything. This is an experience few can ever have."

I withdrew further. I didn't try to make him understand that it was too much of a blow. I didn't want to be aware of it. A man's system can't stand up under such a shock. I wanted to sleep, to leave this terrifying experience.

The phone rang. The doctor handed me the receiver.

It was my mother's voice asking what was happening. It was filled with anguish. I could not speak.

The doctor spoke with her. "Yes, Mrs. Griffin. He's seeing enough to make out colors. He's very upset. His wife is on her way over."

My wife and children. Would I know them? Would I know my parents after all these years? Strange and twisted perceptions came to mind.

Later a car pulled into the driveway. I heard its door slam. Nerves simmered up from numbness. "Tell me who it is," I said to the doctor.

"Your parents."

I prayed vaguely and braced myself, prayed that this not be a deception for them. They had suffered too much, too gallantly on my account.

Then there was a swirl of movement. Faces drew close to mine. They were kissing me, talking in low tones. I had to pull out of it, to reassure them in some way.

"Can you actually see me?" my mother asked.

"I can see that you have on a green dress," I mumbled.

I couldn't control the vision enough to see their faces. I would see a portion of their clothes and instantly the ceiling or a wall—then haze.

Talk went on around me. I retreated into a stupor until the sound of another car aroused me. I stayed seated at the table. At the door, I heard the voices of my wife and children. I staggered up from the chair. Susan ran forward and was the first to appear. I concentrated beyond strength to see all the radiant wisdom of her two-year-old face looking up at me.

"You beautiful little thing," I said, touching her cheek.

I saw her face clearly and then it blurred.

Suddenly, Elizabeth was in my arms, her face beside mine. I glimpsed raven black hair. Johnny was tugging at my pantlegs. I reached down, felt his short-cropped hair, but could not see him. That first clear view of my daughter had been like looking at the sun, blinding me to everything else. That image remained in front of my face during the next dim hours. The effort of seeing her, or perhaps the emotion, had shattered me.

The next clear memory I had was being at the eye specialist's late that evening. The building was deserted. Words detached from context. The doctor probed the eyes and I felt pain.

"The eyes look fairly good," said the doctor. "Tell me, was it a brain injury that caused the blindness?"

"No, doctor, a concussion," I said.

"A concussion is a brain injury . . ."

"Yes, of course," I muttered.

"We must work on restoring circulation to the eyes," he said.

The doctor gave my wife the necessary prescriptions and we went to the pharmacy. Back home, my family watched over me.

Elizabeth and I stayed up late that night because I was afraid to go to sleep. Would I wake up blind again? Finally, I did manage to sleep.

That next morning, awake before anyone else, I was unable at first to perceive color. I feared that what I had gained had been lost. I managed to glimpse only scattered shadows.

Then the colors returned and the day was filled with manic activity.

There were reporters and photographers, and the beginning of the nervous rigors that shook the whole body. I concentrated on the blind, knowing I must say nothing to hurt them or to give them false hopes. I sat numb in the eye of a hurricane of activity. But I had no recollection of their questions or my answers. I was collapsing without realizing it.

I heard my wife talking to my mother. Low voices. The phone kept ringing, and Elizabeth did some telephoning. Little by little, the public was cleared away. It was decided that the doctor would take me elsewhere to spend that night because the public onslaught had to be avoided.

"You're shaking terribly," said the doctor.

"What the hell do you think they called you for?" I uttered nervously and we all laughed.

I was taken to a friend's house, and the doctor gave me another shot upon arrival. He and his friends sat up with me until I fell into a deep sleep. Some day, I told myself, I will do something for all these people who have watched over me.

The next morning I was having hard rigors. No recollection of that day. I was virtually unconscious, although I moved and spoke. I saw a hall full of reporters and photographers, and I think I said yes to everything they wanted, but remembered no specifics. Then I was taken to the eye specialist. The press mob followed us. The specialist said he would have temporary glasses made immediately. My doctor was concerned about the pressure from the reporters and laid down the ground rules.

"You'll have to wait," my doctor told them. "This man's in a state of shock. He doesn't know what he's saying. You must wait a few days."

But they were insistent. I was feeling nothing but a vague pain in my eyes. Eventually, the doctor cleared the room and the specialist fitted me for training glasses, to force my eyes to focus.

I was smuggled out the back door of the specialist's office and taken to my doctor's home for safe-keeping. However, the phone there kept ringing, at our home and at my parents' home as well.

Telegrams came from around the world, including one from Senator Lyndon B. Johnson and another from the American Foundation for the Blind. Senator Johnson had quipped that this was one Texas miracle he could not take credit for. The Foundation for the Blind congratulated me on a fine interview I had given over the phone to the *New York Times*. I had no recollection of it. I sat numb in the midst of a bombardment, vaguely surprised that people should be so interested.

Finally, the doctors decided to sequester me in a distant hospital. No more visitors, telephone calls, or interviews. I requested that I be able to stay with the Carmelites instead of the hospital. The doctors thought that would even be better. So I was taken to Mount Carmel and no one knew where I was being hidden. What the doctors did not know was that the monks would be tougher than they had been. The monks promised that I would be totally secluded and that the drugs would be administered strictly. I knew I would feel safe in the cloister.

I had no recollection of the trip from the doctor's to the monastery, except blankness. In the monastic house of peace I was to continue the most intimately dramatic events of my life.

During those first days and nights I slept around the clock, except to take water and medicine and to use the chamber pot in the cell. But I did not remember any of that, for my brain was numbed by drugs and my eyesight was hazed by glare of light. Several days have been lost in this mental haze, but I began to come around today.

I recall only one experience during these sleep-filled days in the Carmelite monastery. I woke up to see the shadowy figure of a large man standing beside the bed. I spoke to him. He remained silent, motionless. I spoke again and when he did not answer, I became frightened. Finally I reached out and touched plaster. I learned later that it was a life-sized statue of St. Joseph that had been placed in the cell next to the bed!

Many people wondered what it might be like to see again after a decade of blindness. Sight does not return full-blown suddenly. You have to learn to see again, like a newborn infant. You have to learn to use muscles, to focus. The adjustment back to sight was as complex as the adjustment to blindness had been. The simple mechanics of living had to be learned over again. How to eat, how to walk, how to look at people. I kept forgetting that I could see, and that in seeing I could do many things that I had put out of my life.

At the outset, sight was more of a burden than a help. Nothing looked as I had remembered. I could not get around well. Instead of sounds to guide me, there was now a visual confusion of objects and an extreme clumsiness. I knew I was acting in a dream, but I could not prevent it. The monks did not talk about it. They understood that to regain sight after so long was not accomplished quickly, that one must concentrate on other things. Just as I had the support of the Benedictines at the Abbey of Solesmes while becoming blind, I now had the support of the Carmelites while recovering at Mount Carmel.

When they came to awaken me this morning for early Mass, I was amazed when they said that it was already Sunday. I attended Mass from the little cubicle upstairs, looking down on the chapel.

I made these notes because there was no memory from one moment to the next. It all seemed real for a brief time, but disappeared soon afterward. I could not read my handwritten notes. I saw only blurred and jumping lines. The memories were without sequence, fragmented.

Monday, January 14, 1957

This morning I took the medicines handed to me by one of the monks, and I was able to inject myself with insulin for the diabetes. Then I was escorted to the kitchen for toast and coffee. Suddenly, the rigors began to shake the entire body. A shot was necessary.

I was dimly delighted only because the prior would have to give it and I knew that the size of the hypodermic needle was terrifying to him.

"I hate to do this," he said shakily.

"It's nothing. Just jab me anywhere. But hurry."

"Wait a minute," the prior said. He went out and called to one of the Carmelite nuns from the dispensary.

The tiny nun entered the cell. Poor thing, I thought, she will faint when she sees the size of that needle.

Quickly, she grabbed a wad of cotton, dipped it in alcohol, rubbed the arm and then jabbed it expertly.

"Sister used to be a nurse before she became a nun," the prior said with a smile of relief.

Later we had a simple and tasteful lunch of beans, homemade bread, butter and coffee. I experienced slight rigors but we decided against another shot. Instead I went back to sleep for several hours.

I awakened in pain. Nerves gripped and cramped. I went out into the corridor where I was intercepted by the prior. He said it was time to take all the medicines again.

I spoke with difficulty. I said I was wondering if there were not some sort of animal that did nothing but sleep and eat all day. I knew there was such an animal but could not name it. Finally, I thought of it.

"It's a sloth, isn't it? I know what it feels like to be a sloth."

The prior was thoughtful for a moment.

"I think that the sloth moves around a little more than you've been moving these past few days."

We laughed out loud and that broke the tension.

I returned to bed and, as the prior left the cell, he asked: "You don't want the light on, do you?"

"No, but thanks for asking."

Light caused immense fatigue. When he hit the switch, I felt that a great weight were lifted. I felt safe, at home in the dark, and everything relaxed back to a semblance of normalcy. I knew it would take time before light became once again natural.

Tuesday, January 15, 1957

This afternoon I became more aware of sights, but could absorb them only a little at a time. Then sight would click off, banishing awareness.

They had brought me a book of great paintings this morning, opened to *Woman Weighing Gold* by Vermeer. I saw her expression, remote and serene, and the magnificent light that pervades the canvas. My first clear sights were of masterpieces, which was exalting. But also I began to see the monks as living portraits. I looked out the window on this grayish day hinting of snow but saw the rye field as brilliantly green, with black-and-white cattle grazing on it. Everything appeared as a marvelous painting. Then blankness, fatigue, and the need to sleep.

After a nap, I called my wife and later my parents. How excited they all were about the improving eyesight but how strange it was to hear the noise of the world over the telephone. Happiness mingled with a peculiar depression, because I sensed their concern and could not be with them.

After days of silence, I listened to Bach. My heart was almost unable to bear it, for the music was as overwhelming to hearing as the paintings had been to sight. Clarity, enthusiasm. I smiled at things brought gently to life by the music, observing outlines clearly—the brass door-knob, the statue of St. Joseph, the large wooden cross on the wall.

Would I ever forget the colors of Vermeer, the colors in Bach's music, the colors in these silent moments in the cloister? I prayed that I would not, that they would live vividly hereafter to remind me of God's gift.

Thursday, January 17, 1957

Yesterday marked a week since regaining partial sight. The prior drove me through the nearby countryside, discovering things that the sighted take for granted. Even hovels seemed beautiful. I made the prior drive at a snail's pace, so avid was I to observe every shingle, every tree. I gasped at the new homes and longed to go inside to see how they were furnished. Clothes and cars were astonishing and strange.

But most of all I was fascinated by seeing the faces. The women were so beautiful I could hardly bear it. I constantly nudged my guide to say: "Look at that gorgeous girl! Honestly, aren't women the most beautiful creatures you've ever seen?"

By noon—and this happened every day—I was exhausted from nothing more than the intense excitement of seeing new things.

Friday, January 18, 1957

Today it struck me that I had not looked in the mirror. I observed the face of a stranger, a man now graying and lined. I had long ago lost any image of my face, but I knew that this was a different man. It had never occurred to me that a decade would make such a difference in appearance. I did not linger long.

The cloister continued to have a restorative effect. In the calm gray light of rain against the windows, nerves returned perceptibly to health. There was still fatigue and the immense weight of seeing, as though my eyes were being pulled into shape by the training glasses, but that was nothing in light of seeing again.

Saturday, January 19, 1957

This morning the prior brought a phonograph player into my cell. We listened to Mozart conducted by Thomas Beecham. Then the rain poured in a fine rumble at the finale heard down these long dusky corridors.

I thought of the children and Elizabeth and my parents and longed to be with them. In that moment, were it not for the great wash of the invigorating music, I would have been embittered that the world with its impatient news hounds prohibits my being with my family. Instead, I was hidden here, but I knew it was the best way. If I were at home, I think I would weep, but now in this condition, one tear could be dangerous.

I have noticed that I am not alive to all stimuli as I was before. Now, I am blurred to all the senses except sight, which overwhelms all others even in its imperfections.

But sight, yes, it obsesses me. I squint and concentrate and feel it grow better. I look out and see it with wonder. All sights continue to be like paintings. Surely no one had seen the view from atop this monastery as a Florentine landscape. It was the same with the medicine bottles: clear, greenish, amberish, in different shapes.

Yes, to watch the daylight turn into the obscurity of night and to feel nostalgia for that, to see all of this brightness change like a modulation in harmony.

Is this what it means to see? Is this the way other people see? If not, it is surely the way they were meant to.

A man is alone in himself at such a time, filled with intimate discoveries, reinforced by music and silence and the rhythms of objects viewed very still, viewed deep within self, from deep into past memories brought to freshness by renewal.

January 20-22, 1957

I left the monastery secretly. I was fitted with new glasses to replace the training pair, enhancing my vision but increasing the pain.

When I first walked into our home, Johnny came toddling up to me. As I bent down, he put his arms around my neck. We sat on the couch and he put his eye against my glasses and stared in with great curiosity. He realized that something had changed. All evening I watched the children, observing them in all of their moods and watching the play of expressions on their faces. I realized that I had before only the palest concept of how my children really were.

At that moment the full wonder of sight's precious meaning swept over me, and I promised not to let vision ever become stale. The full strength of these years of illness and blindness supported resolve. It had all been worth it to read a whole world of innocence and wisdom in the clear eyes of our children.

But eventually it was learned that I had returned home. Since the phone began ringing at all hours and no one could sleep, the doctor ordered me back to the cloister.

I made no notes during the next few days, preferring to remain in the cell most of the time. Eyes closed, I listened to Bach as memory drifted over the decade of sightlessness. Intuitively I realized that with the great dominance of sight, I would lose the more subtle ranges of hearing I had cultivated. Alternatively, I poured over more art books, indulging in these visions until the eyes grew weary.

By January 25, I began to make notes once more, notes about that time of great interior loneliness.

I struggled through layers, back to realizations. I was not unhappy but I did not feel the sort of bursting joy that others thought I should feel. Rather, it was a lonely, terribly private reality, and yet I could not bear to be alone. I needed life around me, but still felt it necessary to preserve the illusion of solitude. Thankfully, all was taken care of in the cloister.

Later, perhaps it can be explained how at such a time love must allow for this privacy, that indeed the granting of it is the greatest proof of the quality of love. Being home was wonderful but I had to return to the monastery when press people kept showing up at our door.

January 27, 1957

Yesterday I spoke with Lon Tinkle and Decherd Turner, book editors for the two Dallas newspapers. Decherd indicated that he would like to visit. I told him to come for lunch the next day. It was a pleasant prospect, even if against the doctor's orders. He was to be the first outside visitor and the first of my old friends to visit.

Before Decherd arrived for lunch today, I became dizzy with the prospect of speaking to a fellow writer. I was frightened also, because I did not know how to look at people. The prior assured me that I did and that Decherd would understand. Then the monks brought in a chair and a small wobbly coffee table, as I dusted and swept the cell. A dented metal ashtray was placed on the coffee table. Even though the effect was tawdry, I was touched at the gesture.

The prior brought my esteemed friend to the cell. Decherd entered smiling, his eyes peering questioningly into mine. He had a stack of magnificent books with him and presented them to the prior for the library. The prior took them gratefully and departed.

What did we talk about?

I do not know. Scholasticism, Vermeer's light, St. Augustine—names come back, but the words are blocked and the memory stops at the absorbing view of a face with light falling across it from the window.

There was some constraint. I was deeply moved and feared showing it too much. I also wanted to talk, but I did not know how to look at him. Would he think I was staring? Did one look into a person's eyes or did one glance about the room. His dark eyes were fixed on me.

I offered him a cigarette. Did he take it? I cannot remember. A glass of very bad port before lunch? I could not touch it, as I recall, but I believe he had a little, served in a large drinking glass, which he drank without showing distaste, although I felt it.

Then lunch. I had promised him there would be nothing special, that I would not even tell the Carmelite nuns, who prepare the meals, that he was coming. I told them only a moment before we entered the refectory. "Another plate for the professor," I said.

They were horrified. They had prepared nothing special. Immediately they set about breaking eggs. I assured them he expected only what we had. The monks and nuns rolled their eyes—a distinguished guest, and nothing but Carmelite food!

Lunch was a haze. Later, over coffee, we talked. I was making sense, I think, but mostly I was looking, perhaps staring. I know it was absorbing at the time, and I greatly regretted it when Decherd had to leave.

But always on his face there was that strange expression I could not forget, gentle but peering—the way one looks at a wounded animal.

That evening, a gray, icy dusk. In the chapel they made their evening meditations. We were cloistered from freezing rain, closed in, protected. I struggled against the numbness. It was impossible to pray so I spent a time alone in the chapel, thinking nothing, feeling nothing, at peace.

Later, as I was walking past the recreation room downstairs, I saw the ping-pong table. It occurred to me that now I would be able to do things like that. I had passed that room and thought nothing of it, unaccustomed to being able to do such things.

A monk invited me to play ping-pong. The ball was only a white streak at first, but soon I was hitting it. And then we played some billiards. All of the stagnation left. It was fascinating. For the first time since this thing had happened, I felt real laughter within myself. And it was good exercise for the eyes, too.

Back in the cold cell, I indulged in the luxury of reading, although the print blurred and the smaller print was impossible to decipher. Still, to pick up a book and be able to read it was a thrill.

I read those marvelous texts of *Matins*, *Lauds*, *Prime*, and the rest, reciting them aloud and in that recitation there was the intense breaking through of joy for which sight served as the instrument.

The soul's nourishment and normalcy feeling beyond the words to their innermost meaning, melting away all hardness as it awakened love to its proper dimensions. If only these clarities could remain always to erase the numbness, the endless pettiness. Yet the tired brain conceived the idea of reading the clear black type of these prayers and therein found full reason and justification for seeing again.

I have not yet become accustomed to sight and I still feel as though I have an extra hand, since I do not have to carry a cane. And there is much that I have not seen. Everything remains new, fresh. I have not been selective in what I observe. I continue to stare and to mumble in bewilderment that all of this is "too beautiful . . . too beautiful."

— A World of Light —

February 8, 1957

Returned home after interminable sessions with the doctors, and with a new pair of glasses that gave the impression that I can see like a hawk. Overwhelmed by a minutiae of details long since forgotten, by gravel, by blades of dried winter grass, by every stroke of tree branch in the barren trees, and by the light underwebbings of clouds. But it was as though the weather had contrived to ease me gradually into the beauty of sight with as little exhaustion as possible, for these have been mostly gray days, heavily clouded and fogged until today, when the sun came out.

Tonight, for the first time clearly, I looked at the last glow of twilight in the western sky and overhead saw the full clarity of a half-moon in a cloudless heaven. I could distinguish only the faintest pinpoints of stars, since the sky was not yet fully dark. Later, as I turned around in the chair from a cluttered desk, I saw a world of light across the ceiling. At the other end of the studio stood a rumpled bed. I decided immediately to straighten the bed, to sweep the floor, to begin fresh in this new life.

February 27, 1957
HIGH COURT VOIDS OBSCENE BOOK ACT
That was the front page headline in yesterday's *The New York Times*. The U.S. Supreme Court ruled unanimously that readers could not be deprived of literature because it might be harmful to children, reversing the conviction of Detroit book dealer Alfred E. Butler, who sold copies of *The Devil Rides Outside*. Our efforts against censorship in the Michigan case [*Butler v. Michigan*] have been worth the years.

Justice Felix Frankfurter wrote the opinion of the highest court: "It is clear on the record that appellant was convicted because Michigan made it an offense for him to make available to the general reading public a book that the trial judge found to have a potentially deleterious influence upon youth. The state insists that, by thus quarantining the general reading public against books not too rugged for grown men and women in order to shield juvenile innocence, it is exercising its power to promote the general welfare. Surely, this is to burn the house to roast the pig . . . The incidence of this enactment is to reduce the adult population of Michigan to reading only what is fit for children."

A magnificent statement. How sweet is justice.

March 3, 1957
I have been out here in the workroom quietly writing all morning, filled with peace and happiness and a peculiar softness, as I wrote a brief review of a new volume of Beethoven's letters.

The poor harassed man, maddened by the ordinariness of those he loved, suffering the agonies of hell physically, financially, and still translating his sufferings into some of the most sublime music the world has known. He retired to the "divine world of art" but was surrounded by misunderstanding and pettiness in his personal life.

Perhaps genius is something of that—the ability to be faithful to the "divine world" while living in the earthly one; the ability to persevere by returning again to the creative function despite the gall. As I read the Beethoven letters and wrote the review, I listened to his late quartets. His letters will stay in memory for a long time, but his music will be here even longer and right up until the end.

March 12, 1957

I had an experience which I suppose only a few people in the world can understand. My heart is still pounding against my chest from it.

I went into my parents' house to get a cup of coffee. I decided to take some pictures of the children since it was such a magnificent spring day. I went into the storeroom where I keep the camera and there, on a shelf, I saw my dark glasses which I wore when I was blind and my cane lying beside them. Both were covered with a thick layer of dust. It was so unexpected I was jarred. It was almost like walking upon a dead person. I slammed the door and returned to the living room.

"What's the matter?" my mother asked.

"Nothing," I said.

"Why, you're pale as a ghost."

I could not tell her. But all of the horror of these past years exploded, smothering me. I went into mild shock, sweating, going white. I wanted desperately to take those glasses and throw them away with that film of dust on them. Strange, I saw nothing else in that cluttered store room. I saw the cane, too, but that did not matter. Only those terrible black glasses casting a dust-blurred highlight burned in my consciousness. They looked blind, staring.

March 21, 1957

Going through old letters dating from my adolescence in France, seeing reflected there the passionate innocence, the wonderful, unconsciously seminal quality of those days. We lose much as we grow older, into the grind of living. The ardor of affections becomes subdued, our friendships more cautious. It is not a gain, as I realize with this sudden return to the past. And yet it is right, right to replace the friendships with family, no matter how much more grave the responsibilities. We had those days and we used them well, and now they seem remote and hauntingly desirable, but these are better ones.

Scattered Shadows

I go through and read old letters, a casual activity I could not do when blind without someone to read them aloud, which would not be the same experience at all. Many old friends, mostly from France, who wrote long letters, full of leisure and confidence, savored in the writing and in the reading. Now all these friends have gone their own ways, which is natural, and we correspond with a brief note in a Christmas card. How wonderful to have these letters and to be able to reread them in privacy. I can relive those years while living fully these moments with my wife and children, which are the best moments of my life.

During the same hours, I read though the old editions of the Greek philosophers belonging to grandfather Young, my mother's father, who left them to me. For the first time I actually see the pages, his markings, and I see him with a strange new insight. This man ran a store and came home in the evenings to sit before the fire and read. I remember that as a daily event from childhood, but I was too young then to be interested. Now I find his penciled markings around these phrases of wisdom and know him better.

May 29, 1957

I have worked the past two months on a series for the International News Service, writing short articles about the dramatic high points of losing eyesight, the decade of blindness, and my recovery of sight, which was also the basis of a longer piece for a New York anthology.

While it has been agonizing to relive those years, and I have had to put aside writing fiction and keeping a journal, this story has created interest, and the proceeds will support us for at least a year. That has to be the most important thing, because we are expecting our third child and Elizabeth needs security and peace now. The previous deliveries were very difficult, especially the first, and I pray that she will not have to endure such pain and stress next time. I was in a wheelchair when our first child was born, on crutches for the second, but at least I shall be able to walk into the hospital when the third child arrives.

June 16, 1957

My thirty-seventh birthday and Father's Day, celebrated quietly and magnificently here. Mozart symphonies float out over the countryside of a broiling Sunday afternoon; the family rests in preparation for the dinner party later on this evening. I clean up the studio and get all of the material out for the *Look* magazine reporter and photographer who arrive on Tuesday to do a story on us. It is hectic in the good sense here.

Robert Ellis arrives from Mexico this evening to join us at the dinner party hosted by Louise and Penn Jones, our friends in Midlothian.

Ellis will be bringing some of his magnificent paintings, which the Joneses have been collecting. He has always given us works each time he visits, for we cannot afford to buy them. They are the masterpieces Elizabeth always described, and now I can see them with my own eyes. Such serene, graceful works of vibrant colors and sure lines—entirely original.

A torrid breeze enters the window occasionally, and the music, this sublime music, is accompanied by the rustle of wind in the trees.

June 28, 1957

In going through and editing these journals, I notice how often I use the word *strange*; and it is right to do so, for all of life seems strange.

I live each moment as though I could not believe it, as though all of it were new. Each time I take a bath, shave, lie down to rest, it is new, and it is seen and felt vividly. Every discomfort, that too is strange and interesting to a man given a new vision of the world.

And the strangeness, too, of driving a car alone for the first time in twelve years. Before my blindness, I took such things for granted, drove everywhere and rather disliked it. For two days I practiced, going only up the lane to the mail box; but today I had to go all the way into town. The car was easy to handle, and all of the old skills returned naturally, so that there was no nervousness, no pressure. It was enthralling to be alone behind to the wheel. I drove on out the highway a few miles and returned by the back-country road, alternately speeding for the thrill of movement and creeping in order to see all of the wildflowers, the barns, the fields of mown hay, the cotton patches and flower gardens of the farms. A thousand things intrigued me.

How I should love to strike out for an entire afternoon in the car, going down side roads, going anywhere the roads led, for nothing but the wonder of looking. These things, so commonplace to others, fill me with longing to experience them alone. And perhaps this strangeness, this wonderment comes from the fact that most of my friends who are blind have never experienced even the commonest of these things. In a way, I do it for them, too. And certainly, I see it as few others in the world, from this perspective of absolute newness.

August 6, 1957

Today Gregory Parker Griffin was born prematurely but healthily, and Elizabeth is also healthy and radiant, too. Our new son was named after St. Gregory of Gregorian Chant fame, and takes his middle name from Clyde Parker Holland, who was a direct descendant of Quanah Parker, the last Commanche chief. Quite a lineage! For the first time I was able to see one of our children at birth. He is a beautiful child, just like the others, although very small, less than five pounds at the moment.

November 2, 1957

All Souls Day, when we remember the dead and pray for them. The day itself contributes to the radiant and somber mood: heavily over-laden with clouds through which shafts of sunlight occasionally march across fields and woods. Autumn—always majestic, impersonal, detached, and beautiful. And what complex resonances this day evokes, containing simultaneous awe and tenderness, radiance and the type of fear that comes from seeing with sudden clarity those immensities that are not really fearful, but which we cannot encompass comfortably, and therefore which we would prefer to evade.

I came to work with great calm and said the rosary for the departed souls, and in the background, the canaries and parakeets chanted all their joy in an odd counterpoint that was somehow fitting. Now I begin, with great softness in my heart's depths, to read through my requiem list of friends, family, and others who have gone home. I remember them and miss them, and pray for the repose of their souls.

The great clangor of the day, with its dissonances and consonances combining into a strange beauty, floats over the world, drowning out for a moment the rattlings and clinkings of our little lives. It removes from them the callouses that unconsciously develop in our daily exis-tence and it allows them to participate in the emotion of eternity.

Acknowledgments

The Prologue to *Scattered Shadows* draws on a piece published in the anthology *Handbook of Short Story Writing* (Writer's Digest, 1973). Part I of the memoir was composed and polished by the author during the sixties, with only minor revisions by the editor. Of those previously published: "Return To France," "The Blind Man of Tours," and "The False Pearl" appeared in *Ramparts* as *Scattered Shadows*; "Pierre Reverdy" and "Images of a French Poet" were published as "My Neighbor, Reverdy" in *Southwest Review*; and all five were reprinted in Brad Daniel's edition of *The John Howard Griffin Reader* (Houghton Mifflin, 1968).

The first three sections of Part II are based on articles written for a series syndicated by the International News Service in 1957. "The Writing Life" draws on texts from *The Basilian Teacher* and *The Griffin Reader*. Portions of "A True Friend" were in *Catholic World*; Griffin's reflections on writing in "Fame and the Devil" were in *The Nation*; and an early version of "Lost Souls" was in *Catholic Digest*. "Artists and Smut Hunters" incorporates articles from *The Nation*, the *Dallas Morning News,* and *The Griffin Reader*. "A Different Species" appeared in a posthumous book of Griffin's essays, *Encounters with the Other* (Latitudes Press, 1997).

In Part III, "What It Means To See" was published in *Reader's Digest, Jubilee*, and in the anthology, *The Spirit of Man* (Hawthorn, 1958).

◄

Elizabeth Griffin-Bonazzi established The Estate of John Howard Griffin in 1982. Then we worked together as husband and wife, from 1983 until her death in 2000, bringing several unpublished works into print under our Latitudes Press imprint. As John Howard's widow,

Acknowledgments

Elizabeth's witness was invaluable, as were her intelligent editorial suggestions. We worked together on *Scattered Shadows* during 1991-1993, and then put it aside. I revised from our typescript onto the computer during 2000-2002.

Griffin scholars have made useful contributions to this work, but historian Michael Power provided the most insightful commentaries during this long process. Michael has done valuable research on Griffin, published an essay on John Howard's friendship with Father J. Stanley Murphy and a book on the Christian Culture Series at Assumption University in Windsor, Ontario, which Father Stan founded, in 1934.

Two great friends who have been supportive over decades will always have my gratitude. The late Decherd Turner, dearest friend of The Estate, offered astute observations on this book and on my *Man in the Mirror*, which was dedicated to him. Daniel L. Robertson, who accompanied me to interview Griffin for *Latitudes* magazine in 1966, has maintained a rich dialogue on Griffin during our forty-year friendship.

Also I want to recognize authors who have written about Griffin: Studs Terkel, Jonathan Kozol, Brother Patrick Hart, Eugene McNamara, Russell Hardin, Father August Thompson, Bishop Cyprian Lamar Rowe, John Reeves, Stephen Michaud, Bryce Milligan, and Paul Christensen.

Sincere thanks to Robert Ellsberg, Editor in Chief of Orbis Books, for guiding us through a third Griffin-related project together. I have been edified by his insights before, but especially so on this memoir.

Finally, I appreciate the cooperation of the Griffin Estate heirs: Susan Griffin-Campbell, John Griffin Jr., Gregory Parker Griffin, and Amanda Griffin-Fenton. We shall remember always their parents' soaring spirits.

—Robert Bonazzi